Not a Gentleman's
WAR

The University of North Carolina Press ■ Chapel Hill

Ron Milam

Not a Gentleman's
WAR

AN INSIDE VIEW OF JUNIOR OFFICERS
IN THE VIETNAM WAR

© 2009 The University of North Carolina Press
All rights reserved

Designed by Jacquline Johnson
Set in Janson Text
by Keystone Typesetting, Inc.
Manufactured in the United States of America

The paper in this book meets the guidelines for permanence
and durability of the Committee on Production Guidelines for
Book Longevity of the Council on Library Resources.

The University of North Carolina Press has been a member of
the Green Press Initiative since 2003.

Library of Congress Cataloging-in-Publication Data
Milam, Ron (John R.)
Not a gentleman's war : an inside view of junior officers in the
Vietnam War / by Ron Milam.
p. cm.
Includes bibliographical references and index.
ISBN 978-0-8078-3330-8 (cloth : alk. paper)
1. United States. Army — History — Vietnam War, 1961–1975.
2. United States. Army — Officers — History — 20th century.
3. United States. Army — Military life — History — 20th
century. 4. Vietnam War, 1961-1975 — United States.
5. Vietnam War, 1961–1975 — Social aspects. 6. Vietnam
War, 1961–1975 — Psychological aspects. I. Title.
DS558.2.M55 2009
959.704′3 — dc22
2009016602

13 12 11 10 09   5 4 3 2 1

For my parents,

MIKE *and* HELEN MILAM,

who worried, but supported

my enlistment

For my wife,

MAXINE, *and my son,* ALEX,

who provided the motivation

to survive

Contents

Illustrations

Figures, Maps, and Tables

Acknowledgments

I want to thank several professors at the University of Houston for helping me to understand the critical elements of analysis and writing: Hannah Decker, Landon Storrs, Frank Holt, and Jim Martin, all of whom also introduced me to the joys of rigorous research. The Department of History at the University of Houston was also very generous in awarding the John O. King research fellowship in the latter phases of my writing. Thanks to Chairman Joe Pratt and Graduate Advisor Marty Melosi for the opportunity to leave campus for one semester and finish my writing.

I was fortunate to work as a teaching assistant with three professors who helped me develop my teaching style. Many thanks to Professors Tyrone Tillery, John Moretta, and Steven Mintz. Each of you has taught me invaluable lecture techniques that hopefully will help my students in the future.

I was fortunate to have met archivists who not only understood the Vietnam War but shared my passion for the subject. Vietnam veteran Rich Boylan at the National Archives, College Park, Maryland; Vietnam veteran Frank Shirer at the Center of Military History, Fort McNair, District of Columbia; and Vietnam veteran Dave Keough at the Military History Institute at Carlisle Barracks, Pennsylvania, were very accommodating, knowledgeable, and generous with their advice and time. Ericka Loze at the Donovan Research Library, U.S. Army Infantry School, Fort Benning, Georgia, allowed me access to archive rooms as if I were still a student at the school. Thank you for keeping the library open beyond normal closing hours and for the generous use of the copy machine. And thank you to the entire staff at the Lyndon Baines Johnson Presidential Library, University of Texas, Austin, for your generous support in the initial phases of my research.

The first review of my manuscript was conducted by Professors Joe Glatthaar, Robert Buzzanco, and Marty Melosi. Each of them brought their expertise to the process. As a visiting professor at West Point, Dr. Glatthaar provided a military history perspective that required me to change the focus on several sections, which improved the final product.

The recollections of the combat experiences of Vietnam veterans are a major part of this manuscript. The Vietnam Veterans National Memorial at Angel Fire, New Mexico, provided a list of contacts through the "Keep in Touch" program. Dr. Victor Westphall, founder, died in July 2003, and I regret not being able to share my scholarship with him. He is missed by veterans of all wars. Thank you to all of the Vietnam veterans who filled out questionnaires and submitted to hours of interviews, particularly Vernon Lovejoy, Jim Wonsick, Dave Cook, Ed Vallo, John Moore, Mike Hutton, and Bob Ryan. Sharing memories of bad times is never easy, and I appreciate your trusting my intentions and honesty.

My new employer, Texas Tech University, has provided an atmosphere conducive to research and reflection about the Vietnam War. Their reward of a Humanities Fellowship in my first year of employment made trips to archives and to Vietnam much easier. The world-renowned Vietnam Center and Vietnam Archive has embraced my scholarship and teaching in ways that I never dreamed possible. Teaching the Vietnam War to more than 600 students and accompanying several of them to Vietnam during the summers of 2006, 2007, and 2008 has sharpened my focus on America's involvement in that war. I was moved by their responses to walking in the footsteps of American soldiers at My Lai and American marines at Khe Sanh. Many thanks to my students Natalie Swindle, John Southard, James Barber, Rosa Phifer, Beth Mora, Cameron Carter, Juan Coronado, John McPherson, Larry Gaytan, Dana Dang, and Capt. Gary Jones. Dr. Jim Reckner, executive director of the Institute for Modern Conflict, Diplomacy, and Reconciliation and a Vietnam veteran; Dr. Steve Maxner, director of the Vietnam Archive; and Khanh Cong Le have been instrumental in helping me make the transition from Vietnam veteran to Vietnam scholar. Jim Cloninger provided much needed research assistance particularly regarding photos. And my thanks to Amy Hooker, C.A. at the Vietnam Archive, who went beyond the call of duty to assist with both archival and technical support.

The University of North Carolina Press has provided excellent support throughout the publishing and marketing process. Stephanie Wenzel, project editor, and Zach Read, assistant to the editor in chief, were in continual contact and helped me meet the many necessary deadlines, and David Perry, assistant director and editor in chief, expressed confidence in my work from the beginning. Jim Willbanks and John Prados read the entire manuscript and offered critical comments that shaped my ideas and improved the final product.

This work would not have been possible without the support of my family.

My son, Alex, a doctoral candidate in organizational/industrial psychology at the University of Houston, helped me understand some of the testing models found in the literature. My daughter-in-law, Traci, provided technical support necessary for documentation production. And finally, my wife of forty-three years, Maxine: she was my chief research assistant, typist, and editor, but more importantly, my confidante and partner. The impact that she has had on my teaching and scholarship is immeasurable, and her complete support of our new academic life has made the transition remarkably easy.

Not a Gentleman's
WAR

PROLOGUE

October 7, 1970. Somewhere East of Phu Nhon, Pleiku Province, Republic of Vietnam.

The North Vietnamese Army (NVA) reconnaissance unit had efficiently executed the ambush, but the rocket-propelled grenade fired from the B-40 rocket launcher had failed to detonate, and the American radio telephone operator and lieutenant at the center of the patrol had narrowly escaped death. The ensuing firefight had resulted in the wounding and capture of a young North Vietnamese officer, who lay in the jungle clutching his lower abdomen. His brown fingers contrasted vividly with the whiteness of the intestines that protruded between his hands; he was either instinctively trying to push them back into his abdominal cavity or attempting to hide the wound from his captors.

Kneeling at his side was an American sergeant and an American lieutenant. The sergeant removed his survivor's knife from the inverted scabbard on his web gear. The lieutenant shoved him away, saying, "Put it away, Sergeant. I'm not Lieutenant Calley."

Determining the genesis of a research project is always difficult, but the idea for a study on the role of junior officers in the Vietnam War probably originated with this incident. The impact of Lt. William Laws Calley's behavior on March 16, 1968, at My Lai has permeated all studies, attitudes, and observations about company grade officers in Vietnam. And as a young lieutenant on that day in October 1970, I would not tolerate Calley-like behavior, even though the sergeant had meant no evil intentions. "I'm just cutting gauze, L.T. He'll die before the medevac arrives if we don't bandage his guts."

With full acknowledgment of the challenges that a Vietnam veteran has in studying objectively the performance of his fellow soldiers, *Not a Gentleman's War* is based on both the army and civilian reviews of the leadership of junior officers in Vietnam. As an infantry advisor to Montagnard troops, I am all too familiar with the results of poor military leadership. Because my own Mobile Advisory Team (MAT 38) consisted of only five people, my experiences with American casualties resulting from mistakes are, fortunately, minimal. However, combat is combat, and successful completion of the mission with minimal casualties is the goal of any military operation. Since most studies of the war have concluded that the company was the most important organizational unit in most battles, how junior officers led their men was critical. And since there is a vast body of literature about the experiences of soldiers and general officers, a study about junior officers seems appropriate. This book will confirm that these men served, for the most part, with great skill, dedication, and commitment to the men they led.

Most Vietnam War scholarship has addressed elements of geopolitical and home front conflict. I have tried to avoid such discussions in this book, but certain biases exist in all Vietnam veterans, particularly regarding senior leadership. I served in Gen. Creighton Abrams's army, and I admit to a certain element of appreciation for his strategy and tactics when compared with those of his predecessor, Gen. William Westmoreland. Thus, the reader will note disdain and disgust regarding some policies in place from 1964 until 1968. Notwithstanding this issue, I have attempted to minimize discussions about why and whether the United States should have been in Vietnam. While kneeling over that prone enemy officer, I was not thinking of the political, social, or economic consequences of the war. While such studies are important to a complete understanding of the Vietnam War, this project is not about such issues. It is about soldiers and the consequences of poor leadership in a war that was not a gentleman's war.

ONE A THOUSAND CALLEYS

*I thought initially that the loss of my glasses in the explosion
accounted for my blurred vision, and I had no idea that the pink
mist that engulfed me had been caused by the vaporization of
most of my right and left legs. As shock began to numb my body,
I could see through a haze of pain that my right thumb and little
finger were missing, as was most of my left hand, and I could
smell the charred flesh, which extended from my right wrist
upward to the elbow. I knew that I had finished serving my time
in the hell of Vietnam. As I drifted in and out of consciousness,
I felt elated at the prospect of relinquishing my command and
going home to my wife and unborn child. I did not understand
why Watson, who was the first man to reach me, kept screaming,
"Pray, Lieutenant, for God's sake, pray!" I could not see the
jagged shards of flesh and bone that had only moments before
been my legs, and I did not realize until much later that I had
been forever set apart from the rest of humanity.[1]*

*I don't choose the wars I fight in. When people ask me why I went
to Vietnam, I say, "I thought you knew. You sent me."[2]*

In 1981 the BDM Corporation published a voluminous report titled *Strategic
Lessons Learned in Vietnam*. Among the strongest indictments of U.S. failures
was that of the junior officer corps. "We have at least two or three thousand
more Calleys in the army just waiting for the next calamity," said one anonymous colonel.[3] In numerous official studies, academic journals, soldiers' diaries, veterans' remembrances, novels, and even Hollywood films, the lieutenants who served in Vietnam were depicted as bumbling idiots who exhibited
poor leadership, which was responsible at least in part for America's defeat.
The military establishment expected its officers to be gentlemen and to

conduct themselves with decorum like their predecessors in previous wars.[4] "Let officers be men of sense; but the nearer the soldiers approach to machines perhaps the better," wrote Alexander Hamilton.[5] George Washington was even more emphatic about the need to distinguish officers from the men they lead: "If the men consider, and treat officers as an equal; and they are mixed together as one common herd; no order, nor no discipline can prevail."[6] Such was the desire of early American political and military leaders for the kind of men who would lead others into battle. That image would remain throughout America's participation in the next eight wars.

But the Vietnam War was not a gentleman's war. Society chose to defer the induction of those citizens who had more important things to do with their lives, such as attending college, having children, joining reserve or National Guard units, being employed in important vocations such as engineering or teaching, or working in a family-owned business. So by definition, the military consisted of young men who were unable to avoid induction or who, for various reasons, wanted to fight. Some of these men may not have fit the military's definition of "gentleman," but they were the pool from which the military had to choose.

Nor was the war fought like a gentleman's war. The measure of success was an inconceivable military concept known as the body count, instead of the more traditional idea of real estate held, and the military hierarchy tended to exaggerate, if not fabricate, the numbers to indicate achievement more vividly. Junior officers were responsible for the initial reports, since it was at their feet that the bodies lay. But the numbers changed as the layers of officers and gentlemen above them reported success to Nha Trang, Da Nang, Chu Lai, and ultimately Saigon and Washington, D.C.

The rules of engagement established by the military hierarchy were anything but gentlemanly, because civilians were coerced into leaving their hamlets and villages that had served as ancestral homes so that free-fire zones could be established, allowing the more efficient use of air and artillery power. Consequently, anyone who refused to leave such zones was considered to be Viet Cong (vc) and thus eligible to be captured or killed. Such recalcitrance coupled with a military rumor mill that accentuated the active participation of women and children in terrorist activities rendered all civilians suspect. It fell on the shoulders of young junior officers to execute these policies amid these universal beliefs.

This was not a gentleman's war because of the manner in which the enemy fought. He chose to ignore conventional warfare tactics, at least after the

Battle of the Ia Drang Valley,[7] and to concentrate instead on small-unit actions, the deceptive use of land mines and booby traps, and atrocious acts against local civilians to intimidate them into supporting his cause. Crude but lethal booby traps that threatened the lives of their soldiers tested the military skills of junior officers in surveillance and defense against such weapons. Bouncing Bettys, toe poppers, punji pits, and chi-com grenades were commonly used to maim the command posts or point elements of platoons, thus challenging junior officers to motivate and control the payback instincts of their soldiers.[8] Gentlemanly responses were infrequent and often overwhelming when measured against the initial confrontation.

Nor was this a gentleman's war because of the types of troops that junior officers led. The inductees were frequently either society's misfits, malcontents, or rejects from selective social and economic institutions, and they possessed societal ills that were commonplace in the 1960s. Soldiers not addicted to drugs before they entered the army were afforded many opportunities for indulgence in Vietnam. Soldiers who were not racists at home were plunged into integrated units in Vietnam that tested their attitudes toward one another and, compounded with each soldier's personal arms, created volatile situations that often resulted in conflict.[9] Such racist attitudes were also displayed against both the Vietnamese enemy and allies, which infrequently resulted in atrocious acts committed by soldiers.[10]

Finally, the officers and gentlemen who supervised the daily activities of soldiers did not manage it as a gentleman's war. Field- and general-grade officers lived in luxury at battalion, brigade, and division headquarters, which contained air-conditioned billets with movie theaters, swimming pools, and officers' clubs.[11] Often these same officers conveniently sought out limited firefights that involved little real danger but allowed eligibility for the coveted Combat Infantryman's Badge and, if sufficient pressure was applied to a clerk, perhaps a Bronze Star, with "V" device for valor, or even a Silver Star. Since officers only served in a combat role for six months, these senior officers and gentlemen avoided much of the stress associated with the rigors of combat. And yet, it was these same senior officers who collectively blamed the American defeat, in part, on junior officers. Such an allegation is wrong; these junior officers may not have been the officers and gentlemen desired by the military establishment, but they were sufficiently trained and performed efficiently in a war that was certainly not a gentleman's war. Furthermore, because such officers tended to be similar in socioeconomic class to those they commanded, they shared many of the same views as their men about the

Vietnam War, and such attitudes may have led to much of the criticism about their performance in the postwar analysis.

THE VIETNAM WAR HAD not even ended for America when articles and books denouncing the military's performance began to appear. Journalists who had covered the war for newspapers and magazines were the first to offer critiques, followed by field-grade officers who had recently retired. A historiographical essay regarding these "angry colonel" books can be found in Appendix 2.

For purposes of this study, "junior officer" is defined as a 2nd or 1st lieutenant, the lowest-ranking officers in the chain of command. While there will be frequent references to captains, who by military definition are considered junior officers, they are not the principal subject here, since most of them commanded companies. Synonymous terms are "junior officer," "lieutenant," and "platoon leader."

This book is divided into two parts: preparation for Vietnam combat conducted in the continental United States, or in military lingo, CONUS, and experiences in Vietnam. In the CONUS section, the selection and training of junior officers is discussed, and the army's evaluation of its programs is reviewed. Since officers were commissioned through three main sources — the U.S. Military Academy at West Point (USMA), Reserve Officer Training Corps (ROTC), and Officer Candidate School (OCS) — each of these institutions is examined. The Vietnam section reviews the training that junior officers received once they arrived in-country. The accomplishments of junior officers, as well as the detrimental aspects of their performance, are also reviewed. Rules of engagement, junior officers' roles in the commission of atrocities, and discipline problems in the field provide information regarding leadership at the platoon level.

Archival evidence is at the core of this study, with oral histories, diaries, recent personal interviews, and veterans' questionnaires used to supplement government and military documents. To offset any military bias from such materials, other secondary sources were investigated to balance government data. Since the army provided more than 75 percent of the junior officers who fought in the war and since the infantry was the branch that engaged the enemy most frequently and created the greatest number of both friendly and enemy casualties, the bulk of the research has been conducted about army infantry junior officers.

To evaluate junior officer performance in the Vietnam War, we must address the army's perception of what it wanted in its leaders. Field Manual (FM) 22-100, *Army Leadership*, spells out in great detail what is expected of an officer in combat situations, but there is more to leadership than can be described in a manual.[12] The army's responsibility was to select, train, and deploy junior officers to Vietnam who could lead men into battle, direct the destruction of the enemy with minimal friendly casualties, and complete the mission assigned to the unit. All of these tasks are difficult because of the intangibles involved in determining what constitutes effective leadership in combat.

One such junior officer was 1st Lt. Robert Ferguson, 101st Airborne Division, who was wounded on October 8, 1967, near Tam Ky, Republic of Vietnam. He died of his wounds one month after the battle. His actions in his last battle earned him the Distinguished Service Cross, and he had previously been awarded the Bronze Star with V device.

Lieutenant Ferguson's father was Maj. Gen. R. G. Ferguson, commanding general of the U.S. Army, Berlin. Upon hearing of his son's death, General Ferguson wrote a letter to Army Chief of Staff Harold K. Johnson asking for an inquiry into the USMA's Aptitude System, because his son had been terminated at West Point for his "lack of leadership potential." Not willing to abandon his plans to become an officer, young Ferguson had enrolled at Dickinson College at Carlisle, Pennsylvania, and received a commission through the ROTC program. His father's letter to General Johnson contained a dossier of tributes, awards, and personal letters of accommodation attesting to his son's leadership ability. "The West Point Tactical Department, however, was convinced that Bob would not be a leader and an army officer. But as you can see from his record, Bob was convinced otherwise. He was a leader in the ROTC, in college administration, in training, and particularly in combat."[13] General Johnson forwarded the letter and dossier to the superintendent at West Point, requesting that the academy conduct an investigation of its predictive ability regarding leadership. With performance in combat being the best indicator of leadership, the army had to do a better job in this critical area, even though there are multiple intangibles involved.

An army axiom of leadership is that leaders should be trained to do what their soldiers do and should be willing to participate in every combat action in which they elect to send soldiers. This "muddy boots" concept applies to all levels of command,[14] but in Vietnam the field and general grades fought their war from the rear echelon or from the relative safety of a helicopter.[15] Lieutenants fought their war with their troops, so technical skills were an important part of their leadership, as was the courage to readily face danger and death. During the entire war, junior officers led platoons into the most intensive battles and were killed at nearly twice the rate that might have been anticipated based on their relative percentage of troop combat strength.[16] The commonly held and Hollywood-inspired belief that the average life span of an infantry lieutenant was fifteen minutes was probably an exaggerated claim, but the danger for lieutenants exceeded that of other ranks. Early in the war, the Battle of the Ia Drang Valley demonstrated the need for courageous junior officers, and Col. Hal Moore observed in his combat experiences that junior officers would be in the thick of the fight. "There was considerable hand-to-hand fighting. For example, the 1st platoon leader was found later KIA [killed in action] and five dead PAVN lie around him and near his CP [command post] foxhole."[17]

Thus the army had to select, train, and deploy junior officers who were capable of leading men into the fiercest type of combat — not necessarily the style of fighting that had existed in World War II or Korea, where lines of battle were drawn in a fashion similar to the linear warfare style generally practiced by armies around the world. This guerilla style involved neutralizing the effect of artillery and air support by engaging the Americans with close-in fighting. Most platoon leaders and company commanders were reluctant to call in artillery on their own position, thus reducing the effectiveness of technology. "You Americans were very strong in modern weapons, but we were strong in something else. Our war was a people's war, waged by the entire people. Our battlefield was everywhere, or nowhere, and the choice was ours. . . . Being everywhere was the best mobility of all," stated Gen. Vo Nguyen Giap, commanding general of PAVN (Peoples Army of Vietnam) forces, about the Ia Drang Valley battle.[18]

An example of a soldier whom the army selected to be a junior officer early in the war was Rick Rescorla, an adventurer who had served in the Northern Rhodesia Police Force and, prior to that, had seen combat action in Cyprus with the British army.[19] Rescorla had met a U.S. Army ranger in Africa, was impressed with America's military operations, and came to the States to pursue a career in the U.S. Army. As one of the oldest candidates at the "Benning School for Boys," he excelled in OCS and graduated near the top of his class. He was chosen to become a platoon leader of the 2nd Battalion of the 7th Cavalry Regiment, 1st Cavalry Division, which had begun training as the army's first airmobile division. The unit trained together at Fort Benning and deployed together in July 1965. By November they were involved in the Battle of the Ia Drang Valley, where Rescorla distinguished himself as the best platoon leader in the division. He was a "muddy boots" type of leader who knew everything about his men: their wives' names, how many kids they had, and what they wanted to do after their army days were completed. During the early days of the war, unit cohesion was strong because units such as the 1st Cavalry Division had trained and deployed as units, and the combat performance indicated the success of such a method. Rescorla was awarded the Silver Star for his combat performance at Ia Drang, but he was troubled by the loss of his men. The leadership attributes that made him an excellent platoon leader worked against him when he had to make a choice about remaining in the army.

Rescorla left the active duty army because the Vietnam War was not conducive to the use of his leadership skills. Featured on the cover of Harold Moore and Joseph Galloway's *We Were Soldiers Once . . . and Young*, Rescorla became a celebrity when the book was published in 1992. An effective leader who was wounded returning for the bodies of his men at Ia Drang, he later became a vice president of security for Morgan Stanley in New York and was killed when Tower 2 of the World Trade Center collapsed on September 11, 2001.[20] Virtually all of the employees under his supervision survived, but he went back in, as he had done in Vietnam. His sense of responsibility for his men, taught in the army and experienced in combat in Vietnam, stayed with him to the end of his life.

Lieutenant Ferguson and Lieutenant Rescorla represent one extreme of the continuum of leadership taught by the army's schools, one in ROTC with some West Point background and one in OCS. At the other end of the continuum is Lt. William Laws Calley. As the only soldier convicted of murder at My Lai, Calley exhibited none of the leadership traits of Ferguson or Rescorla. That the army chose him to attend OCS should be neither an indictment of the selection process nor an indicator of the demand for junior officers in the summer of 1966. Calley's car broke down in Albuquerque, New Mexico, as he was returning to his hometown of Miami, Florida, to answer his draft notice from the local Selective Service Board.[21] He visited a local recruiter and enlisted. The sergeant accepted his application for clerk school, which he attended at Fort Lewis, Washington, after completing basic training at Fort Bliss, Texas.[22] During basic training, he took the admittance test for OCS and passed, and then he enrolled at Fort Benning in Infantry OCS.

His performance there was not remarkable; but he was not recycled for lack of demonstrated leadership traits, and he did not fail any of the academic curricula.

Rumors persisted during Calley's trial that he failed map reading. But that course was difficult for many candidates, particularly those who had grown up in cities, since the course required the soldier to orient himself to the surroundings. Regardless, lack of map-reading skills had nothing to do with his actions at My Lai. Upon graduation, he was assigned to the 23rd Infantry Division (Americal) in Hawaii, prior to their departure for Vietnam.

Calley was the beneficiary of the same type of unit deployment as that of Lieutenant Rescorla. Rescorla personally killed many PAVN and VC soldiers and saved the lives of many U.S. soldiers with his decision making under combat situations.[23] Lieutenant Calley personally killed sixty women and children and was convicted of murder by a court-martial panel of combat veterans.[24] Both men received training at Fort Benning's OCS, and both men wore the "butter bars" of a 2nd lieutenant. Both felt the stress of combat and the loss of soldiers under their command to mines and booby traps, and each felt the pressures of senior leadership orders, demands for body count, and the loneliness of command. But they reacted differently to their respective environments.

The chapters that follow will deal with men like Ferguson, Rescorla, and Calley, and with the thousands of men who returned with physical and mental scars of their individual leadership. While no specific answers are easily available when dealing with the acts of one individual soldier, as a group the junior officer corps' successes or failures must be examined within the context of a war that was not a gentleman's war. But it was the war in which thousands of ordinary citizens were trained to lead other soldiers into combat. The question of how many were like Calley is problematic and hypothetical, but historians and military analysts have speculated about the answer for thirty-five years. This book will provide some new answers.

PART ONE

The idea that war consisted of more than the practical art of throat cutting — in other words, that it rested on a substantial body of theoretical knowledge that had to be mastered — is largely a product of modern technology.

MARTIN VANCREVELD

The Training of Officers: From Military Professionalism to Irrelevance

CONUS

TWO THE SELECTION PROCESS

I was fucking drafted. Yeah, I became an officer, but I didn't volunteer — I was fucking drafted! [1]

The early years of the Vietnam War found the military in a healthy position regarding the prospects of officer procurement. President John F. Kennedy's stirring words that "the torch has been passed to a new generation of Americans . . . [and] that we shall pay any price, bear any burden, meet any hardship, support any friend, oppose any foe, to assure the survival and the success of liberty"[2] inspired many young men to seek employment in their government, some in agencies such as the Peace Corps and others in the military. When the events associated with the Cuban Missile Crisis caused Congress to reinstate the draft for the first time since the Korean War, many young men accepted their plight and entered the army almost willingly because it was their duty as citizens. Hostilities in Vietnam in October 1962 were minimal, although 16,000 Americans were serving there as advisors, and casualties were "light."[3] Most of the officers had been commissioned through the USMA or through ROTC programs at military-oriented schools such as the Citadel, Virginia Military Institute, or Texas A&M University. In general, the army had no officer procurement problem.

When the marines went ashore at Da Nang in March 1965, followed in May by the army's 173rd Airborne Brigade, army personnel officers recognized immediately that supplying junior officers to the combat arms would be a major challenge. The generals who commanded corps and divisions were sufficiently in the pipeline, as were the field-grade officers who commanded battalions and brigades. Many of these majors, lieutenant colonels, and colonels had combat experience from World War II and/or Korea, and they were considered by the military establishment to be sufficiently trained and ready to command troops on the battlefield. But lieutenants and captains, who would command platoons and companies in combat, were in short supply, and there was no immediate solution. The USMA could be expanded, but even if the input were doubled, which ultimately was accomplished, such officers would not be available for platoon duty until 1969. The ROTC programs could be expanded, and new programs could be launched at schools where none had previously existed, but that would also take years to achieve. The only flexible avenue for increased officer commissioning was through OCS, and most such schools had been severely curtailed after the Korean War.

The need for junior officers was paramount in the minds of the various chiefs of staff when they met with President Lyndon B. Johnson in early November 1965 to propose an alternative battle plan to that being suggested by Secretary of Defense Robert McNamara. This plan, to take the war to Hanoi and Haiphong in North Vietnam through the use of air and naval power, was endorsed by all of the chiefs as well as by the chairman, General Earle Wheeler, but was soundly rejected by President Johnson.[4] This critical meeting launched the decision to rely on ground troops to win the war and was crucial to the issue of manpower planning. Consequently, one can conclude that it was in early November 1965 that the army had to develop plans to fill the junior officer leadership vacuum.

The most obvious solution to the officer shortage would have been a call-up of the reserves and/or the National Guard. Units could have been activated that were capable of being deployed immediately for Vietnam. But the issue of whether, when, and what units to call would cause controversy within the Johnson administration from the buildup through the TET Offensive period. In the early days, Chairman Wheeler opined that calling up the reserves would not be efficient, because reserves could not be moved into combat in ninety days, as had previously been announced, but instead would take four months. Given such a choice, the war managers opted for the use of new troops, some of whom would be draftees, since they could also be trained and made combat effective within the same four months.[5] Gen. William Westmoreland also believed that a call-up was not necessary, because enabling legislation would be required if the reserves were to be deployed for more than one year.[6] President Johnson also resisted, citing the strong pressure to cancel the call-up during the recent Berlin crisis and knowing that political pressure would come to bear on the administration once the war began to affect those who had volunteered to serve in capacities that did not include Vietnam. Thus the general backed the president, ostensibly against the wishes of the secretary of defense, and the draft or the threat of conscription would supply the soldiers that junior officers would lead into battle. Further compounding the decision process was the fear that company-grade officers within these potentially called-up units might not be capable of leading men in combat and, in some cases, were not even occupying positions commensurate with their Military Occupational Specialty (MOS).[7] Thus, for a variety of reasons, most of which were political, reserve units were never called up for combat duty, though certain MOS needs were eventually met by activating soldiers with certain required skills.[8]

The army was faced with filling the pipeline with junior officers who could quickly assume combat leadership roles. To the army's credit, even with a war raging and with personnel needs paramount, it recognized the need to procure as many junior officers as possible who were college educated, or who at least had some college background. The army looked to the campuses across America to meet its needs, either through existing ROTC programs or through the recruitment of college students into the planned expansion of OCS. But the college campuses were teeming with antiwar sentiment.

Figure 2.1 illustrates ROTC enrollment on college campuses across America. At the time of the buildup, there was minimal visible unrest on college campuses, although that would change dramatically as the war intensified. Furthermore, since college students were exempt from military service (2-S deferments) if they maintained satisfactory progress toward a degree, opposition to the war was based more on moral convictions than on fear of being drafted. However, in 1966 the Selective Service changed the rules and required male students who would otherwise be eligible for the draft in the absence of a 2-S deferment to take the Selective Service College Qualification Test to prove their ability to continue in college. If they wanted to attend graduate or law school, they were required to score exceptionally high on this standardized, nationwide exam. In 1967 Congress abolished graduate deferments except for medical fields and allowed student deferments only until completion of the bachelor's degree.[9] An implementing executive order provided a one-year deferment for persons accepted for admission into a graduate program or professional school for their first year of study beginning October 1967, and it authorized deferment of subsequent years within certain specified time limits.[10]

The military was clamping down on this easiest of all deferments, and campus unrest began in earnest across America. Although the antiwar movement was generally widespread, certain areas of the country were more bellicose than others. For example, after the TET Offensive in February 1968,

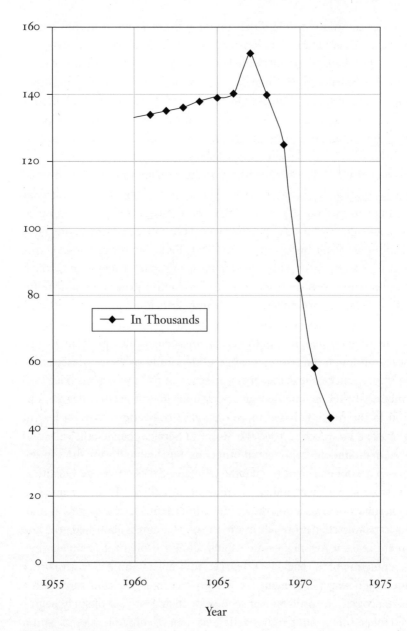

Figure 2.1 ROTC Enrollment

SDS (Students for a Democratic Society) disrupts Cornell ROTC exercise, 1969 (photo courtesy of the Dallas Morning News Collection, Texas Tech University, The Vietnam Archive, VA014058)

protests against ROTC members and facilities took place at the University of Michigan and the University of Maryland, and ROTC buildings were burned at Howard University, the University of Wisconsin, and Michigan State University.[11] Some schools even dropped their ROTC programs completely; Harvard, Dartmouth, Yale, Columbia, and Stanford were the most prominent.[12] Other schools began to cancel their participation, not because of student protest, but because there were not enough cadets to maintain a viable program: small liberal arts colleges such as Franklin and Marshall, Grinnell, and Davis and Elkins fit into this category.[13]

With ROTC programs being curtailed, the army still maintained its desire to attract college-educated men to fill its junior officer ranks. Recruiters visited campuses to explain OCS options to students who might be facing induction or whose college had no ROTC program. In many locations, recruiters were not welcomed on campus. At Whittier College in California, an OCS selection team was heckled by several "hippie types," and at Hamilton College in New York there was a lie-in by eighteen students.[14] Outright bans on recruiting were instituted by Brooklyn College, Hunter College, Herbert Lehman College, and Queens College, all of the City University of New York. The letters to the army in these matters usually stated that while the administration understood the desire of the army to procure college-educated officers, the students and faculty chose to not allow recruiters on campus.[15] Dr. Edwin D. Etherington, president of Wesleyan University in Middletown, Connecticut, wrote to the secretary of defense asking that military recruiters not conduct interviews or tests on campus but, rather, to schedule activities with Wesleyan students at sites off campus. He admitted in his letter that other government agencies and businesses would still be allowed to recruit on campus.[16]

Against this backdrop of campus unrest, the army had to address the problem of finding junior officers. An easy solution might have been to just expand ocs by sending existing enlisted men to such schools, but the records indicate that the army continued to actively seek college graduates. And since deferments had been tightened considerably, potential draftees sometimes sought refuge in army officer candidate schools, particularly during the period when a candidate could choose to enroll in a noncombat-arm ocs program. Such "reluctant volunteers" raised suspicions in the army as to the likelihood of a sufficient desire to obtain a commission.

The army was concerned enough about the motivation for entering service that it conducted a survey in 1969 to determine if the draft was the most compelling reason for enlistment. The study was conducted among soldiers in the United States, of all grades, both officers and enlisted men. Those surveyed were asked, Would you have entered active military service if there had not been a draft or military obligation? Response options were "definitely yes," "probably yes," "probably no," "definitely no," and "don't know." Among 1st and 2nd lieutenants, approximately 65 percent of those questioned answered "definitely no" or "probably no." Even half of the captains who would have reenlisted to achieve their higher rank indicated that without the draft, they probably would not have volunteered. Equally significant were the results from enlisted men whose responses were identical to those of officers, up to the rank of E-6, when careerism set in.[17] One can conclude, therefore, that the majority of the junior officers had joined the army for the same reason as had the men they would command: because their government would have forced them into service had they not enlisted.

The army was also interested in men who waited to be drafted, because this group was also a potential source of officers. The army commissioned a study of men who had been called to the Armed Forces Enlistment and Examination Centers for their first physical examination. Since these men had not yet made up their minds as to how they would handle their obligation, they provided the army with data necessary to effectively recruit them into active duty. For the army, the data was devastating. White, black, and "Spanish American" men all uniformly chose enlistment in the navy or air force before enlistment in the army.[18] By ethnic group, 42 percent of whites, 37 percent of "Negroes," and 35 percent of Spanish Americans were going to wait to be drafted.[19] Among this group, 26 percent had some college experience, with 5 percent having graduated and 4 percent having done postgraduate work. As for the reasons these citizens chose not to volunteer, 35 percent of white respondents and 12 percent of Negro respondents indicated a desire to serve only two years instead of the necessary three associated with enlistment.[20]

These findings had a significant impact on the army's plans for officer procurement. The recruiting study was commissioned in late 1967, just prior to the TET Offensive, and an early indication on the college student situation coincided with the army's desire to increase the number of college-trained officers. The very successful College Option Enlistment Program had been instituted in 1966, and many OCS classes contained more than 50 percent college graduates.[21] In fact, the army changed its policies in late 1967 to allow *only* college graduates admittance to OCS, if they had less than one year's prior service.[22] This policy change would have, for example, precluded admittance for William Laws Calley because he was not a college graduate and did not have one year's prior service.[23] Such restrictions on admission would, according to army theory, enable commanders to evaluate enlisted men for up to eight months before nominating them for OCS. College graduates, however, were allowed to apply for OCS during basic combat training (BCT), and if accepted, they would attend one of the schools after advanced individual training (AIT). The army had determined that college graduates were more capable of learning the skills necessary to lead men in combat, and it would structure recruitment to maximize the opportunity to procure such men.

Even if college graduates did not want to become officers, the army recognized that the institution was fortunate to be receiving so many men with advanced education. This situation became the subject of many inquiries, including that of the assistant secretary of defense, who requested a study as to how best to utilize college graduates, who were expected to be 35 percent of the enlisted accessions in fiscal year (FY) 1969, as compared with only 4.5 percent in FY1967.[24] This increase was the result of the curtailment of college deferments, and the army wanted to develop programs for best utilization of these men. The number-one suggested utilization was officer training, but even where that was not possible, college graduates were expected to assume leadership positions in BCT and to assist instructors with "slow learners."[25]

The army's desire for college graduates as officers led to a critical examination of its commissioning source options. Since most general-grade officers in the army were (and still are) graduates of the USMA, their impact on the procurement problem was apparent when, in 1965, the academy approved a 75 percent increase in the size of the cadet class.[26] Since these cadets would not be commissioned for four years, they could have no impact on Vietnam troop strength at the time of the buildup in 1965–66. But the army was not concerned about an overabundance of West Point graduates because it saw such officers as being the backbone of the service, whether in war or in peace. Eventually, and currently, West Point would provide more than 25 percent of all new lieutenants in the army, whereas during the Vietnam War era, less than 5 percent were from the academy.[27] Thus, from the viewpoint of the buildup, the USMA could provide quality, but quantity would have to be procured through other sources.

Since no additional officers would be obtained immediately through the academy, ROTC-commissioned officers would have to make up the majority of the 28,823 officers to be procured, up from 18,226 before the buildup. One plan was to order officers in reserve units to active duty. This was rejected for reasons of MOS incompatibility, as was a plan to terminate educational delays of those officers who had applied for a deferment of active duty in order to attend graduate school.[28] The only other source left to meet the increase was OCS.

The original plan for OCS accessions from two schools — Infantry at Fort Benning, Georgia, and Artillery at Fort Sill, Oklahoma — was 1,800. With the buildup in 1965, the goal was changed to 6,500, and three additional schools were opened, for the Signal Corps at Fort Gordon, Georgia; for the Corps of Engineers at Fort Belvoir, Virginia; and for a Branch Immaterial School at Fort Knox, Kentucky. The Fort Knox school would provide branch immaterial training for all candidates for thirteen weeks, and then those to be commissioned in Armor would stay at Fort Knox for an additional nine weeks. Or candidates could attend newly opened schools at Aberdeen Proving Grounds, Maryland, for Ordnance; Fort Lee, Virginia, for Quartermaster; or Fort Eustis, Virginia, for Transportation.[29] So the increase of approximately 10,000 OCS candidates would come from the schools and installations identified in table 2.1.

TABLE 2.1 OCS PROGRAMS AND INSTALLATIONS

Type and Location	Number of Troops
Engineer — Fort Belvoir, Virginia	1,200
Artillery/Missile — Fort Sill, Oklahoma	2,900
Infantry — Fort Benning, Georgia	4,000
Southeast Signal — Fort Gordon, Georgia	800
Armor — Fort Knox, Kentucky	525
Ordnance — Aberdeen, Maryland	325
Quartermaster — Fort Lee, Virginia	300
Transportation — Fort Eustis, Virginia	550
Total	10,600

Source: Office of the Assistant Secretary of Defense for Public Affairs, "Army to Expand Officer Candidate Program," NARA.

This buildup in ocs programs could barely keep pace with the military's needs, and particularly with the army's rapid deployments, which by the end of 1965 approached 120,000 troops (see fig. 2.2). The army's growth in Vietnam was the most significant as compared to the other branches, including the Marines.[30]

By 1967, even this increase in candidates fell short of the number required to meet the needs of commanders in Vietnam, because troop strength at the end of 1966 had nearly doubled, with 385,000 troops in-country. By the end of 1967, 486,000 American troops were serving along with an additional 72,000 soldiers from Korea, Thailand, Australia, New Zealand, and the Philippines. American junior officers were required to work as liaison officers for these units.[31] An additional 21,000 soldiers would be required for FY1967, with most of them required in combat arms.[32]

It was at this point in the selection process that the army decided to recruit actively on college campuses, to expand the College Option Enlistment Program, and to train those in ocs for combat duty. Within one year of the aforementioned changes, the army would close all of the noncombat-arm schools and commission virtually all new officers in infantry, artillery, and armor, or in combat engineering if a candidate was a graduate engineer or scored exceptionally high on a math test. The army referred to this as a "cutback" in ocs, but it appears to have been only a change in the mix, to replace officers killed or wounded in combat and to restrict the number of

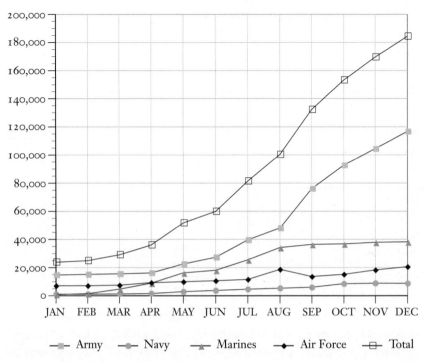

Figure 2.2 Buildup of U.S. Forces, 1965

officers who were not trained to fight. With more than 525,000 men serving, this was the period of highest casualties in Vietnam, and the army had to address the issue of officer candidates turning down their commissions at the end of the ocs program and serving only the balance of their two-year obligation, which could be only one year. Therefore, the army changed the rules and required a three-year enlistment for all ocs candidates.[33]

The news was not all bad for the army's college recruitment efforts. During FY1969, even with casualties from the TET Offensive causing erosion of support across America, there were schools that still desired to host new ROTC programs as well as expand existing ones. Fifteen new schools hosted senior ROTC units as approved by the Department of the Army.[34] Not all schools were approved, however, but the following request from the president of Howard Payne University in Brownwood, Texas, to the president of the United States indicated that the anti-ROTC attitude was not universal across America:

> I asked the people at 4th Army Headquarters if it would be in order for me to write you and ask you to get the blessings of the President, and

they assured me it would be quite in order. So, would you please point out to the President the following facts:

1) Recently I recommended to our Board of Trustees that they pass a resolution prohibiting hippies, draft card burners, or demonstrations on this campus. . . . We do permit, of course, any comments from students, faculty, or others.

2) We also stated in our resolution that we would not permit our student body to do anything that would potentially embarrass the President or the Congress of the United States.

Since we are the first school in the country to pass a resolution prohibiting hippies, draft card burners, demonstrators . . . it seems to me that this would be a fine place for an ROTC regardless of the fact that our college is not a very large one.

Guy D. Newman, President[35]

By FY1970, the army recognized its surplus of junior officers and began a program to reduce the number of candidates by offering inducements for withdrawal from the program. By this time, 65 percent of all OCS candidates were college graduates, yet many of them were not needed, since Vietnamization was fully implemented and American units were rapidly being redeployed. Thus, within a period of approximately three years, the U.S. Army ramped up to meet its needs in ROTC and OCS and then ramped down. It appears that the army met its needs, but when it was satisfied that the war would soon be "settled" at the bargaining table, it did not want an oversupply of officers trained for combat. But the individual male citizen still had to decide which option to take in fulfilling his military obligation.

Although the USMA expanded its class size in the early 1960s, getting admitted to West Point still required high academic standing in high school, demonstrated athletic ability, and in large metropolitan areas, superior performance on a standardized test, followed by a congressional appointment to the school. While some reports indicated that openings existed for some classes during the war and that antiwar sentiments led many qualified students to choose not to apply for admission,[36] few students could opt for meeting their obligation by going to the academy. If a student entered West Point in 1965, after the buildup, he would have watched three classes graduate. And each of those classes would have graduated between 525 and 785 students. Some would have gone to Vietnam, and many of those would have become casualties.[37] The type of individual who would choose to become a cadet would not ordinarily be a "draft dodger" choosing the academy to avoid service. However, of the 600 men who graduated from West Point in 1966, only 98 volunteered for Vietnam, which was 25 percent of those who chose a combat branch of infantry, artillery, or armor.[38] Those who did volunteer to go to war were usually assigned to an elite unit in Vietnam.[39]

College students attending nonmilitary schools had two choices, assuming being an officer was in their plans: They could join ROTC and be confident that they could stay draft-deferred for four years, at which time they could be commissioned and continue their training to become a platoon leader. Or they could reject the opportunity given them by the university and wait until they graduated to face induction or enlistment. This latter choice could include election of the College Option Enlistment Program, which allowed them to finish their degree if they enlisted in the military, with a guarantee of admission to OCS. But ROTC was an option available to more than 200,000 male cadets in 1968.

In the beginning of the buildup, ROTC membership swelled because of the impending draft, and then it began to recede once antiwar activities became prominent on college campuses and casualties began to mount in the war zone. Most military analysts believed that the increased membership was the result of draft avoidance.[40] "I suppose I figured if I was going to go in the army, because the draft was going, then I would just as well go in as a lieutenant as a private, so I went ahead and did it."[41] While postwar analysis indicated that enrollment dropped drastically as the war progressed, ROTC did provide a "safe haven" until about 1969, when many cadets began to drop the program to take a chance with their draft situation.[42] (See fig. 2.1.) And even with campus radicals attempting to shut down programs, students had to decide whether to fight the draft or fight their fellow students, at least symbolically. In the army, ROTC-commissioned officers accounted for about half of the new officers, which meant, by definition, that at least half of the newly commissioned officers would be college graduates. However, many dropped out of the programs after the TET Offensive and took their chances with the local draft board. Students made these decisions even though the army changed the curriculum to be more academic and less militarily oriented.

The army had an additional problem with ROTC, because historically the newly commissioned officers from this source were given their choice of branches in which to serve. This was a concern that had arisen prior to the buildup, because ROTC-commissioned officers typically selected noncombat arms as their branch of service.[43] The infantry was traditionally their last choice, and it was the infantry that was most understrengthened as the buildup began. Said Michael Horton,

> My initial assignment came back infantry. And of course this was after the '67 TET Offensive, and we'd had quite a bit of insight, at that time, into what Vietnam was about, what was going on over there. So as a . . . what I considered at the time a bright young college student I thought I ought to do something to see if I could remedy this Infantry assignment. I'd just completed a letter-writing course in the Business school. So I set down and wrote a letter to the Department of the Army expounding on my vast maintenance background in the civilian area of aircraft and requested a transfer to the transportation corps. And told them that I felt I could better serve their purpose in the field aviation maintenance. Well I promptly got back a transfer, and a nice little letter that said, in essence, "No, we didn't realize you had this vast technical background and based on that we are going to re-assign you from infantry to armor." So that's how I got to be a tanker.[44]

Once the casualty reports began to filter back to the colleges and universities, it became even more difficult to recruit infantry officers. The army had to look elsewhere for the majority of its platoon leaders.

THE TRADITION OF DRAWING on OCS for officers at the outset of a war predates Vietnam. When the United States entered World War I, it had no immediate program in which to secure its officers, other than through the USMA. The 1916 National Defense Act had only been in effect for a year, and few officers were available when the United States declared war on Germany in April 1917.[45] Soldiers were commissioned directly from civilian life after ninety days of training, and these new officers were labeled "90-day wonders."[46] Their mediocre performance during World War I caused the army to change the training for World War II, requiring all officer candidates to complete BCT prior to OCS. Army Chief of Staff George Marshall appointed Lt. Col. Omar Bradley as commandant of the infantry school in 1941, and Bradley's first decision was to develop a program to train up to 75,000 candidates to become army officers.[47] But the disparaging "90-day wonder" sobriquet stuck, and even in 1951 when the OCS program was expanded to six months to facilitate Korean War needs, those graduates were similarly labeled.[48] In 1965, with the expansion of the programs to meet Vietnam War needs, all candidates would already have attended BCT and AIT; hence the "90-day wonder" term would more appropriately be "300-day wonder."

The college student simply had to locate an army recruiter, assuming one had not come to his campus, and arrange to take the Officer Candidate Test, a three-hour-and-five-minute exam covering verbal, quantitative, and mechanical ability, as well as spatial perception and officer quality. If he scored 115 on the test, he was chosen to appear before a three-officer panel that would determine if he was qualified to enter the army under the College Option Enlistment Program.[49] Categories under the officer quality section included current affairs, leadership ability, and general science. And while the test was not as difficult as the previously mentioned Selective Service College Qualification Test, it ostensibly did measure as accurately as possible one's ability to *learn* to lead men in combat. Additional requirements for college graduates were achievement of a score of 300 (of a possible 500) on the Physical Combat Proficiency Test, which would be taken in BCT, and successful completion of BCT and AIT.[50] Thus a college student in his senior year could guarantee his place in an OCS class, forget about the persistent harassment from his local draft board, and begin the planning process for fulfilling his military obligation.

The army would commission approximately 50 percent of its junior officers during the Vietnam War through OCS and, according to the U.S. Army Infantry School (USAIS) commandant, would produce "some of the finest platoon leaders we have sent to Vietnam."[51] But this accolade was not shared by everyone, for a variety of reasons. This school also produced Lt. William Laws Calley.

THE BDM STUDY CONCLUDED that the combination of the three commissioning sources for junior officers caused the corps to be the most ethnically and socioeconomically diverse junior leadership corps in the history of U.S. warfare. The report perhaps oversimplified the selection process by affirming that the "upper middle class was represented by West Point, the middle class by ROTC, and the working class by OCS and direct commissions."[52] Christian Appy, in his book *Working-Class War*, stated that the officer corps "may have been the least privileged officer corps of the twentieth century."[53] The debate regarding the socioeconomic class of junior officers is relatively new, but the issue on enlisted soldiers has raged from the time the first ground forces came ashore at Da Nang. The two issues are somewhat related, because the performance of the junior officers would certainly be influenced by the type of soldiers they were asked to lead.

There is general acceptance of the Appy thesis and the conventional wisdom that the war was fought by soldiers who came from working-class families. However, there is an interesting debate on this issue between James Fallows, author of "What Did You Do in the Class War, Daddy?" (1975),[54] and Arnold Barnett, Tim Stanley, and Michael Shore, authors of "America's Vietnam Casualties: Victims of a Class War?" (1992).[55] While this argument focuses on who paid the ultimate price in the war through battlefield deaths, it has particular bearing on the subject at hand because of the high death rates among junior combat officers. Fallows, in a rebuttal article in 1993, admitted the possibility that even though the American elite was "conspicuously absent" from the war effort, "conspicuously does not mean totally."[56] Fallows wrote that "two of the most dangerous specialties in Vietnam were those of pilot (especially helicopters) and infantry lieutenants. Because of the educational requirements for those jobs and the role of ROTC in providing lieutenants, they drew many men from affluent backgrounds, many of whom died."[57] Fallows failed to mention, however, that OCS was contributing more than 50 percent of the junior officers, and while college graduates made up a large percentage of this group, prior enlistees would have represented a cross section of socioeconomic groups.

The junior officer corps was probably more representative of America in terms of class distinctions rather than ethnicity. Historians of the Vietnam War are familiar with the evidence of African American contributions to the war effort, particularly at the beginning of the war, when more than 23 percent of the fatalities were black soldiers.[58] Secretary of Defense Robert McNamara's Project 100,000, dubbed by him as "the world's largest education of skilled men,"[59] had the effect of increasing the black composition of the military from 12 percent at the end of World War II to 31 percent at the beginning of the Vietnam War.[60] This Great Society program set a goal of 100,000 men per year to be offered positions in the military, even if they failed the Armed Forces Qualifying Test. They would be offered training so that they could acquire skills that would improve their lives after they fulfilled their military tour of duty. Most of them went to Vietnam and served in a combat MOS. They were killed at double the rate of American forces as a whole.[61] Civil rights leaders complained to President Johnson about the excessive casualty rates, and eventually the number of black deaths was commensurate with the proportion of black soldiers in Vietnam, approximately 12.5 percent.[62]

Explanations regarding why the African American death rate was so high at the beginning of the war include (1) blacks were assigned to combat units disproportionately by white officers because their deaths were less bothersome to society, (2) black soldiers lacked education and skills necessary to qualify for rear-echelon jobs, and (3) black soldiers volunteered in disproportionate numbers for both combat units and more dangerous jobs in those units, such as point man. My conclusion is somewhat different, based on personal observation that black soldiers — even those who were drafted — volunteered for Airborne training in disproportionate numbers because jumping out of airplanes paid $65.00 per month hazardous duty pay. With this skill, they were qualified to serve in "elite" units such as the 173rd Airborne Brigade, the 82nd Airborne Division, and the 101st Airborne Division. These units drew the heaviest combat assignments in the early days of the war. Soldiers admitted under Project 100,000 also had twice the number of court-martials and convictions as the rest of the military.[63] The program was a disaster and was canceled in 1972.

Most of the attention on the lack of black officers has focused on field and general grades, where few black officers held rank. This was due to the lack of integration in the armed forces until 1947 and the racial bias that existed in all institutions of society. During the Vietnam War, the total percentage of black officers was approximately 2, with the army's percentage at 4.[64] While the army's record is more impressive than that of the other branches, only seventeen black cadets attended the USMA at the height of the war in 1968.[65] There were fourteen army ROTC programs operating on predominately black campuses, and these were the source of most of the army's black junior officers.[66]

OCS classes enrolled black candidates from prior enlistees and the College Option Enlistment Program, but the numbers were low. While no records were kept, a perusal of OCS class yearbooks indicates that there were usually 8 to 10 black candidates in each class of 200 students, which would be consistent with the 4 percent total.[67] The army had an opportunity to increase this percentage by lowering the requirements on the standardized tests as it had done with Project 100,000, but it chose to not do so.

The army had another opportunity to increase the number of black officers through direct commissions. This was done infrequently, usually as a result of displayed battlefield leadership. While no accurate records of ethnicity exist for such commissions, the number of direct commissions was insignificant in relation to the total number who served.

There is no record of the number of Hispanics or Mexican Americans who served in Vietnam, since the Department of Defense did not offer "Hispanic" as an ethnicity choice on applications until 1972. While surnames that indicate Hispanic ethnicity are prevalent on the Vietnam Veterans Memorial (The Wall), the number who served as officers is probably less than that of African Americans. Mexican American enrollment in college during the Vietnam War was low; hence the opportunity for an ROTC commission did not exist. And OCS classes appear to have had few Hispanic candidates.[68]

The selection process for junior officers used the existing, established institutions to recruit men who the army believed could get the job done. There was no attempt to achieve racial diversity or to create an officer corps that would reflect the nation's demographics. Aided by the pressure of the Selective Service system, even those who had been drafted into the army were coerced into becoming officers, because the army had few options left. The army would grow its own through training, because deferments and the antiwar attitudes on American campuses made recruiting difficult. As Ward Just wrote in 1970, "One senior officer said with some heat: 'Calley never would have become an officer if we were not so short handed.' Why are we so short handed? Because the bastards at Harvard (Harvard is short hand for any student who refuses the war) wouldn't fight, wouldn't step up to their responsibilities. They got their deferments, and left the war to the least competent people. They are the ones to blame."[69] It would be the task of noncommissioned and commissioned officers, many with combat experience, to create leaders who the army believed could lead men into battle, in a war that was not a gentleman's war.

THREE   THE TRAINING PROCESS

Interviewee: Were you a spitter, or a buffer?
Interviewer: I was a buffer.
Interviewee: Oh, you guys had it easy. We heard they changed
it to buffing machines in 1968, so you guys were pussys.[1]

Whether a recruit was black or white, rich or poor, the civilians who were selected by the army to become officers had to be trained to lead men in life-or-death situations. These citizens not only had to learn to be combat leaders; they also had to acquire certain skills that were vital to performance as a leader, such as map reading, small-unit tactics, marksmanship, weaponry, and fire and maneuver. Yet, the three commissioning sources had distinct ways of achieving training results. For cadets at West Point, the army had four years in which to turn students into officers and college-educated men. ROTC would have the same time period, or more, but the army had to rely on mostly civilian schools to teach their prospective officers the skills necessary for success in combat. Only through OCS could the army completely control the training activities of its future officers. An examination of the various techniques used by the three commissioning sources to train officers for combat is warranted, because this had to be the army's main concern while the Vietnam War raged in Southeast Asia. And teaching men to lead other men into battle is a formidable task, even if the trainees are of the highest quality. If the selection process has allowed entrants who do not possess certain learning skills or whose motivation for service is lacking — and therefore they may be less inclined to exert maximum effort toward completion of assigned tasks — the training process becomes even more challenging. Since the army had determined that the three main elements necessary for combat leadership were academic excellence, physical ability, and leadership capability, those are the areas that will be examined within the context of the three commissioning sources.

The greatest controversy surrounding academic requirements of the USMA in the early 1960s was whether to continue to stress engineering as the main focus of a cadet's academic program. West Point was the only engineering school in America until 1824, when Rensselaer Polytechnic Institute was established.[2] Said Neil Creighton, "You are going to be an engineer major? They said, 'The one flexibility was you could choose your language if it fits our priorities.' That lasted for many, many years."[3] The history of the USMA turning out excellent engineers was a barrier to an increase in social science and humanities courses becoming part of the core curriculum. But changes were instituted in 1965 that enabled cadets to choose elective subjects of a nonscientific nature, which could ultimately lead to a degree in liberal arts. During this time, the academy also began to recognize that combat platoon leaders needed an academic background that included social sciences such as psychology and sociology, and that communication skills best learned in English and literature courses were vital to the group dynamics of the platoon. And a department of history was created that stressed military history but that would also teach the role of the military within the context of American society, as well as the historical study of leadership.[4] "Another one I liked very much was military history. That was propitious because that fit right into your profession."[5] These changes were brought about by studies commissioned by the army and in many cases were spearheaded by civilians who tried to make West Point more like civilian universities.[6] Ultimately, the curriculum was changed from a 70 percent/30 percent engineering mix to 60 percent/40 percent, with a 1970 goal of 50 percent/50 percent.[7]

West Point produced many outstanding scholars in the 1960s; only Harvard, Princeton, and Yale had more graduates receive Rhodes Scholarships. But the question of academic relevancy was raised during the Vietnam War. Did the officers in Vietnam need the strong curriculum base of math, science, and engineering when they were performing so many political and social tasks? With frequent life-and-death decisions about civilians and enemy sympathizers being required, perhaps less emphasis on things and more on people would make sense.[8] To the army's credit, it addressed the issue and improved the academic preparation for newly commissioned officers by broadening the scope of their education.

That the USMA produced excellent physical specimens who were capable of meeting the rigors of combat is also indisputable, because part of the selection process for cadets included athletic prowess. The physical fitness regimen required cadets to take part in intramural sports if they were not participating in intercollegiate athletics, and it is inconceivable that cadets could have satisfactorily completed the program if they were not capable of performing rigorous physical duties. The Physical Combat Proficiency Test was given in the fourth year, and one can assume that USMA cadets scored, as a group, higher than those enrolled in either of the other commissioning sources.

The third element of officer training is leadership, which is the most difficult quality to measure in a training program. It would have to be considered the most important ingredient in the training process, a fact recognized by OCS, because the leadership scores there were equally weighted with academics. And since the army has an entire manual devoted to leadership, FM22-100, the subject requires special scrutiny.[9] In 1965, a USAIS review of the manual found it to be lacking in its approach to the applicability of leadership methods pertaining to the Vietnam War, and a section 99, "Leadership for U.S. Forces Engaged in Counterinsurgency Operations," was added.[10] Salient points that the army thought were important to the Vietnam War effort, but that were not otherwise considered relevant in previous wars, included the following:

> Platoon leaders will be required to solve local economic, political and social problems incident to operating within a population. Small unit leaders must be prepared to contend with combined operations with receiving state forces usually conducted at division level and higher. In addition, the small unit leader must insure that he is prepared to make positive decisions on his own without recourse to higher authority and to guard against demoralization of the troops because there are no definitive terrain objectives or because extensive combat operations may produce no tangible results.
>
> Keep the troops informed and instruct them why they are fighting "someone else's" war, while back home the country is enjoying "peace time" conditions. Be alert for insurgent psychological operations and be prepared to counter them.

These words were written in the summer of 1965, within a few days of the 173rd Airborne Brigade being deployed to Vietnam as the first army ground troops. They are prophetic words and set out the myriad of responsibilities that a young, inexperienced lieutenant would assume, whether commissioned by USMA, ROTC, or OCS. Each of these sources would determine the most efficient manner in which to instill these leadership traits in its potential officers.

FOR CADETS AT WEST POINT, their first exposure to the stress that would represent the closest thing to combat in a peacetime setting was "Beast Barracks."[11] This introduction to the military way of life entailed eight weeks of "hell," ridicule and hazing, and complete degradation of the spirit. More than 25 percent of the incoming class would typically resign their admission status and quit before the eight weeks were completed.[12]

> Part of the problem was they basically almost starved you to death. . . . Of course the idea was, which everybody felt was, "We want to get those out who really don't belong here" . . . and hazing was there. The sleep deprivation was there because they made you get up early and you couldn't sleep all the rest of the time. You were so damn tired because you were doing all these things. . . . You had a shower formation where before you could take your shower you had to sweat the form of your body on the wall behind you and things like that. That wasn't hard to do because you'd jam your chin and then you'd be down there for a while. You'd start sweating whether you wanted to or not. I don't want to put it like it was being a prisoner of war or anything like that.[13]

Many Vietnam veterans who graduated from West Point whom I interviewed about their combat experiences described West Point's Beast Barracks as more stressful than the war itself, because new cadets had no control over the antics of upperclassmen leaders. The idea of excessive harassment was to force cadets who could not handle such pressure to resign and not waste their time as well as that of the USMA. If you could not handle Beast, then you certainly could not handle your first year as a plebe; but more importantly, the army believed that you also would not be able to handle the rigors of combat. As Atkinson writes, "Years later, men who had been in horrific combat in Vietnam would wake up shrieking from nightmares — not that they were about to be overrun by the Viet Cong, but that they couldn't find the proper hat during clothing formation."[14] Such exercises were designed to instill in the prospective officer the idea that unforeseen situations would always develop in combat, and one must be prepared to solve an immediate problem with ingenuity. A cadet must always be prepared so that his equipment was readily available, in working or appearance condition, and he must anticipate that such a call would go out at any hour of the day or night. The anticipation of a minefield or a booby trap or sniper fire was the combat equivalent of clothing formation, and the West Point leaders were convinced that battlefield preparation was improved by such harassment.

The cadet was also taught military subjects such as marksmanship and how to assemble field gear, but these issues were secondary to the greater effect of induced stress. The idea of eating "square" meals was designed to eliminate even the pleasure of eating and, instead, to require cadets to get minimal nourishment while succumbing to harassment by upperclassmen. During the 1962 Beast Barracks period, the army finally recognized that lack of nourishment was affecting the ability of some cadets to complete their training. However, instead of changing the dining room harassment techniques, it delivered to each cadet a nightly half pint of milk and an apple or banana. Upperclassmen saw this change as "coddling" and not in keeping with the traditions of the corps.[15] Thus the army, while striving to improve the environment for training, had to fight the tradition that so permeated the academy.

A cadet experienced a pattern of decreased harassment and increasing responsibilities of command over the next four years. As a student, each cadet assumed the role of a noncommissioned officer (NCO) within his company, so that he could experience a hands-on leadership role. And in the summer after his third year, he was assigned as the equivalent of a 3rd lieutenant to a Table of Organization and Equipment unit. This allowed him to observe command, if not actually participate in daily leadership.

Induced stress in the form of harassment was only one method of developing leadership at the USMA. Building character, the inherent aspect of becoming an officer and a gentleman, was based on adherence to an honor code. Consisting of only thirteen words, "A cadet will not lie, cheat or steal, nor tolerate those who do," this code and the enforcement that prevailed at West Point were important to the creation of an atmosphere that permeated all aspects of student life.[16] Officers commissioned at the academy strived to adapt to these simple words because of the importance placed on them during their four years as a student. Vietnam veteran and West Point graduate Howard Boone believed strongly in the honor code: "I'm still romantic enough to think there has to be a certain number of idealists in every profession. You lose the last honest man, that profession is gone, or it's as good as worthless. And for that reason, I've always thought the honor code was and is a great thing. And where else do you find the one they have at West Point?"[17]

Such codes existed to a lesser degree in ocs and rotc, but the enforcement was more critical than the mere existence of the words.

Without self-enforcement, the honor code ceased to fulfill the needs of the army in creating officers who possessed "personal moral codes that will sustain them through a career of army service."[18] The army expected the graduates of West Point to adhere to principles of character as they entered the next phase of their officer training.

All graduates of the usma received Regular Army (ra) commissions and were required to attend Army Ranger School.[19] This opportunity was not available automatically to most officers who generally received reserve commissions if they were graduates of ocs or rotc. Ranger training was arguably the best in the military and was mandatory for usma graduates before they reported to their first duty station.

> I went to Ranger school, which is the best thing I ever did I thought. . . . At the platoon level and patrolling operations it was the best thing I ever did for preparation for Vietnam. I sincerely believe that. I feel it's a great course and everybody ought to go through it because all it is is a psychology course that teaches you how you and other people react under real pressure. I mean they do that on multiple planes because everyone has different hot buttons. Some people can't do without sleep, some can't do without food, some can't do long marches. Everyone's got different buttons. Ranger school is structured so that it can push everyone's buttons (at one time or another). . . . I found that Ranger school was probably the best training I ever received. It was most helpful for me as a combat leader in Vietnam. I don't really remember many times in Vietnam where I was as tired or strung out as I was at Ranger school, because it would have been bad form in combat to abuse your men to that extent. . . . Ranger school was designed to wear you out and show you how people work (when totally exhausted) under different stressors.[20]

This training was so intense that some leaders believed that this excellent course, particularly if accompanied by Airborne training, could be a substitute for the Officer Basic Course (obc) that all non-ocs-commissioned officers were required to attend prior to arrival at their first post-commissioning duty station. Maj. Gen. J. B. Lampert, superintendent of West Point in 1963, wrote that "it is difficult to motivate a cadet for the obc after four years of West Point." He recommended that cadets be "excused from such courses and go directly to their first duty station." Such cadets were also routinely scoring poorly at OBC when compared with ROTC-commissioned officers, and one could assume that such poor performance was due to their lack of interest.[21] This plan was put into place for the classes that graduated in 1964, 1965, and 1966 but was changed for classes that graduated after 1966. This idea had been previously tried in 1950 for the same reasons, and those newly commissioned officers found themselves on the battlefields of Korea within weeks of graduation. A few years later the army repeated its mistakes in preparation for the Vietnam War.[22] One can argue that there may have been a certain amount of institutional arrogance that prevailed in these instances. What could a five-week course possibly teach soldiers who had been training for four years to become officers? It would take a board of investigation, the Haines Board, to force a reversal of this decision.

Regardless of the post-commissioning training, whether academic, physical, or leadership, there was recognition at the highest level of the army that newly commissioned officers needed exposure to peacetime troop command before they were sent into battle. In a letter to Vice Chief of Staff Creighton Abrams, Chief of Staff Harold K. Johnson requested a study to determine what training was required for the West Point and ROTC graduate before assignment to Vietnam.[23] He reinforced the issue previously stated, asking, "Should any other measures be taken to avoid a repetition of the experience with the Class of 1950 at the outbreak of the Korean War?" The study recommended that newly commissioned 2nd lieutenants spend the same amount of time leading troops (four months) that inductees spend in the army, since the lieutenants would be leading these troops in combat.[24] This requirement was statutory, under Subsection 4(a), Universal Military Training and Service Act, as amended, but one has to wonder about the rationale involved in such a comparison. Inductees and enlistees spent all of their pre-Vietnam time in training, and then they went to Vietnam. Officers, on the other hand, received elements of that same training and then were educated more specifically to be officers. But their total time in training was years, not months. However, the military was concerned and recognized that newly commissioned officers needed on-the-job training with troops, and that such experience was essential to effective performance in combat.

HOW DID THE PREPARATION of commissioned officers in ROTC differ from that in the academy? An examination of the academic, physical, and leadership training of men who attended either civilian or military-oriented colleges or universities indicates that the preparation of these prospective officers was less intensive, less rigorous, and less physical. More than 50 percent of the officers commissioned during the Vietnam War era came from ROTC.

When reviewing the academic preparation of ROTC students, one must deal with two separate contexts: the college curriculum that each student would be exposed to for four years at a civilian college or university, along with military training he would receive in summer camp, and ultimately the OBC, which during the Vietnam War became known as the Combat Platoon Leader Course. The attitudes of the universities toward the war and the precipitous drop in ROTC enrollment would affect the role of academia in the training of future officers. Prior to the TET Offensive, few questioned the campus "man in uniform" as he spent hours on the parade field.[25] A national debate had occurred regarding the academic preparation of ROTC cadets, the first such review since passage of the National Defense Act in 1916. In preparation for the passage of the ROTC Vitalization Act of 1964, professors of military science, RA officers, academicians, and congressional leaders were queried regarding the number of credit hours, types of courses, and funding. Their varied opinions on these issues provided evidence that the military's thoughts on important concepts were different from the view of the politicians.

The army had previously concluded that a two-year ROTC program, preceded by a six-week summer camp, could replicate a four-year program at a much lower cost.[26] But congressional leaders insisted on the continuation of only four-year scholarships. A two-year program would be developed, but only a monthly stipend would be offered to the students.[27] And the academic community believed that the military was encroaching on course content that should more appropriately have been taught by regular university departments, rather than by professors of military science who did not hold advanced degrees. This latter issue was of paramount importance to the various host universities, because some professors believed academic credit was being given to course work that lacked intellectual rigor. "It is the contention of some members of the faculty that the subject matter in question (Democracy, Communism, etc.) is purely academic and that an objective presentation of it could not be given by military personnel obligated to conform to established Defense Department policy."[28]

Thus the universities were pressuring the military to improve the academic value of its programs, in exchange for an increase in academic credit. By agreeing to these changes in 1964, the military became an integral part of the academic programs. There was an improvement in the level of course work of future junior officers, and professors of military science were thrust into positions as active members of schools and colleges. When campus rioting and dissent began in earnest in 1966, many of these professors had to choose between their military careers and charges of anti-intellectualism. Most chose silence, which was a way to keep ROTC out of campus debates on the merits of the Vietnam War.[29]

The ROTC Vitalization Act of 1964 attempted to improve the quality of the junior officer being commissioned by providing a better education. With improvements at summer camp and a more rigorous academic experience, the military believed it was producing a well-trained and motivated soldier. But after the TET Offensive in February 1968, unrest at colleges and demonstrations against the very presence of uniformed men on campus caused many college administrators to question the existence of ROTC on campus, or at least to challenge the conduct of the programs. The president of the University of Michigan, Robben Fleming, dealt with the issue this way:

> As to the larger question of whether ROTC ought to be on campuses, I tend to favor it despite my own connection with civil liberties causes. My reasons are that I fear a professional army in a democracy; that I think the infusion of officer talent from non-professional ranks promotes the concept of a civilian army; that in twenty-two years on three campuses which have ROTC programs, I have yet to find the faintest hint that somehow the military is dominating the campus; and I believe that officer standing is a legitimate outlet for those students who must serve some time in the military anyway.[30]

Positions such as Fleming's put sufficient pressure on the military to consider altering the collegiate course of instruction and reducing the number of hours that ROTC students spent on strictly military subjects. Intense negotiations with Department of Defense civilian and uniformed personnel sought to focus "less on drill and more on assuring its (ROTC) place on the campus through congruity of the goals of higher education."[31] The concept of "substitution" was introduced on campuses across America, wherein ROTC cadets were allowed, even encouraged, to substitute courses in history, political science, psychology, and sociology for drill and ceremony. Outside lecturers were invited to address ROTC classes under "the New York Plan," an effort by New York University's National Security Information Center to assist ROTC instructors across America in broadening the academic base of their teaching.[32] Even though the list of individuals on the speakers' bureau included such hawks on the Vietnam War as Walt Rostow and Zbigniew Brzezinski, who could be considered biased on the war issue, this was at least an effort to recognize that the future officer commissioned through ROTC had to be exposed to more than a military education if he were to truly represent the citizenry as an officer. Thus many of the ideas that had been debated a few years earlier in the context of the ROTC Vitalization Act of 1964 gave way to the practical need to avoid campus unrest.

Unlike their West Point peers or even OCS graduates, the ROTC-commissioned officers, particularly in the post–TET Offensive era, had to carry into their military careers the osmotic pressure of the antiwar college campus. This burden may have been greatest upon graduation, when they would be assigned to an OBC at one of the branch schools. There they learned how to act as officers. This post-commissioning school was their first real taste of the army, because the summer camps between years two and three or three and four were too short to form a lasting impression on a cadet who would return to the antiwar campus environment. Using the Infantry Officer Basic Course (IOBC) as an example, one can appreciate the radical departure that Fort Benning must have seemed from the openness of a college campus. But unlike an OCS candidate or a West Point cadet during Beast Barracks, the newly commissioned 2nd lieutenant was welcomed to the USAIS with a cordial letter from the assistant commandant: "We are privileged to have the officers of the Combat Platoon Leader Course and their ladies as a part of our team. With but few exceptions, each officer with further education and training, can be a distinct asset to the army. We need men with the educational background and personal attributes of these officers."[33]

The army had a unique situation with ROTC-commissioned officers. They met the first requirement of a good officer because they possessed college degrees. However, the academic preparation they were offered at IOBC was minimal in terms of skills necessary for combat leadership, because of the short duration of the program. The course was to be a "do-it type," and study assignments were to be kept to a minimum.[34] While fifty-five-hour workweeks were normal, it is interesting to note that the army did encourage the newly commissioned officers to bring their wives to Fort Benning, a privilege that was not encouraged among OCS candidates. The army seems to have looked on the OBC as a "coaching session designed to help the new officer over the shoals of his first six months on active duty."[35]

I found it to be very easy. I mean, I was an honor graduate there. Basically it was academics. I found the whole army educational experience to be . . . well, for two things, I liked it. I liked the shooting, I liked most of what you did, and the bookwork that you had to do was relatively straight forward. I think the Army assumes that you're an idiot and teaches down from there, but certainly the class I went through was not to qualify you in tactics so much or anything else, but really was to qualify you . . . to get you sort of army-ized I guess. Most of us were ROTC, we had no idea how to salute or anything. We didn't know rank. I mean, I knew rank, but I can remember one of our first classes was teaching us how to tell what the rank was, the officers.[36]

A great deal of controversy existed regarding the academic program that would best prepare these newly commissioned officers to be combat platoon leaders, and the fear of redundancy in training was part of the issue. The IOBC was attended by both ROTC-commissioned officers and newly commissioned officers of both the Army Reserves and the National Guard. The assistant commandant of the USAIS took exception to redundancy being a problem when he wrote to the assistant adjutant general of the Minnesota Army National Guard that "the current world situation and demands placed upon our graduates combine to underscore the importance of combat leadership capability. For this reason, I would rather err in the direction of teaching too much instead of not enough. We can not risk the creation of a void when mistakes result in casualties. I hope you agree."[37] It is apparent from the tone of this letter that the army took the IOBC course training seriously, because that was the only course available for newly commissioned officers, and the army did not want to "tinker" with the course, especially to change it to accommodate the needs of the National Guard.

The army also appreciated the quality of the Ranger course as an add-on to the IOBC in training combat platoon leaders. Only those who would receive RA commissions were automatically eligible for the Ranger course, and only those who were designated Distinguished Military Graduates received RA commissions. But the Ranger course was expanded to prepare officers and some NCOs for Vietnam, and the ROTC graduates were at the top of the list of those who could use the intensive training.

Physical training was not stressed to a great degree in ROTC. Since ROTC stretched over a minimum of four years, with summer camp the only concentrated military type training, the army had to rely on the colleges and universities to conduct periodic physical training. Thus a newly commissioned officer would be physically fit if his collegiate program was sufficiently rigorous to prepare him for combat duty. Once he was commissioned, OBC would include physical exercise, but the program was not designed to create a physically fit specimen. It was instead designed "to teach students what a good Physical Training (PT) program is, to qualify them to teach PT and selected combat conditioning subjects and to help the students gain and maintain a good physical condition while preparing them to pass the Physical Combat Proficiency Test."[38] Students were encouraged to conduct physical training on their own time, but there was little group effort or combined programs such as forced marches, morning runs, or harassing exercise. The students were treated as officers and gentlemen and were not subjected to physical stress. The army wanted these men to attend the Ranger course for the physical regimen as much as for any other part of the program, which indicates recognition of the lack of physical conditioning that most IOBC students had.

The army's concern about the leadership training imposed on its ROTC cadets was appropriate, since the summer camps were too short to instill any lasting leadership skills. But their college education was considered to be a minimal substitute for this lack of formalized training. When Gen. James K. Woolnough took over the training mission in 1968, one of his first concerns was the ROTC program and its effectiveness in training half of the army's first line of combat defense team.[39] In the redesign of the academic portion of the program, Woolnough approved a curriculum that, in addition to providing technical skills, was designed to create "a strong sense of personal integrity, honor, and individual responsibility; knowledge of the human relationships involved and an understanding of the responsibilities inherent in assignments within the military service."[40] One can see that his concerns went far beyond the normal leadership tenets as developed and proclaimed in FM22-100. Perhaps this refocusing of concern for ethical behavior from army officers was a function of the My Lai massacre, and perhaps the army reacted by improving on that aspect of leadership with education, which can have the greatest bearing on the actions of officers. With no Beast Barracks to simulate the stress of combat, and no tactical officer harassment as in OCS, the army improved upon that which had the greatest daily impact on the prospective officer: the education program itself. In *Making Citizen Soldiers: ROTC and the Ideology of American Military Service*, Michael Neiberg quotes a military source after My Lai as saying, "We cannot doubt the importance of a high degree of education for our officers. A half hour of immaturity on the part of one ill-educated junior officer can affect our whole national image adversely."[41] Neiberg states that the comment was a veiled reference to Lt. William Laws Calley, who has been cited previously as the only officer to be convicted for the My Lai massacre.[42] He was not a college graduate; thus he had not been a member of ROTC. He was a graduate of Infantry OCS at Fort Benning, Georgia.[43]

THE ACADEMIC TRAINING FOR officer candidates at OCS was different from that for West Point and ROTC cadets, because it would be part of a concentrated training program taught exclusively by the military. The army would be required to develop a program that could be effective for both college graduates and non–college graduates and for those with extensive military knowledge based on several years of enlisted service, as well as for those who had just completed BCT and AIT. Many of these soldiers had been in the army for only five months. The plan offered courses that were important to any program for educating an officer, but it also required courses that would teach skills a newly commissioned 2nd lieutenant must possess to perform the duties of an infantry platoon leader under combat conditions.[44] The candidate had to pass these courses, known as critical subjects, or he would not be commissioned. Table 3.1 shows the required program of instruction (POI).

If a candidate failed the examination (scoring below 70 percent) in any critical subject, he would receive remedial instruction and be given an opportunity to be retested. If he failed the reexamination, he was to be turned back to a subsequent class, commonly referred to as being recycled. If the candidate failed the same subject after being turned back to another class, he would be relieved from the program for academic reasons.

A candidate was not allowed to retake a failed examination in Combined Tactics I or II. This subject was considered to be the most important of the critical subjects for combat performance and crucial to effective leadership. Anyone who did not pass the exam the first time would automatically be relieved from OCS.[45] Mike Hutton, a Vietnam veteran and a course instructor, confirmed that Tactics I and II were important, rigorous, and stressful, and that candidates who struggled to pass were usually the same candidates who scored low in the leadership section of the program.[46]

The army knew that many of the students enrolled as officer candidates would have trouble with the academic section of the program; thus daily two-

TABLE 3.1 INFANTRY OFFICER CANDIDATE SCHOOL PROGRAM
OF INSTRUCTION

General Subjects	Critical Subjects
Leadership	Map and Aerial Photo Reading
Communications	Small Arms
Airborne, Airmobile, Artillery and Air Force Operations	Anti-tank Missile, Mine Warfare and Recoilless Rifle
Counter guerrilla Patrolling	Mortar
Combined Staff Subjects	Combined Tactics I and II
Equipment, Serviceability and Unit Readiness	(Platoon and Company)

Source: *Infantry Officer Candidate Manual*, 6-3 (1968), DRL.

hour study halls were mandatory, and students who were considered academically marginal had to attend mandatory study halls on weekends. Academic failures were not the main source of attrition, so the army's approach to the academic program appears to have been successful. The army infrastructure identified courses that were most important to combat efficiency and made certain that the candidates who struggled with those programs received special help. However, although army research indicated that tactics could be learned by most candidates, those who struggled with the concepts would receive no second chance. Such measures were not put in place without full awareness of the importance of tactics in combat.

The army was also fully aware of the importance of academics versus leadership, because each was weighted equally. In requiring more than 1,000 hours of instruction, the army recognized that these candidates needed the knowledge that was being presented, probably because many of the candidates lacked military training.[47] When ocs-commissioned officers recount their experiences, however, it is not the academic program that they most readily recall but, rather, the harassment and the physical stress to which they were constantly subjected.[48]

The *Officer Candidate Manual* affirmed that the goal of the physical training program at ocs was to "improve [the candidate's] physical condition and maintain high physical standards."[49] Furthermore, the army believed that the infantry officer must be capable of doing everything his men could do so he may lead by example.[50] This type of training reaffirmed the idea of a lieutenant being a muddy boots leader. The army thus constructed a physical training program that required candidates to participate not only in platoon and company regular sessions of rigorous running, calisthenics, and forced marches but also in infantry school physical training exercises. The candidate took three physical combat proficiency tests during the twenty-three weeks of training, and he was required to score at least 60 points (out of 100) on each of the five components: forty-yard low crawl, horizontal bars, run, dodge-and-jump, seventy-five-yard man carry, and one-mile run (in combat boots). It was not enough for a candidate to pass these tests; he had to improve in each category on each Physical Combat Proficiency Test or be subjected to remedial work. The physical training was the part of ocs that frequently caused older enlisted personnel to be recycled, and ultimately to be removed from the program, because they could not handle the rigorous physical demands placed on them.[51] This part of the program was only 10 percent of the candidate's weighted scores for completion of the course, but failure could be grounds for denial of a commission. And the inability to perform at a high physical level was an indication that he might not possess appropriate leadership skills. The leadership part of the program resulted in the most attrition, and that part of the course was also the most subjective.

The army sought to create the most stressful environment possible during the training of its candidates, because it believed that the more stressful the training situation, the more similar it was to combat. Thus ocs was modeled more on the Beast Barracks from West Point than on anything developed in the rotc program. Complete with harassment by senior candidates, a usma type of honor code, demerits with punishment and physical discipline, and the eating of square meals, ocs resembled the extreme harshness of the plebe year at the academy. Said Russel Hiett about his experiences in the "chow line,"

> You get in to eat and you had to eat square corners which meant you had to look straight ahead, you had [to] pick up your fork and move it in square corners to the plate, pick up a forkful of food, and move it up vertically to your eye level and then move it in a square corner across to your mouth, then put it in your mouth. You move back the same way with the fork, you put it down, chew your food and swallowed it. It was the greatest weight reduction program in the history of the human race. We had people lose a hundred pounds easily and I couldn't afford to lose weight. . . . If you got caught eyeballing, shifting your eyes at a tac Officer and if you shifted

your eyes you had to throw your whole tray of food away and you got kicked out of the mess hall. I think I got kicked out once. Of course while you were eating, it was no fun being in there, you would eat as fast as you possibly could go during that stupid square corners stuff because the TAC Officers were constantly harassing and they might call you up and make you sing some stupid song, like the "Benning's School for Boys" song: "Far Across the Chattahoochee to the Yupatoy" — isn't that amazing that thirty some years later I can still remember this stupid song? "Lies our loyal Alma Mater, Benning School For Boys, onward ever, backward never, faithfully we strive, to the shores of embarkation, follow me with pride." Yes, of course because "follow me" was the Benning theme.[52]

The students accepted into the program had an understanding of the section 99 added to FM22-100, mentioned above, because they were typically working-class soldiers like those they would lead into combat, and they knew that the society they had left behind was ambivalent at best about the war. These were the people that OCS was challenged to develop into combat leaders.

To accomplish this mission, candidates were exposed to two sets of external contacts: the USAIS and the Student Brigade. The USAIS was responsible for teaching leadership skills, and the Student Brigade provided the day-to-day laboratory for the candidates to practice those skills. Each candidate was given the opportunity to be a squad leader, platoon leader, and for some, even company commander during the twenty-three-week course.[53] Upon completion of each leadership position, the candidate was evaluated by his peers, subordinates, and superiors who had served in the candidate chain of command, and such ratings were recorded on the Performance of Duty Observation Reports.[54] The tactical (TAC) officer of his platoon would arrange a counseling session in which the TAC officer would evaluate the candidate as to his strengths and weaknesses. All of these reports became part of the candidate's record for determining his score on the leadership section of the OCS program.

Upon what criteria was the candidate to be rated? According to the *Tactical Officer's Guide*, military leadership is an art and is based upon the "development of traits of the individual's personality and upon the understanding and application of sound leadership principles and techniques."[55] The TAC officer was given first-line responsibility for the development of each candidate's leadership abilities. The general framework around which each candidate was measured, which is similar to the Officer Efficiency Report to which each

TABLE 3.2 INFANTRY OFFICER CANDIDATE SCHOOL PERFORMANCE
EVALUATION REPORT SCALE

Adjectival Rating	Score	Disposition of Candidates
Unsatisfactory	10–17	Should not continue in program
Marginal	18–27	Should be turned back
Satisfactory	28–37	Should continue in program
Better than most	38–47	Should continue in program and will make a fine officer
Exemplary	48–50	Should continue in program and will make an officer of highest caliber

Source: *Tactical Officer's Guide*, January 1968, DRL, 4-1.

newly commissioned officer would be subjected, is shown in Appendix 3 and includes a myriad of traits, qualities, abilities, and attributes that would have to be taught to men whose average age was twenty-two and a half, who had more than fifteen years of education, and who had, on average, seventeen months of enlisted prior service.[56] Col. Robert M. Piper distilled this multitude of qualities into those considered most important for effective combat leadership: ability to lead by example, dependability, moral courage, and judgment.[57]

Perhaps more critical than the Performance of Duty Observation Report in evaluating a candidate's leadership ability was the Performance Evaluation Report, which all candidates were required to submit at the end of the sixth, tenth, sixteenth, and twenty-first weeks of training listing the bottom five candidates in each platoon. These "bayonet sheets" were required after the platoon had ranked all members from most effective leader to least effective leader.[58] While Colonel Piper and other senior officers may have been very formal in their approach to evaluation, the typical TAC officer simply instructed the platoon to identify five candidates whom they would *not* want to follow into combat. At the beginning of the twenty-three-week cycle, it was an easy task, but as candidates were forced out of the program, there were fewer to identify with deficient skills, except those who had been "recycled" into a subsequent company. Such individuals had difficulty convincing their new peers that they were worthy of not being at the bottom of the list. The candidates were asked on all rating forms to rank their peers according to the dispositions shown in table 3.2.

The importance of the Performance Evaluation Report was that candidates themselves were able to remove fellow candidates if they felt others were incompetent and not capable of leading men in combat. This peacetime equivalent of "fragging" was taken seriously by everyone and probably had more of an impact than anything done by the USAIS Academic Department; the company, battalion, or brigade commanders; or the discipline system itself.[59]

We had what were called bayonet sheets where at the evaluation period, I keep thinking because we had thirty some people on my platoon and we ended up graduating fifteen, it had to be maybe every other week, maybe every other week, maybe every two weeks, something like that, that we had to rate the bottom four people in the platoon. They would eliminate the bottom two I think, the TAC Officers after they would look at everybody's sheet and eliminate them and one by one, you got rid of the guys who couldn't keep it together, and couldn't think in terms of the other guys, stuff like that, so if you were a real strong individualist, forget it. If you couldn't hold up your end of the bargain to keep everybody out of trouble, and you couldn't help others, you were going to get it. . . . I can remember one time, one of the guys who eventually did get bayoneted out of our platoon marched our platoon through a ditch of water because he couldn't think of the command for platoon halt or column right or column left; he couldn't remember any of the commands and of course we did exactly what we had to do, we marched through that water with our spit shined boots and our perfectly creased pants and whatever else. You better believe that led to his getting bayoneted fairly quickly after that.[60]

OCS was about discipline, much more so than BCT or AIT, and the army developed a highly structured system not only for ensuring adherence to rules and customs but also for teaching the soon-to-be-commissioned officer how to discipline his own troops. By the army's definition, discipline is "the individual or group attitude which insures prompt obedience to orders and initiation of appropriate action in the absence of orders."[61] For OCS, the hierarchy of actions to correct infractions of rules was as follows:

1) On the spot corrections and formal counseling[62]
2) Formal counseling by TAC officers
3) Officer Candidate Program Demerit System
4) Officer Candidate Program Punishment System

5) Administrative turn back for purposes of further evaluation

6) Relief from the program.[63]

If a candidate committed violations to rules that the army considered the most serious, such as failure to perform assigned duties, being under the influence of drugs or alcohol while on duty, being absent from formation or duty, or disrespect for superiors, the brigade commander would respond, and in most cases, these infractions would warrant relief from the program. Most other infractions were considered minor and fell under the authority of the company commander or even the platoon TAC officer. With accumulation of demerits, the candidate would be punished, which normally meant restriction to barracks or the post for hours or the entire weekend. Excessive accumulation of demerits could also warrant serving punishment tours, defined as marching in a military manner at quick time on a prescribed post, carrying rifles at right or left shoulder arms, with equipment and in the prescribed uniform.[64]

> OCS was chicken-shit, at best, if I can say that . . . because what they're trying to do, they're trying to demonstrate combat stress without anybody shooting at you, so they were really nit-picking; I mean, the least little thing. At the end, after you got so many demerits you got restricted or grounded as you would your teenagers on Saturday where you couldn't go anyplace Saturday night; you had to stay in the barracks. If you got more demerits you got to do that Saturday and Sunday, but if you got more you got Saturday and Sunday demerits then you had to run up the MB-4 which was a mountain round-trip fives miles to work off the demerits. If you got a few more, you got to run up there Saturday and Sunday afternoon and Sunday morning, without stopping. The mountain was pretty steep at the end. . . . We had guys we were literally carrying; their feet were running on the ground but all the weight was being carried by other guys because they weren't in as good a shape because they hadn't had to run that mountain. Having been an NCO, I knew what it took to keep me straight.[65]

One can question whether the punishment aspect of OCS truly maintained order within the ranks, which was partially the reason for having such a system in basic training. At the candidate level, it was more likely to instill in the soon-to-be-commissioned officer a sense of the importance of obedience to rules. It was also used to create stress among the candidates and to assist those in command in deciding who could handle such stress and who might "break." In an interview in 2000, Edwin Frazier, an ocs graduate who achieved the rank of major, said,

> It was outstanding training. First of all, you've to go realize that in order to go to officer candidate's school you've got to have the characteristics they expected of a leader. You've got to already have that. What ocs does, it fine tunes these things. It puts them in proper perspective. We used to say that it takes your God given rights away from you and gives them back to you one at a time as discipline or as privileges. It's kind of like the West Point program where they first break them in and then they develop them. Well, they do the same thing but you only have a short period to do it in — nine months.[66]

Colonel Piper, candidate brigade commander in 1969–70, said, "Under these conditions, candidates occasionally lose their temper or otherwise display loss of emotional control. As unfortunate as this might be, the quality of the product turned out by Infantry ocs indicates that the pressure atmosphere achieves the dual result of identifying those candidates who do not have sufficient emotional stability to be leaders, and of sharpening the control and stamina of those who do have the basic stability."[67] Perhaps Colonel Piper was right: the system was designed to see who could handle the pressure. We know Lt. William Laws Calley handled the pressure of ocs to the satisfaction of his TAC and company officers, but he could not respond properly in combat. At what point in the training process did the system fail to prepare Lieutenant Calley for the stress of the My Lai operation and help him distinguish between right and wrong procedures? The army would review and analyze this issue during and after the war, but efforts to evaluate its selection and training processes were continual and were executed by both government and private organizations. With a war raging in Southeast Asia, the evaluation process was critical.

FOUR THE EVALUATION PROCESS

They weren't worth a damn. Quantity v Quality. Guys could go
AWOL and still get a commission. Maybe in 1966 they were OK,
but they got worse as the war went on.[1]

There may be those who continue to attach great significance to the
source of a person's commission, but I rather think that they are
few and far between, after a few years of service. I can assure you
that while commanding the 1st Infantry Division in Vietnam, I
would have been unable to tell you which officers came from OCS,
from ROTC or from West Point.[2]

It is possible that every once in a while we graduate a man who has
nothing more on the ball than the ability to say "Yes" or "No" at
the right time, and again it is possible that we relieve a man for an
infraction of the rules who would be an outstanding commander.[3]

The army has periodically reviewed its officer school system through formal
boards, informal investigations, and academic inquiries. It has traditionally
recognized the importance of all of its schools, with pre-commissioning
being as important as career education, because there are more lieutenants in
the army than any other officer rank. This chapter considers the results of
these studies, as well as the comments of those in charge, to determine if
there was concern during the course of the Vietnam War about the pre-
commission, or immediate education of the junior officer, and whether the
army believed it was falling short in its preparation of platoon leaders. Since
the most important analysis will be the comments of those who interfaced
with officers in combat, this chapter also includes the results of liaison trips
to Southeast Asia as a prelude to Part II, which deals with junior officers in
Vietnam.

The army periodically reviewed training programs for commissioned officers to be certain that its schools were meeting the needs of the post–World War II military. With Eisenhower's "New Look" and the Korean War having made an impact on the army's officer corps, changes that had been made in 1958 now needed review.[4] With the buildup for Vietnam having taken place, Chief of Staff Harold K. Johnson felt that a new study was necessary, and he placed Lt. Gen. Ralph E. Haines Jr. in charge of the review board. Known as the Haines Board, its members numbered eleven and included a three-star, a two-star, and two one-star generals, in addition to seven lieutenant colonels and colonels. Their charge was substantial and included determining the adequacy of the school system for 1965–75 and reviewing the subject matter being taught as to whether there was too much emphasis on command responsibilities versus technical knowledge. In addition, the board was charged with examining the role of the various joint service and Defense Department schools. Those were the broad charges, but there were two additional pages of items, including item number 12: "Examine particularly the training requirements for newly commissioned officers, taking into consideration sources of new officers and the requirement for attendance at the basic officer's course."[5] The latter was a reference to the previously mentioned decision regarding USMA graduates attending OBC.

The Haines Board was required to submit its findings to the chief of staff within four months, and it completed its initial investigation within that assigned time. However, the final report was not published until 1967, well into the Vietnam War. The initial fact-finding phase of the investigation lasted sixteen days and included visits to all of the major posts, including Fort Monroe, Virginia; Fort Gordon, Georgia; Fort Sill, Oklahoma; Fort Wolters, Texas; and of course the largest school in the system, the USAIS at Fort Benning, Georgia.[6] The Benning visit was particularly noteworthy, because the commandant of the school asked each department to write a critique of its contribution to the army's school system, and those records indicate the attitude of Infantry toward training.

The various departments at the USAIS would have been expected to promote attendance in their individual courses. For example, the director of the Ranger Department recommended that all newly commissioned officers attend the Ranger course because "leadership training is inadequate in that the newly commissioned officer does not receive enough practical experience in small-unit leadership before he is required to perform as a leader."[7] The Haines Board partially adopted this recommendation, which recognized that the Ranger course was the best the army offered in terms of leadership. "The Board believes that Ranger training should be mandatory for all RA officers, and regrets that the course does not have sufficient capacity for all non-RA officers as well."[8] The Airborne Department recommended that "all newly commissioned combat arms second lieutenants, regardless of source of commission, attend the Basic Airborne Course."[9] The Haines Board did not adopt this recommendation and surprised many in the army by playing down the importance of Airborne training by stating that the course "provides no training in leadership, and hence is not a suitable alternative to the Ranger Course for the newly commissioned RA officer. After carefully weighing the value of Airborne training to the individual, the Board concludes that with due regard for the needs of the government, it falls into the nice-to-have category, except for officers being assigned to airborne duty. . . . The Army is today overtraining Airborne officers against established requirements."[10] This recommendation established the sincerity of the board, because being Airborne qualified was considered a "rite of passage" for an army officer. (No one wanted to be a "leg," because advancement in the combat arms usually required an officer to wear jump wings, even if he had never been assigned to an Airborne unit.)

The USAIS similarly made recommendations that were controversial and would seem to be contrary to its own best interests. It recommended dismantling the IOBC and replacing it with the Combat Platoon Leader Course, having the course become "more clearly focused on the newly commissioned officers' initial assignment — platoon leader. Emphasis would be placed on the development of basic combat skills, leadership techniques and basic branch qualifications."[11] The Haines Board adopted this recommendation because it believed that such a course would be an improvement to the current POI, particularly when the nation was engaged in a war that required an extraordinary number of platoon leaders.

But the USAIS recommended no changes in the OCS program. General York even went out of his way to state that "there would be no change in the current Officer Candidate School program. Graduates of the two OCSS (Fort Benning, Georgia and Fort Sill, Oklahoma) would not attend the Platoon Leaders' course, because this would duplicate instruction."[12] The director of the Company Tactics Department was emphatic in his recommendations to the USAIS: "Officer candidates classes do possess the stamina to lead men in combat at the completion of their course. My personal observations in the field are that OCs are ready to command a platoon upon commissioning."[13]

Airborne training jump (photo from Airborne Classbook, 4th Student Battalion, Fort Benning, Georgia; courtesy of Jim Cloninger)

These candidates, according to this officer, were considerably more advanced in their military training than were the ROTC officers who were being readied for the same combat roles. The Haines Board acknowledged this recommendation, and OCS graduates were never required to attend any courses between commissioning and first duty assignments. The Haines Board, however, made several comments and recommendations regarding newly commissioned officers.

Whether the Haines Board offered only minimal comments about the USMA because it believed West Point was doing a good job or because it did not want to "ruffle feathers," the ensuing changes were minor; the most significant was the recommendation that newly commissioned officers attend IOBC prior to Ranger training. Noting that the academy's mission was to provide a broad military education rather than individual proficiency in the technical duties of junior officers, the Haines Board wanted all reviewers of its findings to know that these officers were not ready for troop duty upon graduation and commissioning.[14] Considerable discussion was provided on this issue, as if the members knew that it would be controversial. The board agonized over the length of such a course and wanted to recognize the superior quality of the USMA graduate over the ROTC graduate who would attend the same course. As a compromise, the group recognized Distinguished Military Graduates from military colleges such as Texas A&M, the Citadel, and Virginia Military Institute as being equivalent in quality to graduates of West Point, and thus deserving of inclusion in IOBC classes of a shorter length, prior to Ranger training. Other ROTC graduates would be grouped together for a longer version of IOBC, soon to be renamed the Combat Platoon Leader Course.[15]

The other main recommendation of the board regarding the academy was the strong suggestion that West Point broaden its teaching of the social sciences, particularly psychology and sociology. Noting that the only required psychology course was taught under the aegis of the Tactical Department and that sociology was offered only as an elective later in a cadet's academic career, the board questioned why the two were not linked together, since both pertained to interaction with troops.[16] The board suggested offering such courses earlier in a cadet's career, and West Point not only changed its curriculum to accommodate this recommendation but also began the transition toward behavioral science and humanities offerings that were considered by some as equally important to the army's needs as engineering and science. The only other comment by the board regarding the academy was positive recognition of the imminent expansion of West Point, which had recently received congressional approval, and that the Corps of Cadets would grow from 2,529 to 4,417.[17]

While it offered minimal comments about West Point, the Haines Board had considerable concern about ROTC. Recognizing that the army then procured 66 percent of its officers through this program[18] and that it was the least costly of all other commissioning sources,[19] the board delved deeply into improving this program.

Perhaps the Haines Board's greatest achievement was its identification of the primary needs of the newly commissioned officer. The military establishment probably perceived this, but until a prestigious board published its findings, understanding the problems of newly commissioned ROTC officers within a combat environment was difficult.

Some means is needed to assist the new non-OCS officer in bridging the gap from the mental attitude of a college senior to the mental attitude of a commissioned member of the profession of arms, charged with responsibility for the lives of as many as 40 men and for as much as $1,000,000 worth of equipment. Even within the military profession, the Marine Corps is the only other Service wherein the officer is assigned to a leadership position immediately on joining his unit. Standing before a platoon of seasoned soldiers, with a beribboned platoon sergeant in charge, the young second lieutenant faces in that moment a challenge of large dimension. This moment, like many to come, is one of psychological trauma which the new second lieutenant must meet with equanimity. He must rise to the challenge; he must inspire in those with whom he works a sense of respect for his judgment and leadership. He wants and deserves to be treated like an *officer and gentleman*.[20]

How best, then, could the army accomplish this task of preparing, at that time, two-thirds of its new officers for combat missions?

The board recognized that its charge did not necessarily include pre-commissioning education, but it offered comments where such preparation affected its recommendation on army schools. Such was the case with the ROTC collegiate program. The board questioned the reduction in military courses designed to prepare a student for officer branch assignments while instead offering a general military science background to all students. While the board recognized that this change had pleased academicians and college presidents, and perhaps had made ROTC programs more acceptable on college campuses nationwide, such alterations had significantly challenged the army school system.[21] The OBC thus became much more critical to the officer's successful education, because it was the only real training he would receive to prepare him to lead troops in combat. Unit schools or on-the-job training were dismissed conveniently as "not a panacea for the early entry training of large numbers of newly commissioned officers."[22]

So the board concentrated on the OBC. It criticized the current efforts of the schools to teach by lecture and suggested minimal classroom time, because "hands-on" experience was critical, whether dealing with weapons, leadership, or tactics. And it stressed that the schools should not try to teach excessively, confining the curriculum to only those skills that an officer would need in his first six months of duty. Perhaps the board was naive, because with Vietnam looming as the second tour-of-duty station for most graduates of the OBC, the training they would receive in this course would have to prepare them for combat.

The board also recommended an increase in the length of the course: nine weeks for those not attending Ranger school, and five weeks for those attending either Ranger or Airborne school. The one area it did not address was the question of the importance of physical and mental stress on the student. One can assume by its absence of comment that it did not believe that these students required a simulation of combat stress as was provided at the USMA and through OCS. The board did, however, reserve its highest praise in terms of providing officers ready to assume troop command to OCS. And to this source of commissioning it could not have been more complimentary.

While frequently commenting on the army's desire for college-educated officers, the board recognized that OCS did not always get such a man. "Due to the Vietnam build-up, the army has embarked on a greatly expanded OCS program in an effort to remedy the situation [the shortage of platoon leaders]. In doing so, it is accepting a long term disadvantage in the lower educational level of the average OCS graduate as compared to the ROTC graduate. This is somewhat offset by the fact that the OCS program produces well trained and well motivated second lieutenants who generally remain in the service after completion of their obligated tours."[23] In approaching issues of training, the board recognized that only OCS specifically emphasized preparation of soldiers for branch duty.[24] And furthermore, "probably the best prepared of all newly commissioned officers for immediate duty assignment are OCS graduates. After living and training in a disciplined military environment 24 hours a day for 23 weeks, they are clearly ready to assume the duties of a second lieutenant."[25]

An analysis of the training regimen at OCS provided the board with the evidence to support such a claim. Leadership courses were an element common to all three commissioning sources, and the USMA cadets received 727 hours of pre-commissioning instruction; ROTC candidates received 189; and OCS, only 87. However, the USMA and ROTC officers, upon commissioning, received only an additional 29½ hours of leadership instruction. The board did not consider this to be as beneficial as the 87 hours received by OCS candidates, because such instruction was not given in a disciplined environment.[26] Thus the simulated combat stress was considered a beneficial factor that could not be duplicated in OBC.

Nowhere in the Haines Board report is there criticism of the younger age of OCS candidates, although this early in the buildup, the threefold increase in OCS class size had not yet reached fruition. Nowhere in the Haines Board report is there criticism of the inability of the OCS program to teach non–college graduates the rudiments of military leadership. And nowhere in the

Haines Board report is there concern about the quality of the candidate in the ocs program. But there is also no reference to morals, ethics, or other leadership issues that would become a concern when the next board would meet in ten years.

Concurrent with the Haines Board's study, the army's proclivity toward functioning redundancy was apparent when the Department of Defense's educational advisor, Rolfe L. Allen, had to "weigh in" on the subject. Without knowing whether he was asked to participate, he produced a document titled "Trained Manpower in the U.S. Army." A review of his report indicates that few of his recommendations found their way into the final Haines Board report, but the study is particularly noteworthy for a couple of critical points. Allen believed that ocs had been perpetuated for only two reasons: to keep alive the state of the art begun by Gen. George Marshall in World War I and continued under Gen. Omar Bradley in World War II, and because it gave "lip service" to the concept that "every soldier of France has a Marshal's baton in his knapsack."[27] In other words, enlisted men should always know that they can become officers if they perform their duties at the highest level. Allen also stated, "It is quite obvious, considering the varied purposes behind the three sources of officers, and their several techniques, that the input is not homogeneous. Actually, the mix is surprisingly effective. This probably arises from the average high level of ability and dedication of the young men involved, rather than from the uniform quality or policy of the training program."[28]

The Haines Board issued its final report in 1966, but several years passed before its findings made their way through official channels, and there was a certain amount of dovetailing of other education issues. For example, psychology and sociology courses had been recommended for cadets at West Point, and the board believed that students with these majors who were commissioned through rotc should be assigned to combat arms branches, because such educational preparation would be useful for officers in combat situations. Such changes were made, with 29 percent assigned during fy1966, 41 percent in fy1967, and 79 percent in fy1968.[29] Whether these increased behavioral science assignments were driven by the Haines Board or by Vietnam attrition, the result was the presence of more 2nd and 1st lieutenants in combat whose education had included human relationship skills. Thus, the Haines Board's report did have an impact.

Another ten years would pass before the army would again study the education system for its officers. This time the board was known as the

Review of Education and Training for Officers (RETO), and it was created in 1975 to study the army's needs in the post-Vietnam era. While acknowledging the West Point cheating scandal of 1976, and the change from specific-branch OCS programs to branch-immaterial OCS as being studied by other commissions, RETO focused on career officers and ROTC. By this time, ROTC was providing more than 80 percent of the new officer corps for what was essentially a peacetime army, and the greatest concern of the board was what kind of student was joining ROTC. "The winning of a baccalaureate degree sets the proper quality standard for pre-commissioning education, and general education in the liberal arts or sciences is enough focus for most officers. . . . And yet none of this preparation is enough if the officer candidates have not begun to develop a deep respect for the dignity and worth of each human being — even if living in a village like My Lai."[30]

There it was. An official army document recognizing that the selection process was critical to avoidance of the Lt. William Laws Calley issue. Like the previously mentioned study by Rolfe L. Allen, RETO had determined that training can only do so much, and careful solicitation leading to qualified candidates volunteering to serve as officers became the focus of RETO's ROTC section. It focused on concerns that the ROTC programs failed to measure medical status, physical fitness, leadership potential, or motivation for the military, and it recommended that Armed Forces Enlistment and Examination Centers, the same locations that were screening applicants for USMA and the volunteer army, could become centers for ROTC assessment.[31] Such a screening process would eliminate candidates who desired to become officers but who did not meet the army's standards. A program to attract those whom the army wanted but who had not applied was essential.

RETO was an attempt to improve the army's junior officer corps. What was driving this concern five years after the end of the U.S. active involvement in Vietnam? My Lai has already been mentioned, and the Electrical Engineering 304 cheating scandal at West Point was in the news. Even though West Point had expanded its output to nearly 1,000 graduates per year in 1964, it still furnished a small fraction of the officers commissioned each year.[32] But these officers were often the most visible, assigned to the elite units, and the nation's eyes were usually focused on such officers, as well as on the famous institution.

When the cheating scandal broke in 1976, the chief of staff of the army appointed a commission called the West Point Study Group to look into what was wrong with the USMA.[33] The commission's conclusions were sweeping, but one critical assessment was similar to that of the RETO study: the academy had "slackened its pursuit of excellence," which allowed marginal students to still graduate. How did the academy begin to recruit marginal students? In light of the Electrical Engineering 304 cheating scandal, the committee observed that West Point was concerned about attrition; therefore, it was not as demanding of the cadets.[34] All of this, it seems, was an outgrowth of the selection process that began during the Vietnam War. These cadets would have been those selected as the war was winding down.

DURING THE VIETNAM WAR, the army contracted with George Washington University to conduct numerous studies of its activities. Most of the work was focused on behavioral issues and included such diverse subjects as "How to Teach the Use of the M-79 Grenade Launcher," "How to Conduct Small Unit Patrolling," and "How to Avoid Booby Traps and Mines." Working under the name HUMRRO, or Human Resources Research Office, the organization studied anything the army requested.[35] Among its studies, "An Analysis of Seven U.S. Army Officer Candidate Schools" attempted to identify the problems inherent in OCS at the apex of both interest and enrollment.[36] The findings of this civilian organization were consistent with the earlier assessment of the Haines Board, but in some ways the HUMRRO study found that OCS was succeeding in spite of its inherent problems. HUMRRO recognized that there had been a rapid change in the type of candidate that was being trained in 1967 versus 1965, because these later students did not have the enlisted background of previous classes and were likely draftees, and younger.[37] However, the report made this claim:

> Even though the accent on youth has created difficulties, it should be noted that of graduates of the three major sources of commissioning it is the OCS graduate who is considered by senior commanders as the best trained for platoon-level troop duty, in the initial duty assignment. This was the case in World War II, during the Korean Conflict and remains so at the present time. The concentrated six-month program of training that comprises the current OCS schedule is able to focus instruction at the platoon leader level. As a result, the average OCS graduate is a technically trained leader, well qualified to assume an appropriate company-level assignment.[38]

HUMRRO was interested in identifying the deficiencies in OCS, in light of the changing demographics of the student body. It was particularly concerned that more time was spent in the assessment of a leader's ability than in the development of leaders. This created particular problems because more than 50 percent of the assessment process consisted of evaluations by the candidates themselves, and they were not experienced evaluators of leadership. HUMRRO recommended strengthening the TAC officer rating system and allowing the USAIS instructional staff to play a role in leadership evaluation.

HUMRRO was also critical of the reliance on what a leader *is* rather than on what he *does*, which led to the constant use of pressure-induced stress.[39] The army assumed that the ability to handle induced stress was the greatest predictor of effective combat leadership, an assumption that HUMRRO was not able to prove. But the report concentrated heavily on this issue because the inducement of stress was a central part of the OCS experience, dating back to World War II. However, in that era, TAC officers were frequently wounded combat veterans who were sent back to the States from Europe or the Pacific theater to utilize their battle experiences to train new officers. Such combat-hardened soldiers, according to the theory, could easily assess the degree to which stress should become part of the training process. Because of the critical shortage of junior officers during the Vietnam War era, TAC officers were usually recent graduates of OCS, albeit officers who had graduated near the top of their class. They had no combat experience and thus could only imagine the degree of stress that would be required to simulate the pressures of the battlefield. So they created psychological stress to supplement the physical stress that was already a major part of the program. This psychological stress could never duplicate the environment of the battlefield, and HUMRRO's own investigations confirmed this thesis.

In early 1965, as America was planning to send large numbers of combat units to Vietnam, HUMRRO conducted a study for the army to determine how best to train troops for combat. The study, "Confidence Development during Training," focused on the twin drivers of combat behavior: confidence and despair. Confidence was the attitude characterized by anticipation of successful control of one's environment, and despair was the anticipation of the loss of control of one's environment.[40] HUMRRO concluded that behavior in combat was a function of knowledge and skills and the relative strength of the two opposing attitudes of confidence and despair. Nothing in the study concluded that simulated stress was necessary to develop confidence or to decrease the likelihood of despair.

Stress was, however, a predictor of how much a candidate desired a commission, and it was a factor in the "weeding out" process. Those who could not take it quit and were usually labeled as incapable of handling the leadership demands placed on them by the program. And the physical stress was necessary to determine who could handle the rigors, if not the emotions, of combat. HUMRRO recommended that stress continue to be a major part of the OCS program, but that the TAC officers should be aware of the lack of evidence to support the contention that those who could not take it should not necessarily be eliminated from the program if they were able to handle the physical and academic extremes of the course.[41]

The HUMRRO study was an attempt to improve on what the army felt was one of its premier programs. OCS had stress similar to the academy's, and it had academics like ROTC's. What it was most proud of, however, was the ability of the program to "ramp up" to meet the army's needs and to accomplish this with enlisted soldiers, even though most of them had been in the army for only a few months. As the war progressed, it was OCS that began to contribute an ever-increasing percentage of the officers, and the army appears to have been extraordinarily satisfied with its graduates.

The army was confident in its ability to measure performance at its various schools and had commissioned an early study to determine the relative achievements of its graduates. Since all newly commissioned infantry officers attended the USAIS at some point early in their careers, that school was chosen for an evaluation of technical knowledge and skills attained through IOBC, Ranger School, and OCS. The study was done by the Analysis and Review Branch Office of the Director of Instruction at the USAIS in January 1965 and was published as "Report on Survey of Military Knowledge and Skills of Recently Commissioned 2nd Lieutenants."[42] The survey was designed to measure the performance of the instructional staff more than of the students and to help determine whether IOBC was necessary for recently commissioned officers of West Point.

Since graduates of all three schools took similar but not identical examinations, the army felt that comparisons would be appropriate. The IOBC students took an examination called the Basic Officer Course Military Stakes Examination, a five-hour practical exercise conducted in the field at the end of the nine-week course. The candidates in OCS were given a "different version of the same examination," which was two three-hour tests based on the content of the previously identified exam.[43] The tests were given to a population of more than 1,200, or all of the newly commissioned 2nd lieutenants at the USAIS in FY1964 and some in FY1965.

The results must have shocked the instructors of the USAIS, because OCS graduates scored higher than both the USMA and the college graduates in the IOBC programs. The results were USMA, 57.1 percent; IOBC, 48.1 percent; OCS, 70.3 percent.[44] The explanation given for the USMA graduates achieving higher scores than the IOBC graduates was that the Ranger Course that they all attended raised their scores by eleven percentage points. No explanation was offered for the higher scores by OCS candidates. And the army readily identified the credibility of the tests and the study but failed to publish conclusions with the report, other than that the Ranger Course helped prepare junior officers for combat. Perhaps the one-year service as enlisted soldiers prepared these men for the next period of their tour of duty as junior officers.

The army probably made no further evaluations of these scores because it was satisfied that the OCS program was doing its job and that the Ranger Course was necessary for men who had not attended OCS. And the comparative scores satisfied the army that the quality of the soldier attending OCS was equal to that attending the other programs, at least as far as attainment of necessary platoon leader skills was concerned. Although this survey and report was based on soldiers who entered the programs at the outset of the Vietnam War buildup, it did recognize the relative academic achievement of the students of each program. An examination of soldiers who did not make it through the programs would provide an indicator of the army's propensity to make certain only those who were qualified would be commissioned.

ATTRITION FROM THE VARIOUS commissioning sources varied throughout the Vietnam War era. Since West Point provided few officers, statistically (approximately 5 percent), the number who did not make it through the program is relatively insignificant.[45] And one had to elect to leave ROTC, as many did as the war intensified. (See figure 2.1.) The most important attrition numbers would be found in the officer candidate schools, and more important than the numbers would be trends of failure as well as the reasons for such failure. The USAIS kept detailed records of each class of Infantry Officer Candidate School.

Table 4.1 summarizes the increasing and decreasing enrollment at Infantry OCS in the early days of the war, during the buildup, and in the post-TET period. As is depicted, the attrition rate was relatively high throughout the entire war, even though there was a high demand for infantry platoon leaders.

An examination of the reasons for attrition reveals that academic failures were never significant, even though the army kept the entrance exam re-

TABLE 4.1 ATTRITION AT OCS AND REASONS, 1962-1972

	1962-64	1965-68	1969-72
Total students (no.)	3,268	24,682	18,366
Failures (no.)	1,052	6,549	6,012
Attrition (%)	32	27	33
Recycles (no.)	265	1,931	1,681
Recycles (%)	8	8	9
Reasons (%)*	—	1	0.5
Academic			
Discipline	5	6.5	1.6
Leadership	43	30	22
Personal	3	30	58
Physical	11	6	2
Lack of application	29	23	—

Source: Office of Assistant Commandant, "Review and Analysis, 4th Quarter,"
FY62-73, DRL Archives.
*Percentages do not total 100 due to multiple minor reasons.

quirements constant throughout the war. Candidates who qualified were able to achieve scores on ocs examinations in the various skills that were sufficient to keep them in the program, or they were able to take advantage of the remedial offerings to make certain they stayed enrolled.[46]

Physical and medical failures were also rare at ocs. Even though physical stress was significant throughout the eleven-year period being evaluated, the army reported few candidates' failures because of an inability to handle the physical demands of the program. Vietnam veteran Ed Vallo affirmed the army's attitude toward medical issues. He was accepted into engineering ocs at Fort Belvoir, Virginia, on an eyesight waiver in the fall of 1969. After three days, he was pulled from formation and told that he did not meet the physical requirements to become an officer, and he was almost immediately given orders for Vietnam. He filed a breach of contract complaint with the army and, after a four-month delay, was given a new class. Being disenchanted with the army, he turned it down and went to Vietnam as an NCO.[47] Thus, the army dealt severely even with those who wanted to be officers during the 1965-69 period, even though platoon leaders were in short supply in Vietnam.

Candidates who failed to receive commissions at Infantry ocs during the buildup to the war usually had leadership deficiencies. The breakdown of attrition causes does not reveal whether the deficiencies were attributable to peer review or TAC officer review, but the broad category of leadership deficiencies is used throughout the reports for all schools. Obviously, the army placed a high degree of importance on this quality. In the early years, 43 percent of candidates who were not commissioned had leadership deficiencies, and the percentage stayed high through 1968, when it dropped to 30. The number stayed in the 20 percent range throughout the war. Even during the period of greatest enrollment, 1965–68, the army continued to "weed out" the candidates at the rate of one of every three who entered, which was much higher than that at any other infantry school.[48]

Candidates also did not graduate because of personal reasons. While the army does not define "personal," previously cited sources indicate that the army's policy of allowing a candidate to refuse his commission, thus shortening his tour of duty, caused great consternation at the highest levels. This policy was changed late in the war, but it was a concern even in 1965 when the Artillery ocs at Fort Sill, Oklahoma, began to notice a large number of candidates dropping out prior to commissioning. The army's inquiry focused on the longer term of service, two years and ten months rather than only two years. This artillery issue appears to be different from that of Infantry ocs, because these candidates were dropping out before they ever got involved in the program.[49] But personal issues were a reason for soldiers refusing commissions before or during ocs.

"Personal" would be the appropriate category if a candidate could not "take it," whether for psychological, sociological, or physical reasons. This would also be the category if a candidate quit because he did not believe he could lead men in combat, or if he was distraught over the idea of being a platoon leader, or if he opposed the war from an ideological viewpoint. That use of this category increases so significantly at the time of the TET Offensive and afterward gives some credence to the likelihood that reality had set in for these candidates. However, "bayonet sheets" usually eliminated those whose ideas ran contrary to what peers believed were essential leadership attributes, because no one would want to serve with such a person in combat.[50]

Even though the army experienced many terminations from ocs, it continued to turn back or recycle nearly 1,000 candidates per year at Fort Benning.[51] Whether these students ultimately received commissions is not known, but the USAIS recognized that they were not ready for commissioning and placed them in another class, even though the officer shortage was apparent and pressure to produce platoon leaders for Vietnam was being exerted from Washington.

If attrition and turn-back are combined from 1962 to 1972, the rate of those not receiving a commission from their beginning class ranges from a low of 35 percent in 1965–68 to 42 percent in 1969–72 (see table 4.1). Thus a candidate had less than a 67 percent chance of successfully completing the program once he entered. It certainly begs the question that if the army knew that it could not meet the needs of commanders in Vietnam for platoon leaders to lead units into combat, why did it continue to eliminate one of every three soldiers who wanted to be commissioned? Why not make the program easier, or at least eliminate the psychological stress associated with the program?[52]

Candidates who went through ocs after the TET Offensive may have had it easier than their predecessors. An *Army Digest* article in 1970 quoted a colonel in the Pentagon as saying that ocs was "changing with the times," adding, "That means it's getting easier."[53] But with changes that eliminated square meals, low crawling to the mess hall, and shaved heads came an increase in the attrition rate, not the expected decrease.

> Our class started out 169 guys when we started, signed in at noon on Saturday. By Monday night at eight o'clock we had 39 guys resign from the program. . . . When we got into surveying we probably lost 15–20 guys that couldn't pass surveying, and then we started gunnery and every cycle that we went we'd drop some guys. What they did was if you were academically weak but you had strong leadership skills, they would give you the option to recycle; go back to the point where you start having academic difficulty and continue. But, if you were weak in leadership and academics they wouldn't let you do that. They'd just kick you out, and you'd disappear. I mean you'd go to class one morning and then come back and all of a sudden the guy's bedroll was in an S shape. . . . So, we graduated 40 of 169 in 26 weeks.[54]

Said Russell Hiett in a 2001 interview, "I think we started off with 250 men in the company and graduated something like 125. The attrition rate was strong and we played, little did we know, the first survivor game that years later became popular on TV and that is at the end of every month or every week, I'm pretty sure it was every week, we voted somebody 'off the island.' "[55]

The army continued to create physical stress and whatever psychological stress was appropriate for the particular training regimen being conducted, but it attempted to eliminate what soldiers called the "chicken shit"[56] or "Mickey Mouse" stuff. Spit-shining a floor by hand versus using a polishing machine would exemplify this concern. With the increasing number of older college graduates attending ocs, it is reasonable to assume that the changes were made to give the appearance of an army that was interested only in the amount of stress necessary to efficiently create a combat platoon leader.

IT WAS TRADITIONAL AT the usais for the outgoing commandant to assess the performance of the school and pass that information to his successor. This was done through a mass mailing to the commanding generals of all of the infantry divisions. Maj. Gen. John Heintges left the school in July 1965, just as American troops were being deployed in significant numbers to Vietnam. His successor, Maj. Gen. Robert H. York, a Vietnam veteran, was the recipient of many letters, mostly complimentary, about the 2nd lieutenants the infantry divisions were receiving. All of these units were either in conus, Alaska, the Canal Zone, or Hawaii; thus none could yet comment on the efficiency of junior officers in combat. The various commanders were satisfied with their newly commissioned officers as garrison soldiers.[57] Some highlighted the need for more map-reading courses;[58] some were concerned about the need for more courses on the importance of maintenance of machinery and weapons.[59] But in the early days of the troop buildup, the army was satisfied that its officers, whether they were commissioned from West Point, ROTC, or ocs, were doing the job they had been trained to do. "Most newly commissioned officers approach military service with a good attitude and enthusiasm, in spite of the fact that for the large majority of them, this period interrupts their career. . . . I am convinced that the young officers are better trained today than I was on my first assignment as a second lieutenant," wrote Maj. Gen. George A. Carver, commander of the U.S. Army in Alaska.[60] And Maj. Gen. Martin H. Foery, commanding general of the New York Army National Guard, believed that "in light of experience, it is the opinion of the commanders at all levels that attendance at ocs, Fort Benning, is the most desirable method of securing a commission. Graduates are well oriented, versed in fundamentals, and develop leadership and other qualities much more rapidly than officers derived from other sources."[61]

THE ARMY SEEMED SATISFIED that it was "getting it done" at the outset of the war. But combat is different from garrison, and the real test of the selection, training, and evaluation processes would come in the jungles, rice paddies, and villages of Vietnam, where being an officer and a gentleman would be exceedingly tested. To the army's credit, within a few days of the deployment of the 173rd Airborne Brigade to Vietnam, the infantry school began lobbying CONUS for permission to send a liaison team to Vietnam to "establish direct liaison between the United States Military Assistance Command — Vietnam, 173rd Airborne Brigade, 3rd Marine Amphibious Force and the United States Army Infantry School."[62] Maj. John W. Kent, chairman of the Counterinsurgency Committee at USAIS, was to be the officer to conduct this tour of temporary duty. But with typical army bureaucratic "wrangling," the approval for the trip was a major problem: "I am sorry that I was unable to jar the Kent trip loose for you. The matter had gone too far before I got into it, and some noted hard heads had made their minds up. . . . My suggestion would be to justify solely on the basis of producing a problem for presentation to classes now loaded with next summer's replacements for Vietnam."[63] The infantry school wanted the best information it could obtain to determine if its programs were meeting the needs of combat leaders, but the bureaucracy in CONUS resisted a trip that would gather valuable data.

By March 1966, the army recognized the need to send not one man or even a small team to Vietnam but, rather, to dispatch large teams that would meet with commanders, junior officers, and NCOs to evaluate the output of the various schools who were actively engaging the enemy. The responses of the combat leaders and troops reflected the very specific problems that soldiers in combat experienced every day: the need to stress personal hygiene in BCT and AIT, and the use of technical skills associated with hand grenades and avoidance of punji stakes, mines, and booby traps. The visits were conducted each year, and the comments reflected the changing nature of the war: "Stress hand-to-hand combat; a soldier should know how to kill a man with his bare hands. The American soldier has a big advantage against the small and light Viet Cong."[64] Six months after this liaison visit, another team of investigators reviewed the armor, artillery, and engineering school graduates in Vietnam. Commanders reported great satisfaction with both enlisted men and officers who had been assigned as replacements to the various units being reviewed. But there were some comments that indicated that the war was beginning to change, and that the training which previously worked was no longer applicable: "Although junior officer training was highly praised, the independent or decentralized operations in Vietnam require more emphasis in gunnery procedures" and "USMA and Distinguished Military Graduates without the advantage of branch school found themselves seriously impaired to perform required duties."[65] Both of these comments came early in the buildup and represent frustration in the combat behavior of the enemy, which required the U.S. units to fight with smaller units, thus requiring better leadership from its junior officers.

The liaison team that visited Vietnam in December 1966 conducted surveys with several new divisions that had recently deployed, with the largest being the 25th Infantry Division at Cu Chi. The commanders were very complimentary about the platoon leaders being assigned to them: "The young officer replacements are very good — much better than the ones we received earlier at Scofield Barracks. [This was the division's headquarters near Honolulu, Hawaii.] We are not worried about the officer replacements as much as we are the old non-commissioned officer."[66] Since the division had only been in-country a few months, it had not yet had enough time to analyze the quality of its leadership, nor had it begun to sustain leadership losses.[67] The 1st Infantry Division, which had been in Vietnam six months longer than the 25th and had begun to sustain losses, stated that "50% of our casualties are officers, NCOs and radio operators. The OCS graduate normally does an excellent job and seems to be ahead of the ROTC graduate initially."[68] And the commanding general of the 1st Infantry Division stated that "Benning needs to build up the confidence of young lieutenants — don't lead him by the hand."[69]

The army unit that had been in Vietnam the longest was the 173rd Airborne Brigade, and the comments of the commander regarding the use of firepower were particularly revealing: "Much of the war in Vietnam is being fought at the squad and platoon level, thus *all* soldiers should be trained to call and adjust indirect fires."[70] The commander's comments reflected the frustration of senior leadership that knew how efficient the organic firepower of the unit could be, but the officer on the ground had to request it from the rear base if artillery and gunships were to be effective. Since the 173rd had been in some of the most intensive action of the war, these comments were particularly relevant to the kind of war being fought until 1967.

By mid-1967, the buildup was complete, and the visiting liaison teams found an army with very specific recommendations for the training of both officers and enlisted men. "The young replacement officer is fairly well trained with the edge to the OCS graduate in self-confidence. He knows the rules and routine of the platoon. Our young officers and senior NCOs are too aggressive — which makes it hard to keep them alive."[71] Further, "U.S. Army forces in Vietnam are not employing anti-vehicle mines, thus this instruction should be replaced by more practical work on Claymore mines and detection of VC weapons such as booby traps, trip flares and the CHICOM Claymore mine. Bayonets are not used in action; therefore such training should be eliminated."[72] (This recommendation was not adopted then or later because bayonet training has always been considered a major part of instilling ferociousness and in building self-confidence and spirit. Also, at the Battle of the Ia Drang Valley in November 1965, bayonets were employed to stop PAVN regular forces on the attack.)[73]

The most critical comments in the 1967 liaison visit were directed at NCOs, who were called the "weakest link — NCOs should be provided refresher leadership training and physical conditioning prior to assignment to ARVN [Army of the Republic of Vietnam]."[74] This statement was qualified by senior officers who believed that senior NCOs were being "punished" by newly commissioned OCS officers who were in excellent physical shape after the completion of OCS, as contrasted with older NCOs who had not had troop duty for some time. This comment would tend to draw a distinction between the physical preparation for combat that was inherent in OCS and the lack of preparation of soldiers in general, particularly that of older NCOs who would have been sent directly to Vietnam without any courses that would have made them better prepared for the rigors of combat.

By mid-1968 many of the previously mentioned deficiencies had been corrected, particularly those involving NCOs. With more soldiers attending NCOs school at the USAIS and fewer career NCOs in field operations, there would have been a change in the relationships between the squad leaders of a platoon and the platoon leader. The 199th Light Infantry Brigade leaders indicated they were "quite pleased with the NCOC graduate and the junior officer. . . . They were not as strong disciplinarians as we would like them to be."[75] The 25th Infantry Division interviewees were cognizant of the problems they had just experienced during TET, because they were the unit that suffered high casualties as the VC began their attacks on Cu Chi and Saigon.[76] "This battalion averaged two officers per Rifle Company," stated one battalion staff officer, "and we had to rely on NCOs graduates as small unit leaders."[77] None of the units questioned in the summer of 1968 provided disparaging remarks about the junior officers they were receiving as in-country replacements, other than to state that all junior leaders had to be given additional map-reading training once they had arrived at their assigned duty stations. This extensive report, which included all operating divisions in Vietnam, failed to identify any leadership problems that may have arisen from the increase in the intensity of the fighting.

In 1969 the liaison team found respondents aware of the difficulty that junior officers were experiencing in the changing nature of the war. "The switch to small unit operations does not represent a decrease in the tempo of the war. . . . It is much more difficult for a lieutenant or sergeant to operate independently day and night than it is to spend most of the time on operations as an interior element of a company or battalion formation."[78] But the harshest criticism was reserved for junior officers whose motivation to lead was questioned: "Several commanders expressed criticism of the dedication to duty of a significant number of lieutenants. No solution for this disturbing problem was offered, but most units felt that ocs graduates had an edge on ROTC graduates because they were forced to exercise authority in their CONUS assignment."[79] And Maj. Gen. Melvin Zais, commanding general of the 101st Airborne Division, was critical of training that stressed technical skills without the leadership skills so necessary in combat. "One who asserts himself and strongly exercises his authority will be much more effective than one who is more technically proficient but less willing to take charge."[80]

Zais and others expressed some concern over the type of officer that was being sent to them at this later stage of the war. There has been a great deal of research done on the type of soldier that went to Vietnam late in the war, but there have been few studies on junior officers. One such study was conducted by Douglas Kinnard, who had served two tours in Vietnam, his last as a brigadier general of II Field Force Artillery and chief of staff of II Field Force Vietnam. His research was published in 1977 as *The War Managers: American Generals Reflect on Vietnam*, and he was the first to ask senior leadership a variety of questions about their wartime experience. The book was based on a questionnaire that General Kinnard sent to every general-grade officer who had served in Vietnam. With a 64 percent return rate, the generals expressed serious reservations about subjects ranging from objectives to atrocities.[81] When discussing leadership, Kinnard assumed that the junior officer corps was deficient and that senior officers recognized this fact. In his research, he fielded the following responses:

Junior Officer Leadership (Captain and Lieutenant)
1) Improved throughout the war, 34 percent
2) Remained about the same throughout war, 30 percent
3) Deteriorated as the war went on, 32 percent
4) Other or no answer, 4 percent.[82]

Kinnard concluded that since two-thirds of the respondents were positive about junior officer leadership, such officers must have done an adequate job. And if the other one-third knew something was wrong, why was nothing done to correct the problem by changing tactics or training?

In an interview I conducted with Tony Nadal, commander of A Company, 1st Battalion of the 7th Air Cavalry, who fought at the Battle of the Ia Drang Valley in November 1965, he stated that his platoon leaders — all college and ocs graduates — were the "best he ever saw in my entire military career."[83] All of them were killed or wounded in that battle.

Vietnam training did evolve throughout the war. The analysis of junior officer performance, particularly of officers who had just arrived in-country, was mixed, but most commanders appeared to have been satisfied that the junior officers they received were capable leaders. They did, however, bring with them their experiences from the civilian world, whether from the streets of America or college campuses. And these experiences determined how they interfaced with the soldiers they were leading into battle. In the second part of this book, the junior officer's performance will be examined within the context of the war itself.

PART TWO

It was not a simple matter of kill or be killed, I had to think of my men. I could not let them be killed because of a rigid morality on my part. But if I compromised with that morality too often, I would become little more than a war criminal, unfit to lead those men. I had to struggle to keep a sense of balance.

JAMES R. MCDONOUGH

Platoon Leader

VIETNAM

Map 1 Southeast Asia, 1954–1975

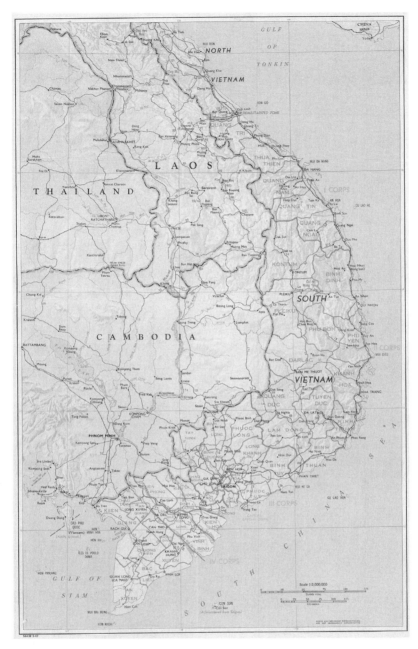

Map 2 South Vietnam, 1954–1975

FIVE TRAINING IN VIETNAM

*The duties and responsibilities faced by today's junior leaders
are perhaps the most difficult challenge that a young officer
has ever had to face in our nation's history. As a platoon leader
or company commander in the counterinsurgency environment —
specifically in the jungles of South Vietnam — where the nature of
the terrain quickly separates battalions into separate companies
and companies into wide-ranging platoons and squads — this
junior combat leader must still exercise control over his unit
and provide effective command direction.*[1]

■

*Due to the existing tactical situation, units rarely knew until
the last minute whether training would be formalized classroom
instruction or an all out practical exercise using the North
Vietnamese as training aids.*[2]

■

Junior officers assigned to a tour of duty in the Republic of Vietnam experienced the same emotional fireworks as enlisted soldiers when they embarked from the United States to the jungle-laden battlefields of Southeast Asia. Except for priority boarding on aircraft, similar to first-class patrons boarding first on today's airlines, junior officers were treated like any other soldier. "Passengers will board the aircraft through gate four in the following manner: all officers and civilians of equivalent rank, followed by all staff NCOs, followed by other enlisted personnel."[3] For most combat arms lieutenants, this would be the first and last time in their tour that they would recognize some bureaucratic favor inherent to their rank, and it would signal the beginning of a year in which they would forget the luxuries of rank and become more like the men they commanded.

In commercial aircraft bearing names such as Flying Tiger, Braniff, and World Airways, with "stewardesses" serving four meals and trying to act cheerful through forced smiles, approximately 2.7 million men and 60,000 women flew from Travis Air Force Base near Oakland, California, to Tan Son Nhut or Bien Hoa air bases near Saigon.[4] This eighteen- to twenty-four-hour flight might stop in Honolulu, Hawaii; Guam; Wake Islands; Marshall Islands; Okinawa, Japan; or Clark Air Force Base in the Philippine Islands, depending on the type of aircraft. But with each stop, the anticipation of battle was heightened among the passengers. And the "stewardesses" were very much part of the acculturation process: "I remember this one stewardess saying to me, 'If you want to know what Vietnam is like, look at the face of the guys that get on the aircraft who've been here a year.' I won't ever forget her saying that."[5]

Most soldiers were surprised that they were not exposed to enemy fire upon arrival. With few exceptions, such as landing at night during a VC rocket attack, soldiers usually experienced a landing similar to that at a major airport in any American city. Hollywood has provided many images of these arrivals, such as that in Oliver Stone's *Platoon* in which the passengers' first visual images are of body bags on the tarmac and bullet-ridden aircraft being readied for repair.[6] And many veterans' journals have described that first experience similarly: "If that's what bullets do to airplanes, what would they do to me? The answer was provided by a forklift off loading supplies nearby. It carried a stack of aluminum boxes that resembled huge tool chests. They were coffins," wrote Philip Caputo in *A Rumor of War*.[7] But most soldiers experienced a much less intense arrival than they had anticipated. "I mean, I suppose we all expected that we were going to be shot at. I mean, we all were pretty dead serious. We had out our steel pots and field gear and everything else and then when you get off there and you find that there are these Air Force guys lying in their T-shirts in the weeds sleeping and drinking cokes, smoking and joking and laughing and telling lies and laughing at us, you look around and after you were there you realized there was nothing happening."[8] Some of the units that deployed en masse were greeted by local women and children, particularly in the early days of the war.[9]

The most revolting sensory perception for soldiers was the smell of the country or, for those who had trained in bases like Fort Dix, New Jersey, and Fort Lewis, Washington, the heat and humidity.[10] "The first thing that strikes you when they open the doors, the heat is just pervasive. It's like putting on a wet coat, a wet hot coat."[11] Said Theodore Mataxis Jr., "As soon as they opened that damn door it's just like you're in a steam bath and someone wraps you in a wool, wet blanket. Just that hot muggy thing. It's just something that hits your skin and stays with you until you get out of country. The overwhelming heat. In fact I was naive at the time and I thought things can't get any hotter. Well, lessons learned in Vietnam, things can always get hotter."[12] But the smell was alien to all westerners and has been described as a combination of poor sanitation, defoliants, rotting dead fish (which was made into a sauce called *nuoc mam*)—and death. Because it was a war zone, the smell of death supposedly permeated the air. The rumor was that the smell was of bodies decaying, but such an odor should not have been prevalent at an airport. More likely it was created by decaying plant life from the jungle, since the triple canopy denied any exit of air, thus creating a sauna-type atmosphere that exaggerated the decay of both plant and animal life. And the smell of burning human waste was prevalent: "The smell of course was from the burning of waste from the outhouses. It seemed to permeate the air almost all the time in the rear."[13] "By the time we got off the tarmac into the Air Force terminal, our uniforms were all wringing wet. That, and the odor from where they were burning all the human waste, the odor of that was a big shock."[14] In an interview with Richard Verrone of the Vietnam Archive at Texas Tech University, Stephen Dant described the odor in vivid detail:

SD: That it was very hot, very muggy, and it smelled weird.

RV: What did it smell like?

SD: You know, kind of a cross between what I had smelled in Guam I guess in terms of tropics and you know I got my first whiff of burning human excrement.

RV: (laughter)

SD: What the hell is that? Then people tell you. You go, "You're kidding."

RV: The shit patrol.

SD: The shit patrol, yeah. You know they set up outhouses around and they would cut up oil drums and sit them under the toilet seat and then somebody would have the duty of pulling those oil drums full of shit out once or twice a day and they would pour kerosene and mix it in and set it on fire.[15]

The sights that greeted embarking soldiers drew sharp distinctions between Western culture and Vietnam. Peering through chicken wire–laced windows, designed to deflect hand grenades thrown by pedestrians, newly arriving men saw things that would shape their attitudes toward the Vietnamese: "At one point, the bus swerved out of the way of a girl riding a bicycle and then the driver jammed on the brakes to avoid running over a half naked Vietnamese kid. . . . We craned our necks to see what he was pointing at. It was a Vietnamese woman with her pants down, urinating in the gutter."[16] Such images remained with officers and enlisted men and ultimately contributed to the racist attitudes that developed over the course of one's tour of duty.

Buses transported incoming soldiers from Tan Son Nhut or Bien Hoa air bases to the 90th Replacement Depots at Long Binh, near Saigon (see map 2).[17] This "repo-depo" was a mammoth facility from which soldiers were assigned to the various units in the Saigon area (III Corps) and Mekong Delta area (IV Corps) that had requested personnel. The 22nd Replacement Depot at Cam Ranh Bay was responsible for requests from units operating in the Central Highlands area (II Corps), and a smaller facility at Da Nang met the needs of units operating near the Demilitarized Zone (DMZ) (I Corps).[18] All of these facilities functioned similarly, with soldiers standing in a line, waiting for orders to be cut to send them to the field. As Thomas Schultz described it, "They cut orders. If you can picture loading a cattle truck — we need ten cattle for steaks; we need ten for hamburger; we need ten for roasts. And the first ten in this line went to the 82d, the ten in this line went to the 1st Cav, and that's how you were cut."[19] Some soldiers even took the opportunity to change their MOS, if they thought doing so might keep them out of combat: "We had a situation where they needed some people in the mortar platoons. They had a lot of Eleven-Bush people, Eleven-Bravos, and if you were curious and wanted to learn to run an 81mm [mortar] or the 'Deuces' [4.2-inch mortars] you could go to a two week school, which was a cram course to familiarize you with the guns. I took that because I wanted to get as much 'sham time' as possible. That's why I was reassigned. The unit I was going to got hit hard and they needed a lot of men."[20] Of course, the military rumor mill was hyperactive, and soldiers dreaded hearing that a large number of 11-Bs were being sent to a particular unit, because they assumed that meant recent high casualty rates. Most soldiers also felt that the farther north they were assigned, the more likely they would experience extensive combat, even though statistically such a hypothesis is difficult to prove.[21]

Junior officers experienced a range of emotions at the various repo-depos, and they had fewer peers with whom to commiserate. Those possessing 1542 MOSS, or small-unit infantry commanders, were in demand throughout the war, and unlike enlisted men, they had little opportunity to change to a different MOS to avoid combat. "There is a shortage of infantry officers in Vietnam. For this reason, officers from the other branches should be used as division staff officers as much as possible. I realize that some positions require the experience of an infantry officer. However, officers in other branches can do an excellent job on the staff—use them," wrote the chief of staff of the 1st Infantry Division.[22] Thus, a 2nd lieutenant at a repo-depo was just waiting for assignment to a particular corps and infantry division; he already knew he would be a platoon leader. "And as you move mindlessly through the replacement system, the whim of an unseen clerk sends you to a unit in a quiet sector—or to a unit that will take its men like lambs to the slaughter," wrote James R. McDonough in his diary *Platoon Leader*.[23] A lieutenant would not know until he arrived at his duty station whether he was replacing a platoon leader who had been KIA, been WIA (wounded in action), or completed his tour of duty. Nor would he know anything about the troops he would soon command, such as their experience in combat or their propensity to fight. He would also lack knowledge about the command structure within the battalion, the logistical strength, aviation and artillery support, and rear-echelon staff duties and responsibilities. In essence, he would know nothing about his future, and he would wait for the decision of an anonymous clerk who would determine his fate.

Once assigned, the junior officer was usually sent to division or, infrequently, brigade headquarters, where he encountered a similar repo-depo; however, this one included a defensive perimeter of mines and concertina wire, artillery and logistics support, and an officers' club. Some units held elaborate welcoming parties for replacements, complete with the unit band playing inspiring battle music.[24] Others were more restrained, with a simple introductory speech by the ranking officer and a tour of the facilities. Regardless of the unit, however, an orientation course lasting several days was required of both junior officers and enlisted men, unless they had accumulated three months of previous combat experience. "With the exception of in-country transfer personnel who have a minimum of three months' combat duty, all newly assigned officers in the grade of lieutenant, warrant officer and enlisted men in grades up through sergeant first-class and platoon sergeant, will attend replacement training."[25] Complete with a packet of instructional materials outlining the duties of leaders, the 25th Infantry Division delved critically into necessary in-country training that it considered to be essential to the successful completion of its mission. "Today the division is actively engaged in combat and civic actions to deny communist expansion in this country. To do these things, you and other men of this division must be physically fit, practice the lessons and habits learned in training and operations, and be motivated to the task at hand. The leader who fails to exercise command and initiative and insure that his personnel are properly led will be guilty of sacrificing American lives needlessly in combat," wrote the commanding general, Maj. Gen. Fred C. Weyand.[26]

THE TRAINING REGIMEN FOR junior officers in Vietnam consisted of three distinctly different programs: orientation, which dealt with the various skills necessary for survival in jungle combat; environment leadership skills, which dealt with transferring that which was learned at either West Point, a civilian college or university, or Fort Benning into traits necessary in Vietnam; and unit training, wherein a newly arrived leader could work with his new command to achieve both confidence and expertise.

Orientation to the jungle combat environment was partially achieved just by time in-country. Some leaders estimated that it took up to one month in the heat and humidity of Vietnam for one's body to be able to function in the rigors of combat. Most divisions had an orientation program that included those items, as directed by Military Assistance Command, Vietnam (MACV), that would enable any soldier, enlisted or officer, to excel in combat:

a. Establishment of partial bases.
b. Saturation patrolling.
c. Establishment of area ambushes.
d. Immediate action drills.
e. Base, camp, and installation security.
f. Convoy organization and protection.
g. Handling of mines and booby traps.
h. Geneva Convention Training.
i. Coordination of naval gunfire.
j. Air-ground support techniques, both combat and logistical.[27]

Training in these key areas was designed to "avoid degradation of effectiveness occasioned by current rotation policies and subsequent loss of experienced personnel in key positions,"[28] but the army did not believe that changing the rotation policy would be beneficial to the war effort. The policy of six-month combat tours, followed by six months of rear-echelon staff duty, had been promulgated in the early days of the war and was never changed, except for junior officer advisors who served their entire year in the field. Six-month combat tours not only reduced the level of expertise in the field; they greatly exacerbated the training requirements of the units. The effect of such rotation policies on unit cohesion was pronounced and will be discussed in Chapter 8.

The MACV suggested training regimen included a POI on the Geneva Conventions, yet the 25th Infantry Division Replacement POI included only one hour of instruction on the Code of Conduct.[29] It appears that MACV was more insistent upon such courses being taught in the training programs of the Republic of Vietnam Armed Forces, where the POI included, "How to earn people's sympathy, confidence and support. Servicemen must respect discipline and good conduct. Codes of conduct concerning discipline and servicemen's conduct toward people. Why the VC try to win the support of people, attitude and treatment toward people, respecting and helping people."[30] This program, titled "Training Schedule for the Course, RVNAF Supports the Rural Reconstruction," was a more extensive POI on the interpersonal relations between soldier and civilian than anything conducted for American soldiers. But when dates of MACV directives are compared, it appears that an emphasis on Code of Conduct instruction began in August 1966 after previously being mentioned only briefly. An examination of infantry division files during this period indicates sporadic mention of such a course, and when conducted, such instruction was usually only one hour in length. One year of intensive fighting and the advent of the search-and-destroy mission may have led MACV to begin such a POI.

One of the more intensive programs of instruction regarding Code of Conduct was held at the headquarters of the 1st Infantry Division. Taught by an officer from the division Judge Advocate Office, the one-hour course addressed specifically the issues of war crimes and atrocities, as well as an individual's responsibilities under the Geneva Conventions.[31]

IF THE LAW OF LAND Warfare, Code of Conduct, and Geneva Conventions took such a small portion of the division training schedule, what courses were considered so important as to require the bulk of the training time? An examination of the replacement training schedule reveals that weapons training, particularly care and maintenance of the M-16A1 rifle, and the section on VC mines and booby traps consumed the predominant place in the POI. Most soldiers, including junior officers, had received training in the use of the new plastic weapon in CONUS, but learning to use the M-16 in the heat, humidity, and torrential rains of Vietnam was a major challenge. Although controversy existed from the outset as to the weapon's efficiency in jungle fighting, Gen. William Westmoreland was convinced that it was superior to the AK-47 that was used by both the PAVN and the VC. "It was admittedly a weapon, a weapon that had to be cleaned meticulously, and ordnance experts were able later to make some adjustments that improved performance;[32] but from the first M-16 in the hands of troops experienced in its use and care, it was a superb weapon."[33] "The M16 is the finest military rifle ever made. It's light-weight, easy to handle, and will put out a lot of lead. If you know it, respect it and treat it right, it will be ready when you need it."[34] The controversy regarding the weapon was, at first, caused by the lack of government-issued lubricant available through logistical support channels. It was known as Lubricant, Small Arms, or LSA, but soldiers frequently requested the more common commercial variety, WD-40, to "make do" until quantities became available.[35] And junior officers who had used the heavier, semiautomatic M-14 during OCS or IOBC were at a disadvantage as to teaching their new replacements to effectively use the M-16.[36] But most troops, at least after 1967, had been trained to use the weapon properly at AIT locations such as Fort Polk, Louisiana; Fort Dix, New Jersey; and Fort Lewis, Washington. Only Fort Polk's weather was similar to Vietnam's. The M-16 also could endanger the lives of troops when it jammed: "If it got the least amount of dirt, it would stop and the bad thing about an M-16, the horrible thing about an M-16 is when one of them quits you, it's not a matter about kicking the bolt back open. . . . You've got to take that gun apart. . . . Time is critical, you ain't got half an hour to stop and fix this thing. We've had guys get killed, and the army lost a lot of guys too because the things quit."[37] So the procedure for relieving jams had to be taught to replacements as quickly as possible.

Soldiers and officers also needed training in how to fire the M-16 in jungle combat, and for new platoon leaders this controversial weapon would require special efforts in training to achieve maximum combat efficiency. The army had experienced apparent neglect by soldiers in firing their weapons at the enemy in World War II, and it was intent on not having the "ratio of fire" problem in Vietnam. S. L. A. Marshall's seminal work, *Men against Fire: The Problem of Battle Command*, stated that as few as "15% of the men had actually fired at the enemy positions or personnel with rifles, carbines, grenades, bazookas, BARs [Browning automatic rifles] or machine guns during the course of an entire engagement. Even allowing for the dead and wounded, and assuming that in their numbers there would be the same proportion of active fires as among the living, the figure did not rise above 20 to 25 per cent of the total for any action."[38] And even though Marshall's thesis would be

M-16A1 rifle (photo courtesy of Americal Division, Veterans' Association Collection, Texas Tech University, The Vietnam Archive, VA050786)

challenged before the outbreak of the Korean War with subsequent changes in training methods, the army wanted to make certain that all American soldiers in Vietnam fired their weapons at the enemy when required to do so.

The M-16A1 was easy to fire, had little or no recoil, weighed only six pounds, and looked and felt like a toy rifle. Firing a 5.56mm round, approximately the same size as a .22-caliber bullet, the weapon was exceptionally light and turned each soldier into a lethal rifleman. But the small round caused problems in some situations: "I mean, the M-16 rifle which was so popular was a rather ineffective weapon in the jungle and we were at a rather big disadvantage against the NVA who we were always bumping heads against because the NVA used the AK-47s which fired a much heavier slug and their slugs could penetrate brush whereas the slugs from the M-16s are very light weight."[39]

Russell Glenn, a retired colonel and combat veteran of the Persian Gulf War, studied soldier responses to combat by questionnaire and interviews with Vietnam veterans of the 1st Cavalry Division (Airmobile). His book *Reading Athena's Dance Card: Men against Fire in Vietnam* revealed that there was no problem with soldiers firing; in many situations, too much ammunition was expended because they placed the selector lever on "rock-n-roll," or fully automatic, which is not an efficient firing method.[40] Weapons training in the Vietnam replacement training centers was designed to teach the soldier how to efficiently kill the enemy and preserve ammunition for a future firefight. Information from *hoi chanhs*, former vc, revealed that as sappers, they had stayed low to the ground because the M-16A1 on automatic tended to shoot high and to the right. Soldiers were taught to place their nontrigger hand on the top of the handguard to reduce the rise of the weapon.[41] For a junior officer leading a platoon, this "fire discipline" was critical to effective combat performance, but he had to learn it himself before he could reinforce such skills in his own troops.

Learning to fire the M-16A1 was not the only weapons-oriented poi; soldiers were also taught how to fire other platoon weapons, even though when they were first assigned to a squad, their primary role was as riflemen. But when a buddy went down, each member of the squad had to be capable of firing the other weapons. Key to maximum firepower of the platoon was the M-60 machine gun, which was essentially a crew-served weapon, since it required an "ammo bearer" who would assist the gunner by helping to feed the ammunition into the weapon. "The M-60 is absolutely a superb infantry weapon, that thing will be around for 50 more years. There was almost nothing that could be done to improve it, I mean, it'll fire when it's full of wet concrete, you almost can't break it."[42] Most soldiers had been exposed to "the pig" in AIT, but in fire-and-maneuver training exercises, the blank ammunition tended to jam; thus most men had never had the opportunity to experience the "wall of steel" that the gun could provide in a firefight. The M-60 weighed twenty-three pounds and fired a 7.62mm round, and many soldiers did not want to be burdened by such a load. Platoon leaders had to be aware of this reluctance and take special precautions to make certain that all squad members shared the agony of ammo bearing and learning to fire the gun, because in a firefight the vc and pavn knew to try to kill the machine gunner first, attempting to gain fire superiority. "Here, you carry this mother fucking pig. No one wanted it. The pig position was the one attacked by the enemy after the co [commanding officer] and the rto [radio, telephone operator]. If they could, they wanted to take out the machine gun because that was where the fire power was coming from."[43] A major part of a junior officer's job was instilling confidence in the platoon's ability to use the M-60.

The M-79 grenade launcher was essentially platoon artillery. Weighing only six pounds and capable of firing accurately up to 200 meters, it could keep the enemy pinned down while rifle squads maneuvered their way

M-60 machine gun, fired by PFC Milton Cook of 25th Infantry Division (photo courtesy of Robert Lafoon Collection [DASPO] Texas Tech University, The Vietnam Archive, VA029696)

into an effective firing position. But junior officers had to convince their soldiers that the M-79 was vital to platoon success, because the weapon lessened an individual rifleman's own protection on patrol. Firing 40mm high-explosive, white phosphorous, smoke, tear gas, and flare rounds, the weapon provided each squad with an ability to place short-range targeted explosives either on advancing troops or on an enemy defensive perimeter.

This "thump gun," or "blooper," was not very effective at close range unless loaded with a shotgun-type round that enabled a soldier to protect himself if he encountered the enemy on patrol. "They had come up with an M-79 canister round so the M-79 guys could walk point if they needed to and basically what it was, it turned an M-79 into a 40 millimeter shotgun and they did it with a plastic cartridge on the front of the round instead of the HE [high explosive] and it had a little small, solid center part that was loaded in double ought buck . . . would go and hit about like a 12 gauge shotgun and it gave the guys something really good for point man in the bush, or to bust something close in."[44] Soldiers who had trained on the weapon in CONUS

M-79 grenade launcher (photo courtesy of Ron Miriello Collection, Texas Tech University, The Vietnam Archive, VAS017809)

were surprised to see that the sights were removed in Vietnam, because they frequently would catch on vines in the jungle. An efficient grenadier could fire and adjust fire without such sights.[45]

The M-72 light antitank weapon (LAW) was also available to rifle platoons. Although it was designed for the European theater for use against Soviet tanks, ordnance experts adapted it for Vietnam by encasing the projectile in a disposable fiberglass tube, thus enabling the shooter to leave the launcher behind. Because of its electronic firing mechanism, the weapon had a high "dud rate" in the humid jungle environment, and platoon leaders had to be diligent in its care and maintenance. If the round failed to ignite and be ejected from the launcher, the soldier who had attempted to fire it was endangered until the entire weapon could be destroyed. If left behind, the weapon became available to the VC to be used as a booby trap against friendly forces. Lieutenants also had to convince their troops to carry the weapons on their rucksacks, because the LAW could be lethal to the bearer in certain situations: "This particular fellow had been carrying this LAW sort of strapped over his shoulder. When he stepped on the mine, the mine engaged the LAW and the rocket fired and blew off part of his head. He was killed, obviously."[46]

While weapons training was the most important offensive POI, mine and booby trap detection was the most important defensive course. Of the 58,479 American deaths in the Vietnam War, 7,471 were caused by enemy booby traps.[47] The WIA records of such incidents are not available but would be significant. For the platoon leader, no enemy contact was more devastating than when one of his soldiers stepped on a booby trap and was killed or maimed, as this indicated VC presence without a visual sighting. In the replacement training programs, great emphasis was placed on teaching both officers and enlisted men the cunning effectiveness of the enemy: "The harmless smoke grenades that we tripped were good reminders that no such mistake would be allowed when we faced the real thing. At the close of the class a young sergeant showed us the twisted, bent barrel of an M-16 A1 rifle, telling us it was virtually all that was left after a soldier's failure to detect a large booby-trapped artillery shell."[48] Such improvised explosive devices[49] could be made from American artillery rounds that had failed to detonate or from manufactured mines and explosive devices that had been provided by the Soviet Union and the Peoples Republic of China, the main arms suppliers to the VC and PAVN. "I mean we just did everything with mine detectors and visual detection. Had all kinds of casualties. Someone was killed almost everyday,

M-72 light antitank weapon, fired by SFC Roger Legget of 198th Light Infantry Brigade (photo courtesy of Americal Division, Veterans' Association Collection, Texas Tech University, The Vietnam Archive, VA050678)

which is really intense when you're trying to do that. I remember one of my medics, Doc Love, saved many people prior to himself getting messed up. These were bad things because some of the booby-traps were (U.S.) 105mm artillery rounds and everything. They weren't the little toe poppers."[50]

Though small in explosive ordnance, the most feared of all booby traps was the Bouncing Betty. "I think it was a Bouncing Betty they used to call it, but which was like a tomato can and had a thousand ball bearings in it."[51] It had a three-pronged firing device that could be seen by an alert point man when rains had washed away the covering dirt. Once the device was stepped on, "the unlucky soldier will hear a muffled explosion; that's the initial charge sending the mine on its one yard leap into the sky. The fellow takes another step and begins the next and his backside is bleeding and he's dead. We call it 'ol step and a half.'"[52] Such a wound would likely kill a soldier, but more dreaded than death was Betty's shrapnel hitting the groin area. "A wound to the genitals was the most feared injury in this war, as in any other conflict. A man's first question to the medic was not 'Am I going to make it?,' but rather 'Do I still have my balls?'"[53]

Toe poppers were also effective booby traps because only half of the foot was blown away, thus enabling the soldier to hop or crawl, with assistance from another soldier, who was then rendered useless in the firefight.

> It was actually just like to blow your foot off. The concussion would just blow parts . . . blow toes off or mess up a foot or something. The chances of it killing you weren't that good unless you fell face down on it or something. But, it would just disable you because one of the tactics later on that was very helpful and worked very well for the North Vietnamese especially was rather than trying to kill guys, they were trying to wound them because then you take at least three people out because you take the wounded plus the other two that are trying to come get him. Or you take a whole bunch of people and when they try to come get them, you just pick them off as they try to come rescue the guy.[54]

The effectiveness of these weapons was dramatic because of the demoralizing effect on the platoon, which meant the junior officer in charge had to deal with the aftermath of such events: "Charlie was very good at putting out booby-traps. They could be anything from punji sticks in the ground to grenades and trip wires. We lost several men doing these sweeps, mostly due to grenades going off. This was very hard on everybody. The men didn't like it — nobody liked it — because they knew they couldn't see the enemy, so we couldn't fight back, and we were having people wounded almost daily."[55]

For the junior officer leading a platoon, there were circumstances when a decision made in haste, and thought to be in the best interest of his men, would have dire results. One such instance was that of Lt. Bob Ryan of the 198th Light Infantry Brigade, attached to the 23rd Infantry Division (Americal) out of Chu Lai in I Corps (see map 2). In February 1968 he was leading his recon platoon on a predawn cordon-and-search operation of a village and was fearful that they would not reach their destination before dawn. Because of his superior knowledge of the area of operations (AO), he elected to walk the point position, rather than his usual position at the center of the formation, near the RTO.

> I halted the squad and took the lead myself; we were close to our assigned spot and I knew the way. I doubt if more than a minute passed before I set off what was a small booby-trap . . . probably a Chi-com grenade. My RTO was also slightly wounded. I was in intense pain immediately and went in and out of consciousness before the medevac arrived to take me to the hospital ship Sanctuary, and then to Manila, Japan and home. I don't think

anything of military import was found in the village. . . . Certainly the element of surprise was lost. It was my first and last time on point![56]

THE TRAINING THAT JUNIOR officers received when they first arrived in-country was designed to familiarize them with the combat environment of the jungle and teach them critical skills. There was little leadership training offered. Few infantry divisions developed training schools for leadership, treating the newly arrived lieutenants like the grunts they would become. Late in the war, the 101st Airborne Division conducted a school called the Combat Commanders Course. The POI included many of the subjects previously taught in the general replacement course, but there was some emphasis on leadership. For reasons not clearly obvious in division records, the 101st Airborne divided its in-country training into three courses under the general POI of the Screaming Eagle Replacement Training School, which included the following:

1) Replacement training for all new in-country personnel, except for EMS in the grade of E-9, and officers above O-4 (Major).
2) Combat Commanders Course (CCC), as mentioned above.
3) Combat Leader Course (CLC), for junior non-commissioned officers and potential non-commissioned officers.[57]

Beyond these general courses, there were specialty programs available, such as that offered by the British army at Ulu Tiram, Malaysia. With quotas for U.S. personnel in important advisory or division roles in Vietnam, the five-week Junior Leaders Course was designed to "teach basic techniques required to live in a jungle environment, with emphasis on jungle navigation and movement." An advanced course, the Officers Tactical Course, was also offered that required the Junior Leaders Course as a prerequisite.[58]

The training programs the army considered most important for combat effectiveness promoted unit cohesion and afforded an opportunity for officers and NCOs to perform their duties in a controlled environment. As emphasized by Col. Sidney B. Berry Jr., CO of the 1st Brigade, 1st Infantry Division, "The need for training does not cease when a unit enters combat; it becomes more important."[59] An example of such a course was the Lightning Ambush Academy of the 25th Infantry Division at Cu Chi. The program was incredibly intensive and required platoons to be at 100 percent assigned strength in order for that unit to be included in the training program. Even platoons with soldiers absent on R&R (rest and relaxation) were not allowed to participate. The course was conducted both inside and outside the division perimeter; thus the unit participated in a night ambush in enemy territory as a final exam. After four days of classroom and field exercises demonstrating such techniques as night navigation, artillery support, fundamental patrol planning, medevac, ambush site set up, and rehearsal, the unit would leave on ambush patrol at 6:00 in the evening and return at 6:00 the next morning. After a debriefing and critique, a formal graduation ceremony was held, which gave credibility to the entire unit's performance. This type of training was designed to enhance the roles of the junior officer and NCOs within the platoon and to create small units capable of performing efficient ambushes.[60]

Since most contacts with VC or NVA were initiated by the enemy, American soldiers had to learn defensive operations. No greater responsibility existed for a junior officer than that of teaching his men how to protect themselves when not patrolling, which was normally at night in a defensive perimeter (NDP). At such times enemy forces were able to inflict casualties that ultimately resulted in the deaths of 4,879 American men and one woman.[61] The number of wounded soldiers in such assaults was very high because mortar, rocket, and ultimately sapper and ground attacks could be conducted in the relative obscurity of darkness, which made counteroffensive operations difficult. Furthermore, calling in supporting artillery, gunships, or airpower was complicated because of the close proximity of friendly troops.

Junior officers were challenged at the end of a day of patrolling in enemy territory, because American soldiers hated to "dig in." Infantrymen were not lazy or careless, but they doubted the need to construct foxholes, because they usually believed in their own immortality. If a soldier constructed a two-man foxhole with overlapping fields of fire, he improved his chances of surviving the night. Only a mortar round that landed directly on top of his foxhole or a ground attack that penetrated the defensive mines and trip wires could send him home in a body bag or require a medevac trip to the rear. A platoon leader had to require the use of the entrenching tool at dusk if his men were to survive the night. In training exercises, he had to teach his men to dig fast, to place the very effective M-18A1 Claymore mine along the perimeter, and to plot artillery fire in advance to protect the flanks of the perimeter. Firing 700 steel balls upon detonation, the Claymore mine was the most effective deterrent to a ground attack, because it would obliterate anything that came into the 120-degree-arc killing zone.[62] Soldiers had to be

M-18A1 Claymore mine (photo courtesy of James Padget Collection, Texas Tech University, The Vietnam Archive, VA008902)

taught how to rig the mine and how to carry it in their rucksacks so it was readily available for use. Firing it on demand with a hand-held electronic device was simple, but if a soldier was scared and not able to handle his emotions, he might squeeze the detonator prematurely. Platoon leaders had to decide if the troops manning such devices were capable of controlled detonation, or whether they were better served by utilizing uncontrolled trip wires to avoid enemy penetration of the perimeter.

> I think that's a critical dimension for any leader. But at the same time it's also all that mocks, nicks stuff [attention to detail] that gets people killed. You know like the equipment checks. I made a statement of charges out on a couple of the guys who'd been using their claymore mines to pop off the back and use the C-4 to heat their c-rations. So, I made them pay for them just as a teaching point. The claymore is a system that you rely on. You can't think you've got 14 of them and only have two or none because everyone wants to heat rations with them. . . . We really got good with the claymore booby-traps we used to set. . . . You know so that claymore was a really awesome weapon. It really did the job. The sensitive part about the claymore's right at the blasting cap when you run your wire up there, there

are two little copper wires that go into your cap. Right there would invariably over time with the cap being taken out and put back in you know every time you set up your claymore they would have to be checked out.[63]

If the VC or PAVN got through, then the integrity of the perimeter was compromised, and the entire unit was in danger of destruction. "The men from the 4th Platoon threw tear gas grenades in an attempt to stave off the enemy soldiers, and a few of them had to engage in hand to hand combat with their foes to keep them out of the perimeter."[64] No lieutenant wanted his men engaging in such close encounters with the enemy, because American firepower was compromised when the enemy was "in the wire."

The army's Vietnam training program for the junior officer was based on the premise that he had been trained to lead in CONUS and that his adaptation to the jungle combat environment was all that was needed to prepare him for duty; hence, individual replacement training was deemed sufficient. But the "baptism of fire" that awaited him on his first combat assignment to his unit would be the most important training he would receive. For some, being assigned to a unit where the outgoing platoon leader had not become a casualty was a plus, although some incumbents could create havoc in the mind of the new lieutenant. "He smelled of heavy sweat that had seeped from his pores and dried many times over a long period of time. But the smell was more than a body odor; it was a smell of death: strong, pungent and repulsive. 'It's wonderful,' he said, 'nothing like it in the world. You'll get more than your share of killing. The bodies are everywhere, and in no time at all, you'll have a collection of ears that will make those rear echelon mother-fuckers green with envy.' "[65] This is a replacement lieutenant in a war like few others in American military history, with different rules of engagement and measurement of success. For this incumbent platoon leader and his replacement, this was not a gentleman's war.

SIX RULES OF ENGAGEMENT

The whole war effort was built on three pillars — the free-fire zone, the search-and-destroy mission, and the body count. The free-fire zone means shoot anybody that moves. The search-and-destroy mission is just another way to shoot anything that moves. I call it the portable free-fire zone — you tote it around anywhere you go. And the body count is the tool for measuring the success or failure of whatever you're doing.[1]

■

In CAP [Combined Action Platoon], the highest rank was E-4, we made our own Rules of Engagement and Survival, we were all one command, higher-ups never came around.[2]

■

Junior officers were usually introduced into combat on an individual basis, without the benefit of extensive training with their unit. From their first contact with the enemy to their last day in the field, they were responsible not only for the efficient destruction of the enemy force but also for adherence to the rules of engagement established by their unit command. These rules were not always clear and easily understood, and conflict frequently existed between the interpretation of the rules prescribed by the company; battalion; brigade; division; U.S. Army, Vietnam; and MACV.

The Oxford Companion to Military History defines "rules of engagement" as "laws laid down by governments and command authorities governing the circumstances in which their armed services may use force, and to what degree. Rules of engagement are designed to prevent the inadvertent escalation of a situation, and strive to follow general precepts of law."[3] Unfortunately for soldiers, and particularly junior officers, the rules established by the command authorities in Vietnam failed to meet this standard, particularly in preventing the escalation of a given situation. The two aspects of infantry operations that affected a junior leader's ability to observe rules of engagement were the search-and-destroy mission and free-fire zones. While these concepts were developed as part of an overall strategy to "win" the war, no understanding of the impact of such tactics is possible without a discussion of the Vietnam War's controversial measurement of success: the body count, which drove strategic and tactical decision making at all levels. And all of these terms can only be understood within the context of the war's chronological development, because the conduct of the war was not static. Search-and-destroy missions did not begin with the first U.S. troop deployments but, rather, developed over time as events in the war caused strategy to change.

Once the United States decided to launch massive air strikes against North Vietnam, the issue of introducing ground troops to protect the necessary air bases created controversy within the Johnson administration. Sorties would be flown from Da Nang (see map 2), although such raids could have been launched from Okinawa or from aircraft carriers at sea with just additional fuel expenditures. Nevertheless, two marine landing teams were dispatched to protect the air base at Da Nang in what would eventually be called I Corps.[4] Thus developed the "enclave strategy" favored by Ambassador Maxwell Taylor, in which the ground forces were assigned to base protection and restricted to offensive operations within a fifty-mile radius.

But Taylor was a soldier, and he recognized that once the troops were in place, offensive maneuvers would follow. "It is a fact of military life that soldiers do not thrive on a continuous defensive; the fine edge of their training becomes dull, and the aggressive spirit and morale decline. . . . It was inevitable that, considering the desperate shortage of a central reserve, sooner or later Gen. Westmoreland would want to use the American ground forces on mobile strike missions without any restrictions."[5] However, at this time there was no need for a body count to measure success; Operation ROLLING THUNDER would hopefully bring the North to its knees, while allowing time to build up the ARVN forces to enable them to withstand the National Liberation Front (NLF) and PAVN troops being deployed into the South. No search-and-destroy missions were authorized and no free-fire zones were contemplated, because bombing in the North would inflict sufficient damage to cause North Vietnam to capitulate.

However, two marine units would not be enough protection for all of the planes necessary to inflict substantial damage on North Vietnam, and Da Nang would not be the only air base requiring protection. In May 1965 the

173rd Infantry Brigade (Airborne) was ordered to Vietnam, ostensibly to protect air bases at Bien Hoa, near Saigon, and at Vung Tau on the South China Sea coast (see map 2). The NLF forces in the South responded to this buildup by launching small-unit actions against the 173rd, and in July the 2nd Brigade of the 1st Infantry Division and the 1st Brigade of the 101st Airborne Division were deployed. More Communist offensives were launched against these brigade-sized units, and eventually full division deployments were completed by sending the remainder of the 1st Infantry and 101st Airborne, the 25th Infantry, the 9th Infantry, and the 23rd Infantry (Americal).[6] All of these units were deployed by the end of 1965, as was the 1st Cavalry Division, Airmobile, which would for the first time test a new concept in American warfare: the delivery of troops into combat via helicopter. This major revision to infantry tactics made possible the aggressive nature of combat that would follow.

The "1st Air Cav" was trained at Fort Benning, Georgia, and deployed as a unit with its helicopters and all equipment. Witnessing the inability of American ground forces to engage the elusive enemy on foot, Gen. William Westmoreland, commanding general, MACV, decided that inserting troops rapidly from a staging area would enable such forces to destroy much of the NLF infrastructure. But mobility was the key, and a troop delivery system utilizing the helicopter allowed the rapid introduction of massive quantities of personnel into an area to engage the enemy.[7]

With sufficient troops stationed throughout South Vietnam, Westmoreland became more offensive minded, but he was not yet committed to what ultimately would be referred to as search-and-destroy missions. Intelligence reports indicated the presence of large forces of PAVN troops in the Central Highlands, particularly elements of the 320th, 33rd, and 66th regiments.[8] Most analysts believed that the military strategy of Hanoi was to split South Vietnam into two pieces, along Highway 19 from Pleiku through An Khe, to the coast at Qui Nhon (see map 2). This accomplished, the marine units north of Highway 19 in I Corps would be isolated from most of the U.S. ground forces, thus allowing PAVN units to come across the 17th parallel and destroy the air bases from which planes were bombing the North. And with the recent PAVN attack at the Special Forces camp at Plei Me, located just southwest of Pleiku, it seemed plausible that Hanoi was ready to launch its strategy. Maj. Gen. Harry W. O. Kinnard, the 1st Cavalry Division commander, was ordered to engage the enemy near the Ia Drang River, southwest of Pleiku.[9]

On November 14, 1965, a platoon of Col. Hal Moore's 1st Battalion, 7th Cavalry, captured a North Vietnamese soldier who turned out to be a deserter and who had been "living on bananas" for five days. Eager for decent treatment, he divulged the existence of three battalions of PAVN troops anxious to kill Americans.[10] By the time this information could be acted upon by intelligence, lead platoons had already engaged the enemy, and death and destruction had begun in earnest. Over a three-day period, 234 Americans would die in battles against PAVN troops who outnumbered the Americans by a five-to-one margin. In Alpha Company, all of the junior officers and NCOs would be killed or wounded, and only 40 of the 120 enlisted men would survive without wounds.[11] This was the first big battle of the Vietnam War, and it was won by American forces who employed overwhelming technology to avoid defeat. It was also one of the few battles of the war that had a decisive conclusion and "established the inability of the Communists to conquer South Vietnam as long as the Americans were there."[12]

Both American and North Vietnamese military leaders learned lessons from this important battle, and both would change their tactics, if not military strategies. The U.S. military recognized that the helicopter was of limited value once the troops had deplaned, and that if the opposing force surrounded the landing zone, new tactics would be necessary to infuse troops into a "hot" LZ. Furthermore, once on the ground, U.S. troops were at a distinct disadvantage as a fighting force, because they were in a jungle environment that was not conducive to use of heavy weapons and equipment. The U.S. soldier carrying a seventy-five-pound rucksack loaded with heavy c-rations was no match for the PAVN soldier carrying a light pouch of rice. And the American soldier walked noisily through the jungle, with his "steel pot" making sounds that were much louder than those created by the lightweight pith helmet worn by his adversary. Only in physical strength did the U.S. soldier have an advantage, which he used extensively in this battle since much of the fighting included hand-to-hand combat.

Hanoi leaders recognized their errors and subsequently made three changes to their tactics. First, they recognized the need to close with the enemy and to "cling to the belt" to discourage Americans from the use of air and artillery power.[13] Second, they also recognized the need to discontinue the employment of regimental-sized units and to deploy company-sized and smaller units, so that casualties from air and artillery power could be minimized. Military historians have now concluded that after this battle, 95 percent of all PAVN-initiated contacts were made by battalion-sized or smaller units.[14] Finally, PAVN leaders realized that they could be more effective in fighting Americans if they chose the time and place of engagement. Various studies during the war and research conducted after the war concluded that the enemy initiated between 65 percent and 75 percent of all contacts.[15]

General Westmoreland's response to the Battle of the Ia Drang Valley was to assume that the enemy would continue to fight in large units, and that the United States could win each battle as it had achieved victory in this pivotal Central Highlands fight. So he adopted the now famous policy of search-and-destroy missions, which were designed to "win the war by seeking out the enemy's military forces and eliminating them."[16]

THE ORIGIN OF THE TERM "search-and-destroy" is attributable to Gen. William DePuy, who served as deputy commandant of MACV, and he used the term to describe what infantry units were designed to do: search out the enemy and destroy him in place.[17] But the term became synonymous, at least among the general public, with burning down villages and inflicting civilian casualties. General Westmoreland considered the term as one of three tactics that made up the overall military strategy: "clearing," which meant either destroying or driving out the guerillas and other military forces so that civilian agencies could begin their assignments; "securing," which meant holding on to a cleared area by patrolling and uprooting secret political infrastructure; and "search-and-destroy." Only the latter would be recognized as a failed strategy.[18] And, search-and-destroy missions were more efficiently conducted in free-fire zones, because artillery and air assets could be more readily employed when only the enemy existed in an area. However, the controversy surrounding search-and-destroy had more to do with the measure of success used to determine the efficiency of the operation: the body count.

"On one wall hung a large poster headlined CHARLIE KILLS. It was my first look at a body count chart. Tick marks in squares denoted the number of kills for each day of the month. I added them up. So far in February it seemed Apache Troop had killed, wiped out, greased, exterminated, or otherwise got rid of more than sixty enemy soldiers. Gooks, dinks, slopes."[19] Every unit in Vietnam had a similar chart in its briefing room, and visiting commanders and dignitaries were shown the data, along with an explanation as to why the number was so large — or small. Where did such a concept originate? Neither in Korea nor in World War II was the measure of success the number of enemy soldiers killed. And for junior officers, who would be the first level of command responsible for reporting the deaths of enemy and friendly soldiers, the emphasis on such would affect the way they conducted their operations.

General Westmoreland did not take the credit or blame for the term "body count," but he did identify Secretary of Defense Robert McNamara's constant "prodding for statistics" as causing commanders to be overly conscientious of the need to keep track of enemy kills.[20] Assistant Secretary of Defense for Systems Analysis Alain Enthoven had developed statistical goals for 1966–67 that had been accepted by key members of the Johnson administration, including Westmoreland, at the Honolulu summit conference in February 1966. In addition to percentage goals for opening roads and railroads and for pacification and creation of food-producing areas, "our military units were to destroy enemy forces at a rate at least as high as the enemy's capability to put more men in the field."[21] So even though commanders had previously reported enemy KIA as a matter of standard operating procedure (SOP), there was now a stated government goal of attrition: the United States could win the war when KIAs and seriously wounded WIAs surpassed the number of PAVN and VC who were trained and ready for combat. Westmoreland conveniently blamed Enthoven's office for the incessant inquiries about enemy deaths, but it was the general who pushed the concept of a war of attrition.

This book will not address the folly of the concept of a war of attrition, but the stated goal of killing as many of the enemy as possible violates even the tenets of the great military strategist Sun Tzu. In *The Art of War* he said, "Generally in war, the best policy is to take a state intact; to ruin it is inferior to this. *Do not put a premium on killing.* To capture the enemy's army is better than to destroy it; to take intact a battalion, a company or a five-man squad is better than to destroy them."[22] Yet the U.S. Department of Defense adopted a military strategy that made killing the institutional goal. And with such a goal, individual soldiers would eventually adopt the concept naturally, thus creating another leadership challenge for junior officers. With the firepower available at all levels of command, it was a natural course of events that would cause abuses of the process. Although Westmoreland eventually claimed that he "abhorred the term," "body count" became the expression used by all combat soldiers to explain why they were in Vietnam.[23]

Since the stated goal was the killing of as many enemy soldiers as possible, setting individual unit goals was a natural outcome. There was nothing more important than getting those kills and then recording them, as Brig. Gen. Douglas Kinnard remembered:

> One time, standing in line for refreshments after a change-of-command ceremony, I overheard a senior general talking to a colonel, an up-and-coming brigade commander. They were discussing the body count and the colonel said to the general, "Well, the vc are getting harder to find." And the general said, "Well, brigade commanders aren't." What he meant, of course, was — you better get off your ass and get some kills or you might be replaced. Well, it may have been absolute coincidence, but a day or two later the young brigade commander was out supervising a squad-level action, going for kills and he was killed himself. Jesus Christ, the guy had a wife at home and a lot of children.[24]

The idea of a colonel participating in squad-level operations, which would normally be led by a sergeant, is contrary to all military training.

The emphasis on body count also affected operations, particularly creating an incentive for senior officers to "rush to the sound of a gun, take command from their subordinate commanders and run the battle themselves. Certainly the commander in the air may see things the commander on the ground cannot see and should advise him of them. On the other hand, the situation on the ground may be entirely different from its appearance in the air. . . . To rush in and take control each time a shot is fired is hardly the way to inspire confidence or to give junior officers needed experience."[25] Senior officers flying overhead would often see fleeing enemy soldiers, and rather than using their air and artillery assets, which were available to them immediately, they would make contact with the platoon leader on the ground and order pursuit. This endangered the infantry soldiers' lives, because there was no ability to detect ambush and booby traps from the air. "If there was something that impacted on morale, I guess it was the 1,500 foot mentality of some of our senior leadership. It was not leadership by example."[26] It was all because of body count. Whether a senior officer became so involved that he participated in squad-level operations or tried to exert influence from the relative safety of his chopper, he was doing so to improve the body count. Even Army Chief of Staff Harold K. Johnson took umbrage with the behavior of some of his commanders who wanted to become warriors: "I note in a cable and news release that reached here yesterday that you and Holly are out chasing vc in your choppers. If I had wanted a lead scout in command of the 1st Division, you would not have gotten the job. Your value and Holly's is proportional to the responsibility that you have for something over 15,000 men. Your job is not to shoot vc. Your job is to see that other people shoot vc. At least that is the way that I look at it."[27] Johnson was expressing his displeasure about the reports of generals trying to increase the body count.

There were ways to improve the body count of a unit other than by trying to kill more enemy soldiers through ground operations. Inflating the numbers was a common practice; it was so prevalent that MACV issued directives that specified how KIAS would be reported. According to the regulations, before reporting confirmed kills, squads or platoons must count the bodies of "males of fighting age and others, male or female, known to have carried arms."[28] The junior officer in charge was responsible for body count verification. In assessing enemy soldiers killed by artillery or air power, such numbers would have to be verified "upon debriefings of pilots or observers which substantiate beyond a reasonable doubt of the debriefing officer that the body count was accurate." Lt. Philip Caputo was, as he described it, "The Officer in Charge of the Dead," and he had to "count them to make sure there were as many as had been reported."[29] But since most units abandoned the bodies in the field, the verification process was left to the junior officers; therefore, the count should have been accurate because the bodies were physically accessible, with all of the gore and odors present. "I can't recall any time I was there that the body count was ever misrepresented — by us anyway. It was honest coming in from the field. If there was cheating, it was done by those in command farther up the line."[30]

But "fudging" was likely to occur. "If somebody had been blown in half and you didn't know which piece went where (you) made it two instead of one. And if somebody would say 'I know I got him, but they must have dragged him away,' then we'd count that. If there was any feasible way to raise the count without getting to be absurd, it was done."[31] Other units set up elaborate ways of determining KIAS, such as a "six inch patch of blood on the ground was one body" or a "two week old cadaver was a KIA."[32]

The impact that this emphasis on body count had on soldiers and junior officers was critical to their ability to function in combat. With senior officers asking for KIAS of the enemy before that of friendlies, platoon leaders often responded without confirming the number of kills. "The desire to have your unit look good and knowing nobody would check. Every once in a while somebody would go out and check, you know, a conscientious company commander, a battalion commander would go out and say, 'Where are the 20 bodies?' and, 'Well here's one and there's one and the others were dragged away,' and the guy would say, 'You don't have 20, you have 3.' 'Well, no, we saw them before they dragged them away.' 'But where did the . . .'"[33] When headquarters began to question the accuracy of the body count, some soldiers began to cut ears from the dead to verify that enemy soldiers had been killed, or they took pictures of the dead posed with the victors. (More information on ear souvenirs will be presented in Chapter 7.)

Even if junior officers had desired to be accurate in their reporting, the enemy often controlled how many of their dead were left behind to be counted. Near Saigon, in the village of Cu Chi, elaborate vc tunnels stretching for miles housed hospitals, ammo dumps, conference rooms, and burial grounds. "They were generally buried in a fetus-like position in the walls of tunnels and covered with a few inches of clay or wattle. It was offensive to leave a dead comrade unburied above ground; furthermore, it helped frustrate U.S. body counts if the dead were hidden inside the tunnels, and there they were at least laid to rest near the ancestral home. The vc also hid bodies of killed Americans in the tunnels to demoralize their comrades, who regarded it as an absolute priority to retrieve their dead for decent burial at home."[34] Many of those who were dragged away were probably taken into these underground labyrinths.

At the conclusion of the war between South Vietnam and the North Vietnamese and Viet Cong in 1975, PAVN troops were sent on burial detail to find the remains of those who had been buried hastily by their fellow soldiers. Bao Ninh, one of only 10 surviving soldiers of the 500-member Glorious 27th Youth Brigade, was assigned to burial detail for two years after the war, traveling throughout South Vietnam searching for shallow graves. In his book *The Sorrow of War* he writes, "The fallen soldiers shared one destiny; no longer were there honorable or disgraced soldiers, heroic or cowardly, worthy or worthless. Now they were merely names and remains. After some final touches with the shovel, their graves would be done, their remains laid out. Then, with their final breath their souls were released, flying upwards, free."[35] None of these soldiers would have been officially part of the body count, but they might have found their way into the numbers as six inches of blood, an ear, a photo — or an exaggeration.

In a recent interview with novelist and former PAVN soldier Bao Ninh in Hanoi, I asked him how accurate he believed American body counts to have been. While he agreed that Americans exaggerated the body count that was caused by American infantry units, he believed that the body count caused by artillery and B-52 bombing was underestimated by as much as 70 percent. He based this on his knowledge of PAVN unit troop reductions after American operations where he was serving and on his discussions with fellow soldiers.[36]

Finally, the body count was inflated at the higher echelons even after big battles where the bodies were readily available for inventory. I was a junior officer detailed to count bodies at the siege of Phu Nhon, March 15–16, 1971; my MAT team (38) counted just over 100 enemy KIA, and our after-action reports reflected this information. However, an American artillery unit, the 1/92nd Artillery stationed nearby, wrote an after-action report stating that 387 enemy had been killed, with 178 killed by artillery. That report went through American channels all the way to the Pentagon, where it became part of the overall body count. Those numbers were a complete fabrication of one of the fiercest battles fought in the later stages of the war, particularly since friendly KIAs were nearly equal to those of the enemy, although the after-action report indicated only 70 friendly KIA and 137 WIA. Perhaps to make the American artillery unit look good or to impress the brass that the officers were doing their job, enemy KIAs had to be greater than friendlies, and the American artillery unit's report reflected such. I knew exactly how many bodies had been recovered, and even with some allowance for deaths by Cobra gunships, napalm, and artillery called in on our own position, 387 enemy KIAs is a "stretch." We were MACV officers, and our body counts were never estimates.[37]

It was within this context of body count frenzy that U.S. infantry junior officers led their men into combat. And the U.S. Army would adopt the search-and-destroy operation as its main way of interdicting PAVN forces from the North and VC regulars from the South. On these operations, the platoon leader was ultimately responsible for reporting the body count to headquarters, even if it was a squad size or ambush patrol under his command. He had the least to gain with an inflated body count, because he was probably not going to stay in the army and did not have to be concerned about promotion. But some units rewarded confirmed kills with in-country R&R. "Anyone who got a confirmed kill got a three-day pass to China Beach in Da Nang," according to Bryan Good.[38] And Charles Gadd claimed that his unit was "constantly under pressure to turn in a body count, and the word was out that companies with the greatest number would get to spend more time at Cocoa Beach. It was an accepted thing to cheat on a body count report—all of us had been guilty of this."[39] So there was considerable pressure on even the junior officers to inflate the numbers.

Thomas C. Thayer, director of the Southeast Asia Division of the Office of the Assistant Secretary of Defense for System Analysis, collected the body count data from 1967 through 1972. After the war, he published a statistical record titled *War without Fronts: The American Experience in Vietnam*. While not criticizing the body count as a measure of success, he believes that not properly analyzing the data was a critical mistake. "The quantification of the war was often criticized as excessive and misleading. The body count was a prime example. The problem was that quantification became a huge effort but analysis remained a trivial one. This was unfortunate because the limited analysis that was done produced much useful insight into the war and lots of questions during the war about the prospects for winning, given the way it was being fought."[40] But the knowledge that policy makers would be looking at the numbers caused military leaders to adopt tactics that would make the numbers appear positive, but not necessarily reflective of progress.

SINCE THE MILITARY establishment had adopted the strategy of waging a war of attrition, the decision to employ search-and-destroy as a tactic to achieve victory took little thought. Once the enclave strategy had been discarded in late 1965, the number of troops in-country was sufficient to take the war to the enemy, both PAVN and NLF, and to utilize the American superior firepower to overwhelm him. But because the PAVN had learned important lessons in the Battle of the Ia Drang Valley, the U.S. military would find few large units to engage. Intelligence gained from captured documents, from prisoners of war (POWs), and from civilians frequently indicated the movement of large forces, but when U.S. units patrolled a specified area, they seldom found the enemy. Or the enemy had left the area and had mined, booby-trapped, and set up ambushes on the trails leading into and out of the identified staging area. Frustration set in among American troops who were being killed and maimed by an enemy who seldom appeared.

In August 1967, MACV became concerned about the sporadic nature of the fighting and instituted a study to determine whether the available "free world forces" were being employed properly. The records of enemy contact showed that American forces spent 80 percent of their time on search-and-destroy missions, with half of that time engaged in fighting regional targets, defined as PAVN or VC main forces. Only 20 percent of operations were involved with security, defined as protecting political, economic, or military installations. ARVN, ROK (Republic of Korea), and other free-world forces were operating as security forces; thus the United States was sustaining most of the fighting against the organized units of the enemy.[41]

Yet the aggregate body count was not satisfactory to the military establishment, even though the kill ratio was an acceptable 1:15. From April 1966 through February 1967 in operations such as ATTLEBORO, CEDAR FALLS, and JUNCTION CITY, the ratio of U.S. to enemy KIAS was between 1:10 and 1:15 — "the daily body count was looking good and the 'kill-ratio' was excellent."[42] Without cooperation from the enemy to make himself more readily available on a battlefield chosen by the United States, the crossover line in a war of attrition would be difficult to achieve. And infantry junior officers were reluctant to send their men into areas that were considered enemy territory without first launching air or artillery strikes. Harassment-and-interdiction fire (H&I) could be brought against such targets, thus eliminating some of the hostile force before an infantry attack. Such shelling had to receive clearance from South Vietnamese authorities, since no actual sighting of the enemy had taken place. H&I clearance was usually routine and accounted for nearly two-thirds of the total ordnance tonnage dropped or fired during the Vietnam War.[43] Junior officers typically had authority to call in such H&I, particularly if fired from their own organic guns. The heavy weapons platoon of their own company could also fire 60mm, 81mm, or 4.2-inch mortars prior to an infantry attack. And on the platoon level, even 40mm grenades fired from an M-79 grenade launcher could be used in an H&I manner. Obviously, the closer to the attacking unit the ordnance was fired, the greater the likelihood of the enemy locating a unit's position, so prudent use of such firepower was necessary. But the concept of firing first then attacking, even when no target had been sighted, was SOP in many units.

In another method of enemy surveillance, infantrymen were introduced into a known VC or PAVN area, waited for contact, and then unleashed massive air and artillery firepower: "Military commanders with poor or insufficient training, such as ground troop officers in the army and marines, often pushed their own troops out into the bush, hoping to draw fire so that retaliation could then be made; usually using air or artillery supporting fire. This method was very costly in both lives and material, and was entirely ineffective. . . . The U.S. troops? They were used as cannon fodder."[44] And in some instances there was not time to call in the artillery before a ground contact began:

105mm artillery rounds being fired at FSB Debbie in support of the 11th Infantry operations (photo courtesy of Americal Division, Veterans' Association Collection, Texas Tech University, The Vietnam Archive, VA050784)

Lieutenant Griffith, the 2nd Platoon Leader was killed shortly after reaching the 3d Platoon positions. The NVA forces pinned down the Company with machine gun fire from the front. Meanwhile, NVA soldiers climbed trees to the flanks and started shooting down at U.S. soldiers. The Company began taking casualties, and at 1635H, Captain Isom reported to the 3rd Battalion, 8th Infantry CP [command post] that he was in contact with a battalion-size force and was receiving casualties. A short time later, the RTO was wounded, and Captain Isom, going to his aid, was killed. This left Lieutenant Williams and Lieutenant Flannigan, the FO [forward observer] as the only surviving officers. . . . The entire 3d Platoon Weapons Squad had been killed. The Company reached their night location at approximately 1800H. They had suffered 17 KIA and 10 WIA or MIA.

This account, taken from an after-action report of the 4th Infantry Division, recommended under lessons learned that "when units move into an area where contact with a superior force is probable, company-sized elements should operate within reasonable supporting distance."[45] For the junior officers involved in this operation, most of whom were killed or wounded, the search-and-destroy mission resulted in disaster, because they failed to use H&I artillery prior to insertion and because intelligence indicated that only a small force was in the area. Nothing in OCS, ROTC, or the USMA could have prepared them for a battle where they were outnumbered four to one, and where support from air and artillery assets was minimal or had not been properly planned.

The use of artillery as a preparation before insertion was not always an option for the junior officer because of civilians residing in the area. "I tried to get artillery into prep in front of us, but would not give it because of the civilian population. . . . Our artillery and gunships we cannot get support unless in heavy fire. [*sic*] On February 5, our first element ran into a horse-shoe ambush. Our co was hit seriously and two other men were killed and two wounded. I begged the Battalion Commander for artillery to get us out of this mess. I went in with 23 men and came out with 9. We were refused gunships and artillery. [He is crying at this point.]"[46] This soldier's frustration was not with the war itself but with rules of engagement that prohibited firing when civilians were in the general vicinity of American troops.

MACV'S RESPONSE TO THE concern about civilians was to develop rules of engagement that were designed to protect civilians who were in the villages being searched, but before destruction took place: "Care must be exercised to return the area to its normal state of order and repair as in those cases where no evidence of enemy complicity is found."[47] But platoon leaders were challenged when leading scared and excited soldiers into a village of suspected vc or vc sympathizers, and keeping property destruction to a minimum was usually not a high priority. The best way to avoid civilian casualties, said MACV, was to avoid civilian contacts with U.S. soldiers whenever possible. The military leadership's answer to this was the creation of the free-fire zone. If civilians got in the way, they would be told to move — the U.S. Army would even move their livestock and meager possessions, and a USAID (U.S. Agency for International Development) unit would help them build a new home in a more secure location, which was defined by MACV as one nearer a free-world unit. Never mind that the new home was far removed from their ancestral dwellings, and particularly from the sacred burial grounds where their relatives lay. But once civilians were relocated, the U.S. could unleash its massive firepower without concern for inhabitants who had been warned to leave; thus those who stayed were assumed to be vc. And once the free-fire zone had been created, commanders in the ao had less concern for the MACV rules of engagement. Westmoreland even believed that while the rules were important but nearly impossible for commanders to adhere to, the relaxing of such would enable more efficient use of American firepower.

That it was necessary on some occasions intentionally to raze evacuated villages or hamlets apparently fed the misunderstanding. Some populated localities were so closely entwined with the tentacles of the vc base areas, in some cases actually integrated into the defenses, and so sympathetic were some of the people to the vc that the only way to establish control short of constant combat operations among the people was to remove the people and destroy the village. That done, operations to find the enemy could be conducted without fear of civilian casualties.[48]

This operations plan led to the oft-quoted phrase "We had to destroy the village to save it."

For junior officers in the field, the ability to call in artillery without civilian casualty concerns was welcomed, but it created other problems. The dud rate of artillery ordnance was roughly 2 percent of all shells fired; that of bombs dropped by B-52s, 5 percent.[49] Thus when junior officers called in a fire mission, some of the rounds would fail to detonate and thus did not provide the death and destruction to the enemy that was expected and often necessary to save an American unit. Furthermore, this unexpended ordnance became the improvised mines and booby traps used against American soldiers by the vc and pavn units.[50] And a 155mm artillery shell rigged to fire upon tripping a wire or set to detonate electronically on command killed and wounded many American soldiers, who became victims of their own weapons.

Free-fire zones also created circumstances in which infantry soldiers were forced to make decisions regarding whether civilians they came into contact with were enemy or friendly. By the very nature of the designation of the zone, any civilians found there were assumed to be vc, at least until inter-rogated. But the logic often evaded soldiers' better reasoning.

A recon patrol spotted a thatched hut and a garden plot with a dozen banana trees. The company got on line, and we cautiously approached the humble rotting abode. As we got close, a feeble old man was spotted trying to escape up a knoll beyond his house. Dressed in nothing but a loin cloth, he pawed at the earth, making little headway. Several soldiers retrieved the man. He couldn't have hurt anyone. Skin hung from his bones, he weighed maybe sixty or seventy pounds. This was our enemy? The man was put on a bird bound for Pleiku, where he would receive medical attention. Rules were rules. We burnt his home, destroyed his garden. An hour or so later, word came that the Montagnard had died. His heart must have failed under all the stress.[51]

Such encounters were frequent, since many villagers refused to leave their homes, particularly the Jarai, Hmong, Bahnar, and Rhade tribes of Montagnards who were indigenous to the Central Highlands.[52] Winning the "hearts and minds" of the people, which was ostensibly a military goal, was difficult if villagers were constantly being questioned, herded into frightening helicopters, and taken to large cities for intelligence gathering.

Civilians, if encountered in free-fire zones, were often used in the search-and-destroy missions to assist in clearing operations. They were sometimes used to help clear bunkers where vc were likely to hide. "The same results are obtained by indicating in the presence of villagers that a grenade will be thrown into the bunker. This will encourage villagers into taking friends and perhaps the enemy from underground shelters."[53] While such tactics may seem harsh and inhumane, for the junior officer trying to gain control of an area while minimizing both civilian and American casualties, prospects were enhanced if he used all available assets.

The search-and-destroy, free-fire-zone, body-count, war-of-attrition policy of General Westmoreland was an army strategy that was not supported by all of the joint chiefs.[54] Marine Commandant Wallace Greene supported the enclave concept, and even though marine units participated in the same type of operations as the army, their approach to the daily fighting was different. Operating mostly in I Corps, near Da Nang (see map 2), they organized their forces into CAPs, which included local Vietnamese militia. The platoon would move into a village and stay, "getting to know the people, winning their trust, and working closely on civic action projects."[55] The concept was effective, and few free-fire zones existed in the marine AO. While Westmoreland lauded the Marine Corps tactics, he believed that his army forces were not equipped for such duty. "Although I disseminated information on the platoons and their success to other commands, which were free to adopt the idea as local conditions might dictate, I simply did not have enough numbers to put a squad of Americans in every village and hamlet; that would have been fragmenting resources and exposing them to defeat in detail."[56]

Although Westmoreland rejected the CAP idea, MATs from MACV performed similar duties throughout Vietnam, and their success was recognized by American units operating in AOs. Having served with MAT 38 in Phu Nhon District, Pleiku Province, I know that such an approach was more conducive to "winning the hearts and minds" than search-and-destroy and the establishment of free-fire zones.[57]

Thus, the military establishment continued to operate in a manner consistent with maximizing the body count to achieve the infamous crossover point. As the body count rose, the rules of engagement were changed to accommodate more use of lethal firepower. Infantry units were sent in to "mop up" and count bodies after B-52 carpet-bombing raids. And junior officers would strive to maintain military order within the ranks of their platoons, which were becoming jaded with death and destruction. There was an increasing tendency for platoon leaders to become more like the men they led: frustrated and angry, but protective of the men whose lives were their responsibility.

These junior officers had not established the body count as a measure of success, nor had they set rules of engagement that allowed such carnage to take place in remote areas of Vietnam. But they were men on whom Westmoreland and others had to rely to achieve victory in this war, which after 1966 was becoming more brutal each day. By March 15, 1968, in Son My Village, hamlet of My Lai (4), that brutality would peak, and a young junior officer would epitomize the ever increasing evidence that this was not a gentleman's war.

SEVEN

ATROCIOUS BEHAVIOR

I have been in My Lai. Everyone that lived there was a V.C. or supporter. On the other hand, there was no excuse to shoot the people.[1]

■

My Lai was caused by an ill-trained, immature officer who probably wouldn't have been an officer if not for the war.[2]

■

That poor lieutenant was screwed by his superiors — it was poor leadership from the top.[3]

■

My opinion was that Calley committed an unspeakably unprovoked, barbarous act that should have been punished before a firing squad. I know of no military man who condoned it. Small town Georgians believed that he was railroaded.[4]

■

The opinions of Vietnam combat veterans concerning Lt. William Laws Calley at My Lai on March 16, 1968, are as varied as the combat experiences of each former soldier. Virtually every book on the Vietnam War has a section on, or at least a reference to, what has been referred to as an "incident," "massacre," "mistake," "operation," and "cover up." It was all of those things as well as a gross failure of leadership from the bottom to the top.

Military historians and scholars from various fields have debated the extent to which My Lai was an anomaly, or whether it was military SOP. "We intend to demonstrate that My Lai was no unusual occurrence," said Lt. Bill Crandall, former infantry platoon leader and Ohio State ROTC graduate at the outset of the "winter soldier investigation" sponsored by the Vietnam Veterans Against the War (VVAW) in Detroit, Michigan, January 31–February 2, 1971. "We intend to show that the policies of the Americal Division, which inevitably resulted in My Lai, were the policies of other army and marine divisions as well. We intend to show that the war crimes in Vietnam did not start in March 1968, or in the village of Son My or with one Lt. Calley. We intend to indict those really responsible for My Lai, for Vietnam, for attempted genocide."[5] The efforts of the VVAW and, later, of California congressman Ronald V. Dellums's ad hoc committee hearings would reveal numerous acts of "atrocious behavior" by infantry soldiers. These preposterous statements invited scrutiny by the press as to their validity. "A reporter from a Detroit daily asked if, in lieu of documentary proof, all the veterans would sign affidavits of their veracity. Other reporters asked for the names of the officers or non-coms who had ordered or permitted the atrocities." The vets refused, saying "that fogged the issue of cultural and political responsibility for the crime of the war by finding a scapegoat," and that all of them "were equally guilty or innocent with Lt. Calley, and that the responsibility for the atrocities rested with the policy makers who kept the war of atrocity going."[6] Nevertheless, investigations by government agencies that had a vested interest in the validity of such statements revealed that, in some cases, the names of the veterans who testified were bogus.[7] But the issue had become part of the national discussion on the war, and as Peter Michelson wrote, "The veterans' strategy paid off. They came to tell their story, not to debate whether it was true."[8]

The extent to which American soldiers committed atrocities continues to be debated as part of the discourse on the Vietnam War. And the role that failure of leadership contributed to such atrocious behavior must be discussed. Since a junior officer was usually present whenever twenty to thirty soldiers were patrolling or on an operation, he would have been responsible for the conduct of his men. And contrary to the comments of Lt. Bill Crandall, Lieutenant Calley was guilty of the most egregious acts: first-degree murder and failure to lead responsibly. And "not all of us" were equally guilty or innocent, because leadership in combat is an individual responsibility, no matter how just or unjust the war. Michael Walzer, in *Just and Unjust Wars: A Moral Argument with Historical Illustrations*, writes, "We are concerned now with the conduct of war not its overall justice. For soldiers, as I have already argued, are not responsible for the overall justice of the wars they fight; their responsibility is limited by the range of their own activity and authority."[9]

The range of activity and authority for the platoon leader was his platoon's AO, but more significantly, as the junior officer in a battle, he was often the *only* officer and represented all levels of command. He was the enforcer of the rules of engagement, murky though they may have been, and the person who could pass judgment on the morality of an action. At that moment all of his education, training, and moral fiber became critical to the life-and-death situation he and his men faced. And the rules that he operated under had been reinforced many times since he had arrived in Vietnam.

The first MACV directive that dealt specifically with war crimes was Directive 20-4:

> A war crime is the willful killing, torture, or inhumane treatment of, or willfully causing great suffering or serious injury to the body or health of persons taking no active part in the hostilities, including members of the armed forces who had laid down their arms or who were not combatants because of sickness, wounds or any other cause. Other acts specified as war crimes were maltreatment of dead bodies, firing on localities which were undefended, and without military significance, pillage or purposeless destruction, killing without trial of spies or other persons who committed hostile acts, and compelling prisoners of war or civilians to perform labor prohibited by the Geneva Conventions.[10]

These rules were periodically updated and sent to all commands, particularly when leaders heard that the rules were being violated. "It has come to my attention that certain members of this command have treated enemy dead in a manner inconsistent with the Geneva Conventions. Although mutilation or maltreatment of enemy dead is prohibited by the 1949 Geneva Conventions and by MACV Directive 27-5, dated 2 November, 1967 (the updated version of MACV Directive 20-4, dated April 20, 1965), it appears that there is a general lack of understanding of what constitutes 'maltreatment.'" This letter addressed the issue of the "cutting off of ears," a somewhat common practice of many troops.[11] Such acts were considered by senior officers to be gross violations of the war crimes directive, yet other seemingly more important issues, like the treatment of civilians, got less attention.

MACV Directive 20-4 and all subsequent directives dealt with atrocities, which can be defined generally as the killing of a noncombatant, either an erstwhile combatant who is no longer fighting or has given up, or a civilian.[12] To understand how soldiers respond to the stimuli of killing and to fully comprehend the magnitude of responsibility that junior officers encountered when the carnage commenced, I use Dave Grossman's model in his book *On Killing: The Psychological Cost of Learning to Kill in War and Society* as a framework. Grossman views killing in combat as a spectrum of occurrences, from the simple act of killing the noble enemy to execution. Along the path will be gradients, which can best be described by referencing historical military events.[13] Each of these categories will also be tied to combat experiences of soldiers in Vietnam.

SLAYING THE NOBLE ENEMY

At one end of the spectrum is the act of killing an armed enemy who is trying to kill an opposing soldier. This would be considered the "least atrocious" act once we absolve soldiers of the responsibility of fighting in just or unjust wars, as previously discussed in reference to the Walzer book, and we accept the premise that killing is what states require soldiers to do. This behavior is the most fair, "grand and glorious" that any soldier will encounter. It may be one-on-one or it may be unit-to-unit. We know that in antiquity, hoplite warriors met on familiar battlefields to fight in phalanxes with identical weapons and shields. With a series of thrusts from their seven-foot wooden spears, the warriors would attempt to wound or kill enough enemy soldiers to move the phalanx off the battlefield. If his spear were to break, the warrior had a sword or small dagger for close combat. Or he could use the butt-spike on the broken end of his spear to inflict a downward thrust on a fallen warrior.[14] This final blow was not necessarily dealt against an armed warrior; therefore, is this the first gradient of atrocity? Thucydides' account of the Peloponnesian War does not indicate that wholesale execution of the wounded took place, although certain battles were given special priority by leadership and more draconian measures were employed.[15] But generally there was respect for the enemy and reverence for the dead on both sides of the battle lines.

Modern warfare has not really changed the one-on-one relationship, particularly at the infantry level. Even in World War II, where conventional battle lines could be drawn, unit-to-unit fighting occurred with the mission to achieve victory by killing enough enemy soldiers to move the line or by causing enough disarray to scatter the troops. During the Vietnam War, after battlefield preparation with artillery or aerial bombardment, VC, PAVN, and U.S. soldiers would engage the enemy in firefights with automatic weapons. No phalanxes were necessary, but squads of men attempted to kill the enemy and overrun his position.

The Battle of the Ia Drang Valley was one of the few operations in the Vietnam War that was somewhat similar to the skirmishes of the Greek and Roman armies. But even there, once the U.S. Army was near defeat from the overwhelming force of PAVN troops, air power was called in to destroy the remaining enemy forces. Since many of the soldiers were wounded, one could argue that the final devastating blow was analogous to the ancient downward thrust of the butt-spike.

The respect for the enemy was also shown in Col. Hal Moore's after-action report on Ia Drang. "These enemies were aggressive and they came off the mountain in large groups. . . . They were good shots. . . . In caring for my men who had been killed and wounded, I was struck by the great number who had been shot in the head and upper part of the body — particularly in the head. . . . He fought to the death. When wounded, he continued fighting with his small arms and grenades. He appeared fanatical when wounded and had to be approached with extreme care. Many friendly were shot by wounded PAVN."[16]

Another Vietnam War battle that generally fits into this category was the Siege of Khe Sanh in 1968, when two PAVN divisions surrounded a U.S. Marine base in Quang Tri Province, near the DMZ, and threatened to overrun it at a time of their own choosing. The first attack happened on January 22, 1968, just a week before the TET Offensive, causing General Westmoreland to concentrate all of his logistic and air support at the besieged base. General Giap, commanding general of the PAVN forces, never launched the impending massive ground attack but used self-propelled artillery and rounds fired from tanks to harass the stationary marines. The shelling continued for three months. This battle ended essentially in a stalemate, with the U.S. Marines experiencing 205 KIAs while killing more than 5,000 PAVN troops with artillery and air power.[17] But the battle was between two military units that could see each other, and each could plan on slaying the noble enemy with its respective weapons. While the U.S. firepower was superior because of tactical air and B-52s that could launch strategic strikes on massed troops and equipment, the PAVN troops outnumbered the Americans by a ratio of at least ten to one. It is doubtful that the marine base could have held if there had been a heavy ground attack, at least in its initial phases.

President Johnson was so concerned about the likelihood of another Dien Bien Phu that he asked Joint Chiefs of Staff Chairman Gen. Earle Wheeler to look into the use of nuclear weapons, which would have "tipped the scales" in slaying the noble enemy. "Should the situation in the DMZ area change dramatically, we should be prepared to introduce weapons of greater effectiveness against massed forces. Under such circumstances, I visualize that either tactical nuclear weapons or chemical agents would be active candidates for employment."[18] They were never used, and the PAVN pulled out, having succeeded in distracting the U.S. command for three months.

There were probably other "big battles" during the pre–TET Offensive period when the two adversaries, the United States and North Vietnam, squared off in "grand and glorious" encounters, but they were rare, particularly when the NLF troops were involved. These battles found the belligerents reasonably respectful of each other's tactics, weapons, and most important, fortitude and courage. Little racism existed between the warring factions, because the battles were fought with a certain degree of warrior ethos. But as the war heated up and the PAVN changed its strategy from large-unit offensive operations to small-unit ambushes and combat avoidance, the continuum of killing began to change.

THE GRAY AREAS: AMBUSHES AND GUERILLA WARFARE

The ancient Greeks seldom used the element of surprise as a tactic. It was not considered "noble" to sneak up on an opponent or to kill him when he was unsuspecting. Clashes had to be in the open, in daylight, and each fighting unit had to be allowed to see the other. Even hippeis, the ancient Greek cavalry, which had maneuverability, did not ordinarily employ ambush techniques. They were used more as a means to project force onto the battlefield against massed infantry troops than to surprise fixed armies with mounted charges.[19] With the advent of guerilla warfare, sneak attacks were probably understood but not tolerated among leaders due to the ethos of war. The ancient Chinese military strategist Sun Tzu wrote of the use of deception in battle, but not of ambush. He believed that knowledge of the enemy was as important as courage, but he did not endorse outright killing by surprise.[20]

Ambush, therefore, may be considered a more "modern" tactic, and all military units employ some type of surprise maneuver designed to lure an unsuspecting enemy into a trap. Native Americans used such tactics against the overwhelming firepower of European settlers in the seventeenth century. It presents a new gradient on the killing scale because the enemy soldier, while still armed, will be surrounded in a killing zone and destroyed before he can make effective use of his weapon. The infantry soldier is confronted with killing a combatant who momentarily is a noncombatant. This kill will not have the same exhilarating "feel" to it that a frontal confrontation would have, because the noble kill of combat requires fairness and equality of risk, which could not exist if the enemy never knew the attack was imminent. But ambush is effective and decreases the likelihood of casualties on one side.

But is ambush of a military unit an atrocity? The victims are by definition armed. And any soldier who wants to achieve victory in modern warfare knows he must seize the advantage wherever it may be found. During the Vietnam War, the guerilla tactics of the vc, which included ambushes that were often initiated by booby-trapping trails, were absolutely necessary if they were to succeed against the superior firepower of American forces. And the American response to vc ambushes was to use the same tactic whenever possible to gain the element of surprise. But it was considered one step closer to destruction of a noncombatant, even though a weapon was seized after the kill was completed. The use of the ambush in Vietnam presented other issues that ultimately led to racial attitudes that U.S. officers and soldiers developed toward the enemy. "The hit-and-hide tactics of the Viet Cong were seen as cowardly rather than competent and resourceful and the Viet Cong were viewed as 'not real soldiers.'"[21] Reminiscent of colonists' attitudes toward Native Americans who fought from behind trees rather than engaging the Europeans in the linear warfare style developed on the Continent, the vc were seen as the modern-day "savages."[22] "They were called madmen and animals and were said to lack any emotions. In addition to being dirty and smelling bad, the enemy were puny and ugly, perhaps an outward sign that they were enemies of God."[23]

In interviews with Vietnam combat veterans, there is a noticeable difference in their attitude toward the vc enemy as opposed to the pavn enemy. "We were constantly harassed by small bands of Viet Cong hit & run tactics [*sic*]. North Vietnamese chose their battles carefully and only engaged 'in force' when odds appeared in their favor."[24] Since "hit and run" has a connotation of illegality, such tactics were viewed, when done by the enemy, as less than honorable. "Both were effective in types of battles they fought — Viet Cong were good at hit & run and (North) Vietnamese were battle oriented."[25] The distinction between being "sneaky" and facing down the Americans was paramount in the eyes of the infantry soldiers. And for one combat veteran, the vc crossed the line. "The nva were well armed and trained; Viet Cong were retaliation driven, not concerned with Rules of War or Vietnamese people — just kill gis."[26]

Should the American search-and-destroy mission be placed in this gray area on the spectrum? To be successful, it had to contain an element of surprise, and it was necessary that the enemy soldier be caught without his unit's capabilities at their maximum efficiency. There was also the destruction of property to lessen the likelihood of future sanctuary by the enemy. All of these operations led to soldiers encountering civilians and prisoners of war, the treatment of which is next on the Grossman model.

THE DARK AREAS: SLAYING THE IGNOBLE ENEMY

The execution of enemy prisoners, whether civilians or soldiers, crosses the line because it is simply the murder of noncombatants. In antiquity, negotiated truces allowed for the exchange of prisoners, or enslavement of the vanquished by the victors might occur. Rarely does one find reference in ancient warfare to the slaying of unarmed soldiers or civilians once they had surrendered their weapons.

In modern warfare, expediency is frequently cited as the reason for not taking prisoners. Units on the move cannot be held up by the requirement of logistical support for feeding and securing prisoners. Moving them to the rear requires support groups to handle the care and feeding, and frequently the unit has not made such a provision. This is the first time in our spectrum analysis that we have encountered an opportunity for an institution to enter the decision-making process in the gradient of killing, because a decision to "take no prisoners" should be made by the units' commanders, not the troops and their local leadership.

Events in Nanking, China, in 1937 provide a stark example of the decision making required to affect this dark area of our spectrum. The local leadership ordered all prisoners to be executed, ostensibly because there was not enough food in the city to feed both the Japanese and Chinese troops. An elaborate plan was put forth that detailed the schedule of executions, the procedure for moving prisoners from holding pens to killing sites, and how the bodies would be destroyed. Memoranda were sent out to the regiment commanders. "All prisoners of war are to be executed. Method of execution: divide the prisoners into groups of a dozen. Shoot to kill separately."[27] Once this order was issued, the gradient point on the killing spectrum moved beyond the slaying of the ignoble enemy into one of stark execution.

The German army in World War II was presented with a similar dilemma. On the eastern front, Operation Barbarossa was intended to inflict great hardship on the Russian military and civilian infrastructure. The soldiers were ordered to execute local leaders, or "commissars," and to "shoot certain categories of POWs and civilians." They also took to indiscriminate shooting without regard for the particular categories that had been singled out for murder by their superiors.[28] Again, institutional decision making regarding how to kill led to this form of atrocity. The German soldier, after a campaign across frozen turf and after many days of intense combat, was faced with committing acts that were considered atrocious in comparison with what he had encountered previously.

But the killing of POWs sometimes occurs with "hazy" institutional direction, and U.S. troops have been guilty of such actions, even before the Vietnam War. Members of the 83rd Chemical Mortar Battalion (4.2 inch) fought alongside and in support of American infantry divisions in the invasion of Europe. Several of these elderly combat veterans prepared a collection of their stories in a book titled *Mark Freedom Paid: A Combat Anthology*, in which they recounted their experiences with POWs:

> We and the paratroopers had been ordered to take no prisoners before seaborne troops arrived. Late that first afternoon, a half-dozen Jerries walked into our position weaponless, with hands held high. Not knowing where their weapons might be, we couldn't let them wander loose. Some FFI partisans came along then, a group of about ten men led by a young woman, all armed with light American-made grease guns. We told them of our "No Prisoners" order, and the woman said, "Don't worry; we'll take care of them for you." The Jerries were then marched away, around a bend in the road, and a couple of minutes later we heard automatic weapons fire.[29]

The unit collaborated in allowing the French resistance to carry out their American orders; thus institutional input resulted in the slaying of these ignoble enemies. Whether the orders have come from above, or whether the soldiers or officers act on their own, the results can be devastating for those who have been disarmed, as related to Stephen Ambrose in his tale of the exploits of E Company, 506th Regiment, 101st Airborne Division, in *Band of Brothers*: "They were under guard and were digging a road side ditch. Lieutenant Spiers stopped, broke out a pack of cigarettes, and gave each POW a light. He stepped back up on the road and watched them inhale and chat. Suddenly and without warning he unslung the Thompson .45-caliber submachine-gun he always carried and fired into the group. He continued raking back and forth until all the POWs were dead."[30] This junior officer personally slew the ignoble enemy; by the Grossman standard, that is an atrocity. If logistical expediency was the reason for the atrocious behavior, it is still in violation of the rules of engagement and is morally wrong.

The taking of prisoners during the Vietnam War rarely presented junior officers with a logistical dilemma. Medevac and resupply choppers were usually available, thus affording opportunities to remove prisoners to a fire-base where valuable intelligence could be gained. The decision for the junior officer should have been an easy one, because such intelligence might contribute to the safety and security of his men. Yet there are instances where violations of the MACV directive occurred. "Sometimes we had them out walking point . . . looking for booby traps or snipers. If they were getting down, or ducking, or looking a little bit funny, we knew something was going to happen. We used them as decoys — something to give us a little advantage. But as far as beating them or anything, we never did that."[31] While such action was technically a violation of the Geneva Conventions, forcing a prisoner of war to walk point was inhumane only if he had no knowledge of the area and would be subject to tripping a booby trap inadvertently, thus killing himself and his captors. And unlike the contemporary suicide bombers in the Middle East, VC and PAVN soldiers seldom killed themselves in order to kill American soldiers.[32] A POW could usually be trusted to try to avoid his own death, thus enabling the American troops to survive the patrol.

But junior officers were challenged to keep their troops from harassing prisoners, particularly if the "payback factor" was at work. "Frietag was shot today. It is his spine so he should be going home. Davis was also hit. Both by the same sniper. And we captured the sniper (three others too). I got hold of the VC that shot Jack. I went out of my head and almost beat him to death. I felt mixed up afterwards. I was glad I did it, but felt I had no right to. He was blindfolded and his hands were tied behind him, and I beat him with a rifle butt."[33] The junior officer in charge that day failed in his duties because he should have separated the POW from the entire platoon after a VC sniper had been so successful in wounding members of the unit.

Officers themselves frequently had to control their emotions about POWs because it was often their soldiers who had been killed in battle. James McDonough's memoir *Platoon Leader* contains an honest account of his over-reaction to the knowledge that a Revolutionary Development cadre was VC and had crawled into the ammo bunker within their NDP in order to blow it up.

Somehow he had palmed a razor blade which we had not found when we searched him. As I spoke, his right hand smashed toward my throat, the blade aiming at my jugular vein. My reflexes were quick enough to catch his hand as it reached for my neck, and I twisted his hand violently until the razor dropped at his feet. Enraged, I grabbed him around his throat with both my hands, pressing my thumbs deeper and deeper into the mass of tissue and cartilage at the base of his neck. . . . I was like a mad animal whose only goal in life is to kill its enemy. . . . I hunched over him, trying desperately to squeeze the last of his life from his body. "Sir, you're killing him. You can't do that."[34]

McDonough was reacting the way many men would have under the same circumstances, but officers had to set examples for the enlisted men they led, especially in combat situations where everyone was armed and each man was a trained killer.

It is difficult to assess the degree to which U.S. soldiers killed POWs without first obtaining intelligence information. To execute a prisoner made little military sense, particularly under the *Chieu hoi* program, which provided American units with valuable soldiers and information. *Chieu hoi* means, in Vietnamese, "to come over," and the soldier who defects is a *hoi chanh*.[35] These former VC could eventually be trained to operate as "Kit Carsons" and lead U.S. units into VC-controlled areas. For a platoon leader, these men could assist the platoon in avoiding mines and booby traps, helping with prisoner identification and interrogation, and navigating the trails in VC-controlled areas. Every prisoner that was mistreated or executed was one less potential *hoi chanh*. The program was considered one of the most successful of the war, with 200,000 defectors changing sides.[36]

The Vietnam War has produced a body of mythology about the treatment of prisoners by U.S. soldiers, and since junior officers were the responsible persons in virtually every instance, the burden of proof regarding the truth has rested on those who were there. A notable myth, at least when first reported, was the incident that was pictured in U.S. newspapers of an alleged live prisoner being dropped from a helicopter. The army chief of staff ordered an investigation of the allegation, and the results indicated that the body was that of an NVA soldier who had been killed on an operation involving the 173rd Assault Helicopter Company near Lai Khe. A pilot had taken the pictures and stored the prints in a fellow soldier's air-conditioned hooch to preserve the developed film. Another pilot saw the prints and mailed them to his girlfriend in the States, with the caption, "This is how we get prisoners to talk."[37] The investigation showed that there was a POW aboard the helicopter as well as a KIA. The KIA was thrown overboard at a location several kilometers from where he had been killed, ostensibly to lower the morale of other PAVN troops in the region. The POW was taken to a rear base for interrogation. This "airborne funeral" had been ordered by a major. But the myth of this act being SOP in American units continued throughout the war, because it seemed logical, though brutal, that prisoners would talk if such a threat was made. However, prisoners talked anyway, without such a threat, and if a POW were thrown out of a helicopter, he could no longer offer any valuable intelligence. Officers flying the helicopters knew the value of intelligence.

Turning POWs over to the ARVN authorities for interrogation and disposition was SOP in many units, but the South Vietnamese often treated them with great brutality. "They would beat them upside the head a little bit and then shoot them. Or they would take and . . . I've seen them put prisoners in a push-up position with a bayonet on the ground: stick a bayonet in the ground under them and drop a sandbag on their shoulders — see how long he can stand it . . . before he ends up on top of that bayonet. Weird sight."[38] Or in some cases, U.S. troops entered an AO that had been recently vacated by ARVN units on a search-and-destroy mission.

> As we got close to the ocean we spotted bodies on the ground, directly in front of us. I warned the platoon not to move the bodies. If they were VC, they might have a live grenade in hand. When we reached the bodies we had weapons at the ready and held up. There were about a dozen corpses scattered across the ground. We looked closer and someone said "Look at their hands. They are tied behind their backs. What do you think, chief?" It seems they were all executed. Someone shot all of them in the back of the head. . . . I would assume we chased these gooks into the ARVN's lap. Then they were executed by them. These people treat each other far worse than the GIs treat them.[39]

Such executions were common in Vietnam, by ARVN, VC, and PAVN, but the degree to which U.S. units participated in such tactics was probably minimal. However, David Grossman's spectrum at the extreme end of civilian executions was reached by American units on a few occasions, particularly at My Lai, and with the more recent revelations of Tiger Force, a reconnaissance unit of the 101st Airborne Division that has been accused of committing atrocious behavior in 1967.

Grossman defines execution as the close-range killing of a noncombatant, either a civilian or a POW, who represents no significant or immediate military or personal threat to the killer. The effect of such murders on the killer is intensely traumatic, since the killer has limited internal motivation to murder the victims and kills almost entirely out of external motivations.[40] Of course, if such an act is traumatic for the killer, it is more profoundly so for the victim. Now we are entering the realm of extreme violence, perhaps characterized by institutional intent and resulting in no immediate military benefit.

Again, there are only a few references to this type of atrocity in antiquity. If a particular Greek polis was trying to send a message to another polis, then perhaps a representative phalanx might be executed, but this type of military unit behavior was completely abhorrent to the Greek warrior ethos.

The notable exception was the destruction of Melos by Athens in 416 B.C.: "The Melians surrendered unconditionally to the Athenians, who put to death all the men of military age whom they took, and sold the women and children as slaves."[41] Larry Tritle, professor of classics at Loyola Marymount University and a Vietnam veteran, writes in *From Melos to My Lai* that the Athenians had been embarrassed by the actions of the Melians, who had staged a great battle against the most powerful military force in the world. Athenian leaders made an institutional decision to destroy the city and either kill or enslave its residents, as a form of payback.[42] But such references are rare in ancient military history because of the ethos of the warrior. Typically institutions, not soldiers, direct such atrocious behavior.

There are, however, many examples of such annihilation in modern warfare. Iris Chang's book *The Rape of Nanking* reports that the execution of more than 100,000 POWs preceded the execution of another 200,000 civilians. Furthermore, the only reason that the execution of the POWs was included in the previous section dealing with a gray area of ignobleness is because of the events that followed. The tragedy at Nanking defies literary description, not only because of the sheer numbers involved, but because of the brutality of the killing. At the core of this behavior was institutional direction and sanction. The carnage was so pronounced that the Nazi ambassador to China reported that even Adolf Hitler was outraged.

During World War II, the German military atrocities were not confined to concentration and death camps. The Holocaust reigns supreme among crimes against humanity, and there is little debate about that issue. But the behavior of Reserve Police Battalion 101 in Poland in 1942 remains the single most abhorrent account of sheer brutality among World War II atrocities. The mission of the battalion was to round up the Jews of certain rural villages in Poland, send the men of working age to work camps, and execute the elderly men, women, and children. This order was sent down from "the highest authorities"; thus it was institutional.

This type of deviant behavior was ordered by a government that had already begun the destruction of the European Jewish population, but this particular action was unique because it singled out a unit of soldiers to carry out the murders of the "least combatant of the non-combatants." No military significance can be argued, and even the value of a terrorist's exhibition and the instilling of fear in the populace seems not to have been a factor, since no traces were left for discovery.

THE MY LAI MASSACRE would probably be at the top of the list if Americans were asked to name the most atrocious act ever committed by soldiers of a U.S. military unit. The number of victims was never completely established, but on March 16, 1968, Charlie Company of the 11th Brigade, 23rd Infantry Division (Americal), massacred noncombatants in two hamlets of Son My Village, Quang Ngai Province, Republic of Vietnam. The Peers Commission Report would place the number of dead between 175 and 400. One American soldier was wounded. This incident became known as the My Lai massacre, and the lone convicted perpetrator was Lt. William Laws Calley.[43]

The My Lai massacre focused attention on the junior officer corps in the Vietnam War because of Lieutenant Calley's conviction as a murderer. The evidence of his culpability was overwhelming, but the defense's responses to the buildup provided evidence that Charlie Company "and the situation in Pinkville was ripe for the animal to emerge."[44]

The My Lai massacre has been discussed previously as the defining moment in the military's criticism of the junior officer corp. To understand the events of March 15–16, 1968, one must examine the background of the unit that assaulted My Lai (4). The hamlet was part of the village of Son My, located near the South China Sea in the province of Quang Ngai (see map 2). The area was considered a VC stronghold because elements of the 48th NLF Battalion had retreated to the village after attacking Quang Ngai City during the countrywide TET Offensive. The unit had actually overrun and briefly held the Regional Forces/Popular Forces Training Center there until driven out by counterattacking 2nd ARVN Division forces.[45] So the unit withdrew to the mountains in the western part of the province to "lick their wounds," to reorganize and refit a unit that had lost more than 150 men during TET, including the battalion commander, two company commanders, and one company commander who was captured. With its strength reduced to 250 men, it combined forces with two other companies in the region so that overall guerilla strength in the My Lai area on March 15, 1968, was approximately 700 fighters.[46]

The local hamlets in Son My had supported rebellion forces dating back to the French occupation. My Lai (1) had been burned to the ground by ARVN forces before the U.S. Army was deployed to the province in 1965, and the villagers retreated as refugees to Quang Ngai City on numerous occasions. The government of Vietnam (GVN) had tried to relocate them to refugee centers, but because of the depressing life in such centers, villagers constantly drifted back to their old hamlets, and into VC control. So on March 15, 1968, the GVN considered all who continued to live in Son My Village to be VC or VC sympathizers.[47]

The NLF units operating in Son My were highly motivated and reasonably well equipped to obtain detailed intelligence about U.S. Army operations. Although they were woefully understrengthened as a fighting unit, they took great advantage of the sympathy of the local villagers to effectively deny American military superiority in the area. In addition to ambushing small convoys, attacking GVN district headquarters, and assassinating local Vietnamese officials, they had established an effective system for the extensive use of mines and booby traps on both trails and forested areas around the hamlets. Since their own forces were understrengthened, they used the local villagers to help construct incredibly lethal homemade death traps: punji pits, swinging hinged traps suspended from abandoned hooches that could effectively drive sharp objects into the groin area of a soldier, and command- and trip-wire-detonated unexpended ordnance. These booby traps and mines had been rigged and maintained by old men, women, and children, or at least this appeared so to the soldiers of the 11th Infantry Brigade, 23rd Infantry Division (Americal), on March 15, 1968.[48]

The American soldiers who would enter My Lai (4) hamlet were similarly understrengthened like their VC counterparts. The 23rd Infantry (Americal) was a patchwork organization that had been put together with units of the 196th Infantry Division in Vietnam in 1967, the 198th Infantry Division in training at Fort Hood, Texas, and the 11th Infantry Division in Hawaii. As these units were separately sent to Vietnam, leadership asked for, and was granted, a month of in-country training before committing any of the units to combat. This included exercises on how to properly load and deplane from helicopters, as well as how to effectively use artillery and Cobra gunship support. But personnel turbulence once the units were in Vietnam created many leadership holes in both noncommissioned and commissioned slots. This was not, however, unusual, and the Peers Report believed it to be a common occurrence when compared to other units that had previously deployed to Vietnam. As the war heated up in mid-1967, all units were faced with a "rotational hump."[49]

At the company level, both C/1-20 Infantry and B/4-3 Infantry received further unit training in the "5Ss" of handling prisoners: search, silence, segregate, speed, and safeguard. This was, however, instruction only in the handling of armed and usually uniformed prisoners, and no instructions were provided on the handling of civilians.

Prior to the Son My operation on March 16, Charlie Company had not been involved in any operations that resulted in combat, although it had patrolled in the Quang Ngai Province and conducted base security. Casualties were 4 KIA and 38 WIA, with only 1 of the KIA and 2 of the WIA having been caused by direct enemy fire; the others had been caused by mines and booby trap explosions.

As to the American soldiers themselves, two-thirds of the NCOs were enlistees and had scored above the army average on all evaluated tests. They also exceeded the army average in high school graduation rates and college courses attended.[50] As to the officers, Capt. Ernest Medina, the CO of C/1-20th Infantry, was a twelve-year veteran who had served eight years as an enlisted man before attending OCS in 1964. His OCS test score of 108 was too low to gain him admittance, but a retest raised his score to 118, which exceeded the requirement by 3 points.[51] He had taken freshman-level courses in history, psychology, English composition, sociology, and accounting at the University of Maryland extension service and had received high Officer Efficiency Report scores from his superiors. "A man of high morals, and professional competence . . . he should continue his exemplary performance in any higher grade." "Capt. Medina is without question the most outstanding officer of his grade and experience I have ever known." Three weeks prior to the My Lai massacre, Medina received the Silver Star for leading his unit against the enemy, although the Peers Report indicated that C/1-20th had not been on any combat operations.[52]

Lt. William Laws Calley, 1st Platoon Leader, C/1-20th, had tried to enlist in the army in 1964 but was turned down because of "faulty hearing." He passed his subsequent draft physical and was assigned as a clerk after basic training. He scored 115 on his test, the minimum score allowed for ocs; however, his reviewing officer recommended a branch assignment of Adjutant or Intelligence, rather than Infantry. His Officer Efficiency Report ratings were "very satisfactory," but Captain Medina noted in Calley "a weakness in his ability to express himself orally to both his subordinates and his superiors alike." This rating period included the time of the My Lai massacre, and his ratings went downhill thereafter; after Calley left Vietnam, however, one rater said, "I could ask no more than to have men of this caliber beside me in combat."[53]

Except for the fact that most of the chain of command involved in the My Lai massacre had attended ocs, the only common thread that the analysts could discern when they first learned of the March 16 tragedy was that most of the officers were "short in stature."[54] But Lt. William Laws Calley became one of the most infamous figures of the Vietnam War, regardless of his physical attributes, when he failed to exercise the kind of leadership he was taught in ocs. His failure to set a proper example for his troops meant he would be personally responsible for the deaths of many of the 175–400 who were murdered at My Lai (4).

The command structure of Task Force Barker, which conducted the search-and-destroy mission at Son My, issued orders that violated MACV directives. Artillery and gunship preparatory fire was ordered on hamlets in which noncombatants likely lived. While the Peers Report indicated some discrepancy as to whether coordinates had been given on the edge of My Lai (4) or directly on the hamlet, between 60 and 120 high-explosive rounds had been fired in preparation for the ground attack that would follow. The burning and destruction of hooches was also ordered, which can be done under MACV directives only if weapons, uniforms, and large quantities of rice are found that indicate substantial enemy support. Livestock and foodstuffs were also ordered to be destroyed because Son My was considered to be VC territory. While the intelligence supported such a concept, the troops were told to destroy "everything" *before* they had been able to confirm the intelligence.

The most controversial command order involved the handling of civilians or noncombatants. The Peers Report stated, "Lieutenant Colonel Barker intentionally or negligently provided false intelligence that civilians would be out of the hamlets in the Son My Village area by 0700 hours, March 16,

1968 and indicated that only vc and vc sympathizers would be in the village, thereby contributing to the killing of numerous non-combatants on that date."[55] No further instructions were given regarding noncombatants who may have decided *not* to go to market that day, and the lack of further instructions required company commanders to decide for themselves as to what actions should be taken.

When elements of C/1-20th entered My Lai (4), the soldiers reacted the way most troops would react after preparatory bombardment of artillery: people who ran were considered to be vc and were pursued. According to sop, persons who had been ordered to halt were to be detained, searched for weapons, and then removed to a holding area where they would be inter-rogated. In My Lai (4), those who ran, even if they were women or children, were shot. Although both the 1st Platoon, commanded by Lieutenant Calley, and the 2nd Platoon, commanded by Lieutenant Brooks, worked through the village in overlapping patrols, the behavior of the units was not identical. While virtually all of the soldiers began to shoot pigs, chickens, and cows and throw fragmentation or white phosphorous grenades into hooches, the reac-tions of the two units differed in that the 1st Platoon under Lieutenant Calley tended to take civilians prisoner and herd them into a holding area. Lieutenant Brooks's 2nd Platoon had "run berserk." After one group of Vietnamese had been killed in front of a hut, the first squad leader, Sgt. Kenneth Scheil, began telling the men with him that he did not like what they were doing but that he had to obey orders. "The villagers had huddled together for safety, but the Americans poured fire into them, tearing their bodies apart, one man firing a machine gun at random, others using their M-16s on fully automatic."[56] According to Thomas Partsch, a member of the 2nd Platoon, Lieutenant Brooks had "totally lost control."[57] His reputation was of a leader who identified with his men and who wanted to be considered "one of the boys."

Lieutenant Brooks had also failed in the "lead by example" category prior to the operation at Son My. He had allowed his troops to seek sexual release in villages where they had patrolled because "they've got to get it someplace and they might as well get it in the village."[58] Having demonstrated his acceptance of such atrocious behavior before the Son My operation, he was powerless to enforce a stricter code of behavior when his 2nd Platoon en-tered the subhamlet of Binh Tay, 500 meters north of My Lai (4). "A number of the men violated the same girl. . . . When a girl was being raped; the others moved in quickly to get some of the action. Several men saw three GIs with the girl. One had penetrated her, one was having oral sex with her, and she was fondling the penis of the third."[59] Lieutenant Brooks had participated with his troops in several sexual encounters in previous patrols, and any words he may have offered discouraging such behavior in My Lai would probably have been rejected by his men because of his previous activity.

For Lieutenant Calley's 1st Platoon, there was some indiscriminant firing into hooches and the cold-blooded murdering of innocent civilians. But his platoon appeared to have been more concerned with rounding up potential POWS than with exerting pure brutality, as was being done by the 2nd Platoon. Calley's men had acted according to SOP learned in unit training regarding the "5Ss" of search, silence, segregate, speed, and safeguard. This may partially explain why the court-martial board found him guilty, because he had an opportunity to move the detainees to another, safer and more secure, location. His platoon had collected about sixty Vietnamese and had ordered them to squat down. Calley appeared with his RTO and asked why these civilians were being held. "We're watching over them," replied Sergeant Meadlo. "No, I want them killed," replied Lieutenant Calley. "We'll get on line and fire into them." Calley turned to Meadlo and said, "Fire when I say 'Fire.' " Calley and Meadlo, standing side by side, blazed away. Mothers had thrown themselves on top of the young ones in a last desperate bid to protect them from the bullets raining down on them. Calley fired at both the mothers and the children, killing them one by one. Then he calmly said, "OK, let's go."[60]

This episode of individual killing was led by a junior officer demonstrating to his troops how to kill efficiently and, according to Calley, how to follow orders. Nothing in his OCS training at Fort Benning had prepared him for this. He took command, killed, and expected the same from his men, or as the Peers Report charged, "He directed and supervised the men of his platoon in the systematic killing of many non-combatants in and around My Lai (4) and he personally participated in the killing of some non-combatants in and around My Lai (4)."[61]

Lieutenant Calley's horrendous leadership did not stop with these first rounded-up victims. His platoon had managed to secure fifty more detainees by a ravine. The record does not indicate that they were being shepherded together so that they could be killed, but when told of their aggregation, Calley went to the site. A member of the platoon was questioning a monk, and Calley intervened. When the monk failed to answer appropriately, Calley struck him in the mouth with his rifle butt, completely ignoring his religious

Bodies of women and children, My Lai (4) at Son My Village (photo taken by former U.S. Army sergeant Ronald L. Haeberle; courtesy of the Dallas Morning News Collection, Texas Tech University, The Vietnam Archive, VA014353, and Getty Images/Time & Life Pictures)

position. And when a two-year-old child crawled to the top of the ditch crying, probably because he had been separated from his mother, Calley picked the child up, shoved him back down the slope of the ditch, and shot him, without interrupting the interrogation of the witness. He was not mad or out of control. He was doing what he thought was necessary to handle the situation.

But this junior officer still was not finished. He shot the monk he had been interrogating and then an elderly *mama-son* who had been wounded earlier and had crawled to Calley's feet. Then he told the two soldiers standing next to him that he wanted everyone killed. When they refused, he and one other soldier began firing into the irrigation ditch, killing all who were there.[62]

The story of the My Lai massacre cannot properly be told without recognition of an officer who performed heroically amid the carnage of March 16, 1968. Chief Warrant Officer Hugh Thompson landed his helicopter in the middle of the massacre and confronted Calley about what he had witnessed: "I asked him if he could get the women and kids out of there before they tore it up, and he said the only way he could get them out was to use hand grenades. 'You just hold your men right here, and I'll get the women and kids out,' I told him." Another soldier said of this heroic pilot, "He told us that if any of the Americans opened up on the Vietnamese, we should open up on the Americans. He stood between our troops and the bunker. He was shielding the people with his body. He just wanted to get those people out of there."[63] Chief Warrant Officer Thompson was a junior officer in the U.S. Army, and he had been subjected to the same selection process and training as Lieutenant Calley. But Thompson understood his job and the importance of effective leadership in a time of crisis.

Three years after the My Lai massacre, the vvaw defended Calley's actions because they believed that his behavior paled in comparison to "the high ranking officials of the Johnson and Nixon administration."[64] Jan Barry, writing in the *New York Times*, said, "To kill on military orders and be a criminal, or refuse to kill and be a criminal, is the moral agony of America's Vietnam War generation."[65] Perhaps when one views warfare in the political sense, such a statement is somewhat credible. But no one at My Lai was prosecuted for refusing to fire into a ditch full of old men, women, and children, nor, to my knowledge, was anyone during the Vietnam War ever prosecuted for refusing to kill noncombatants. Calley's position of leadership, however, demanded that he perform his duties in a manner consistent with the orders he had been given through his chain of command. His platoon had delivered detainees who had been secured and who posed no military threat to his unit. He initiated the killing en masse. He should have been the officer who stopped the frequent but isolated killing by those in his platoon who had become enraged. He was the one responsible for the hundreds of deaths in My Lai (4) on March 16, 1968, although one can make a strong case that others above his rank should also have stood trial and, based on the evidence in Calley's trial, should have been convicted and punished.

Every combat platoon leader in Vietnam had the opportunity to kill noncombatants or to lead his men into actions that would have produced high civilian body counts. Yet there is nothing in the military records or in journalists' records that indicates any atrocious behavior on the scale of that in Son My Village. Many reported instances of war crimes were brought to the attention of the army, and after the My Lai massacre, there were more brought forward than prior to the event. Only 50 allegations were brought against U.S. soldiers before the massacre was made public, and 191 were brought after that date.[66] And in none of these incidents did a platoon leader lead his men into a frenzy of killing noncombatants.[67]

Dave Grossman's black area of execution is at the extreme end of the spectrum, and it is rare in military history. One can make the case that dropping 500-pound bombs from 36,000 feet and killing innocent civilians is the equivalent of many Son Mys. But infantry officers have a unique responsibility because they frequently look the enemy in the eye prior to pulling the trigger; thus they can usually identify those whom they kill with small arms fire. Civilians, children, and noncombatants are not the intended targets of rapid-fire weapons.

For his failure to lead his platoon properly at My Lai (4) and for the murders that he personally committed, Lt. William Laws Calley was judged by a jury of combat veterans to have committed atrocious acts serious enough to warrant maximum punishment under the Uniform Code of Military Justice. His egregious actions cannot be condoned under any circumstances, whether in a just or an unjust war. William Peers, in an oral history after his retirement, said, "That young man was very fortunate to not have served life in prison."[68] President Richard Nixon's commutation of the sentence was a travesty of justice that denigrated the sacrifices of all who served honorably in combat roles and who exercised restraint in the face of the enemy.

As a postscript to the My Lai massacre, the army revised its training in the law of land warfare and doubled the amount of time, from one to two hours, soldiers must spend on matters of the Geneva Conventions. It did, however, require a combat veteran to be part of the process, in addition to a Judge Advocate General Corps officer.[69]

"WE . . . BOILED THE FLESH off enemy skulls to make table ornaments for sweethearts, or carved their bones into letter openers."[70] This passage from John Dower's seminal work *War without Mercy: Race and Power in the Pacific War* describes activities that most Americans find abhorrent but that were associated more with soldiers in Vietnam than with "the good guys" who fought in World War II. But soldiers have taken trophies from the enemy dead throughout history, and Vietnam was no different. Junior officers were constantly reminded of the need to closely supervise the activities of their troops, particularly after contact with the enemy. In one of the most bizarre incidents, a senior NCO forced one of his troops to do the unimaginable:

> On or about 18 February, 1968, MSG E7 Durwood W. Ashbaugh, D Troop, 17th Cavalry, 199th Infantry Brigade (Sep), ordered Sp4 James R. Choquette, a member of MSG Ashbaugh's platoon, to cut the head

off a Vietnamese corpse, near the platoon's bivouac area, and bring it back to him. MSG Ashbaugh, who was the platoon sergeant, threatened SP4 Choquette with jail unless he complied with the order. SP4 Choquette reluctantly and with personal anguish, used a machete to sever the head from the corpse. He gave the severed head to MSG Ashbaugh, who then boiled it until all of the flesh fell off. It was alleged that MSG Ashbaugh traded the skull to an unknown third party for a radio a few days later. 1st Lt. Delbert L. Ehler, the platoon leader, heard MSG Ashbaugh order SP4 Choquette to sever the head, but he took no effective action to prevent the incident from occurring. He was also present during the time MSG Ashbaugh was boiling the severed head and again took no action in the matter.[71]

The soldier violated MACV Directive 20-4, specifically the section related to "defiling or ridiculing enemy dead."[72] While most incidents regarding the dead were not as despicable as this one, which was reminiscent of the acts committed by U.S. soldiers in the Pacific during World War II, these types of behavior constitute war crimes. But they were often considered nuisances by junior officers who were expected to keep such things from happening.

In Vietnam, the most common form of body defilement was the "cutting of ears." The origin of this atrocious behavior is not known, but some believe it was caused by the emphasis of commanders on verifiable body counts. "Cat, what's the deal with the ears? The gooks are very superstitious and believe that when they die, if any part of their body is missing, they won't go to be with their ancestors — it is also a way to prove body count, which higher-higher wants lots of."[73] Since most commanders inflated the reports of junior officers anyway (see Chapter 6), it is improbable that those at the rear were more likely to believe the body count just because ears were provided as evidence.

On the contrary, most units discouraged such activities and punished the perpetrators.

I cut the clothes off and then took my knife and cut both the ears off the dead man. I did this because a close friend of mine, like a brother, had been KIA in Vietnam. Later, a friend wrote to his family and said he had been beheaded. . . . I decided to do the same to them. I put them in a hand-kerchief and then in my pocket. . . . I put the ears in a peanut can in my hooch and went to chow. When I came back they were gone. . . . I didn't care that much about the ears as such. My intent was to cut the man's head off, but I couldn't bring myself to do that. . . . I had heard that in some units this practice was common. . . . I was never told anything in the company specifically about treatment of enemy bodies.[74]

This soldier was replaced in the unit but was not disciplined. The concern on the part of the platoon leader was that his behavior might be infectious and cause others to perform similarly. Junior officers had to decide if this kind of violation was serious enough to warrant discipline, because some men who participated in such atrocious behavior were very good infantry soldiers who performed well in combat situations. "If a guy would have a necklace of ears, he was a good killer, a good trooper. It was encouraged to cut ears off."[75] But if a unit had strict rules against such behavior, as apparently the L/75th of the 101st Airborne Division (Airmobile) did, then junior officers were forced to train their men to avoid such activities. This was particularly true when replacements came to a unit from in-country, and they had operated with less discipline in the field.

They had, the platoon sergeant had told us this one soldier that you know, to be a part of this platoon, to be a man, you've got to bring me a set of Vietnamese ears. My . . . the defendant, the particular fellow involved was a, I think a fairly typical American soldier. He took that word at face value and he went in a friendly village, shot a friendly Vietnamese and cut off his ears and took them to the platoon sergeant. The platoon sergeant was absolutely shocked and the lieutenant was shocked and ultimately the private, the lieutenant, and the sergeant were all court marshaled. That to me was, you know, a mini My Lai situation. This was a law of war type crime. It was tried within the corps headquarters. The soldier got his punishment, he did go to jail. The sergeant got some punishment as did the lieutenant but it was never what My Lai became, granted the numbers were small. One of the legal ironies of that case was that the command structure was so incensed, so upset about the mutilation of the corpse that they never charged the soldier with murder and in fact it was a murder. He killed this fellow, and they only proceeded on the mutilation issue, so sometimes things in the combat zone do get a little fuzzed up but at least the system was resolved within the combat situation.[76]

Similarly despicable activities included taking pictures of the dead after a successful operation, propping the bodies into poses reminiscent of holding an eight-point buck and rifle across one's lap after a successful hunt. "The next morning we took turns taking pictures of the dead, propping them up against rice dikes and putting cigarettes in their slack mouths. We even put our arms around them and helmets on their heads."[77] Such behavior also invited an arrogance that was not healthy on future operations. But this behavior, to most units, was on the low end of atrocious behavior.[78]

THE U.S. ARMY TOOK some steps to improve the training that officers received regarding atrocious behavior in combat. Exercises that required students of IOBC and OCS to decide how to handle particularly delicate situations were added to the POI in 1972.

> You are the battalion commander and one of your company commanders approaches you with the following problems:
> While on a company size operation his unit was taken under fire from an enemy machinegun. Three of his men were killed in the initial burst and several others were wounded as they assaulted the gun position. Just as one of the men worked himself into a position to bring effective fire on the enemy position, the enemy gunner with hands raised moved into the open and shouted "I surrender." The man who had worked himself into a position to bring effective fire immediately killed the surrendering enemy. The company commander states that one of the men killed was the best friend of the soldier who killed the surrendering soldier and he feels that due to the mental stress involved nothing should be done and the whole incident should be forgotten. What guidance do you give him?

> You have captured three enemy soldiers. It is imperative that you find out the location of their unit. Several alternative methods of interrogation have been suggested. Discuss the legality/illegality of each situation.
> A. Take them on a sightseeing ride in a helicopter while the questioning is going on.
> B. Do not feed them until they talk.
> C. Get them drunk in hopes that the whiskey will loosen their tongues.
> D. Refuse to give them medical treatment until they give you the information.
> E. Administer mild shock treatment so that there is no danger of death.
> F. Have a doctor administer truth serum.[79]

Such challenges motivated students to at least understand the problems they might face in battle and to develop options for action that were reasonable within the context of war. Once commissioned, junior officers had to decide how far they would let their troops stray from appropriateness and still maintain an effective fighting unit. It was a fine line between ear cutting, picture taking, and murder at Son My: "Someday there would be vc with sticks and stones and frying pans and weapons: someday soon, and the gis would need a high fighting spirit. A high morale, and if just cutting hair off a Vietnamese or beating hell out of a prostitute or just being with a prostitute or throwing away an empty water can, a bandolier, or a rifle: if just being human beings did it, I would forgive it. Or hell, I wouldn't have had a gi left."[80] These are the words of Lt. William Laws Calley, a platoon leader speaking about the days leading up to the My Lai (4) massacre. However, other platoon leaders saw their roles differently: "War is, at its very core, the absence of order, and the absence of order leads very easily to the absence of morality, unless the leader can preserve each of them in its place. The leader has to set the standards for morality as clearly as he sets the standards for personal hygiene or weapons maintenance. He must allow no cutting of corners. A bottle of soda stolen from an old peasant woman leads gradually but directly to the rape of her daughter if the line is not drawn in the beginning."[81] These are the words of Lt. James McDonough, who was also a platoon leader. Their contrasting approaches to their respective jobs are noteworthy and indicate that some junior officers were gentlemen, but others "crossed the line."

EIGHT

DISCIPLINE

The drug smoking within our unit was terrible, as it was always done on guard duty. This always left me with a very insecure feeling at night.[1]

My troubles began when a new captain was brought in and started giving everybody a hassle. He came in talking shit about haircuts, clean fatigues and bullshit like that. Everybody was coming down on him, and he was a black guy at that.... They were talking about fragging him.... During this time I was strung out on BTS *[barbiturates] real bad. One night I was all messed up on* BTS *and I was passing by the captain's hooch where he was sleeping. I had that case of grenades handy under my bed; so I just went over, got one, came back to his hooch, and threw it in. I fucked him up. I regret doing that, but I was fucked up at the time.... It didn't blow his leg off; he recovered pretty good because he was there at my court-martial.*[2]

Junior officers in Vietnam were responsible for morale and enforcement of discipline in their platoon. Because the war was fought on a squad, platoon, and company level, the responsibility for the day-to-day behavior of the troops was most often without senior officer review. In previous wars, soldiers were surrounded by large numbers of troops from other units, but in Vietnam an infantryman might go weeks without seeing another unit. So maintaining morale and enforcing discipline in the rear was often more challenging than directing the day-to-day combat operations because the lieutenant was, in some elementary way, just another member of the primary group with some of the same group dynamic limitations of the other soldiers.

The junior officer was sent to a unit in Vietnam as just another soldier. His identity as an officer had been diminished at the 90th repo-depo at Long

Binh, where he had stood in line like other soldiers to receive his duty assignment. Once he arrived at his unit, he was trained like any other soldier and learned how to function in a jungle, combat environment. And once he received his specific assignment, he was "choppered" to the unit, usually in the field. There he became the latest FNG (fucking new guy) and the newest member of the primary group.

A term borrowed from sociology, the primary group concept is particularly useful in analyzing combat situations, because of the isolation of a platoon from the rest of the battalion. The term is defined as those small social groupings in which social behavior is governed by intimate face-to-face relations.[3] Studies conducted in World War II had revealed that soldiers were more concerned about those around them than about those with whom they were engaged in battle. "The men seem to be fighting more for someone than against somebody," wrote psychiatrists Roy R. Grinker and John P. Spiegel.[4] Such comments were consistent with S. L. A. Marshall's observations in *Men against Fire* that "the thing which enables an infantry soldier to keep going with his weapons is the mere presence or the presumed presence of a comrade."[5] Marshall was not a sociologist, but his remarks reflected an understanding of combat situations: a soldier functions at maximum efficiency when he likes, respects, and is comfortable with the men in his unit. Such intense affection within the fighting group is referred to as unit cohesion.

Sociologist Charles Moskos studied unit cohesion in various military units in the Vietnam War, and he found that it derived from the desire of individuals to survive. Each soldier was fighting a "very private war"; thus unit cohesion was a "mandatory necessity rising from immediate life-and-death experiences."[6] To the extent that this danger was realized on a frequent basis, such repetitive exposure to carnage banded the group together, even if one or more of the unit was eliminated from the battle by wound or death. In World War II, where soldiers were assigned to a unit for the duration of the campaign or until the end of the war, the only way out of the unit was by an action of the enemy. In Vietnam, the yearly DEROS (date of expected return from overseas station), or in the case of marines, thirteen months, allowed soldiers to leave the unit, thus destroying for the moment the unit cohesion. "It would be hard to overstate the soldier's constant concern with how much more time — down to the day — he had remaining in Vietnam. Barring his being killed or severely wounded, every soldier knew his exact departure date from Vietnam; his whole being centered on reaching his personal DEROS."

This rotation system also deprived the unit of the most important ingre-

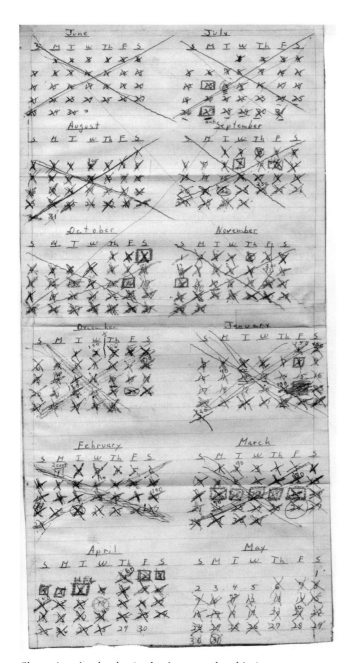

Short-timer's calendar (author's personal archive)

dient in successful combat operations: experience. Depending on his personality and background, a soldier usually felt a certain degree of exhilaration when first assigned to his combat unit. This usually lasted until the first serious contact with the enemy, particularly if there was a loss of life among his unit. However, with this encounter came the beginning of a confidence plateau that continued until about the ninth month in-country. Then he became an "old soldier," when he was most effective as a fighter, teacher, confidant, and leader. Beyond about the eleventh month, he developed "short-timer's fever" and became almost a danger to his unit because of his desire for avoidance of contact with the enemy.[7]

This description of rotational impact on units can be supported by an examination of U.S. soldiers' deaths by time in-country. Table 8.1 shows the number of soldiers who died, by service, according to the quarter of their tour that had been completed. Twice as many soldiers were killed during the first six months of their tour as in the second six months. Or, the longer one stayed alive after arrival, the better one's chances of survival.[8] Thus, the twelve-month tour affected unit cohesion not only by constantly interrupting the experience level of the unit but also by increasing the odds that an individual soldier would die in battle.

For the junior officer, the rotation policy caused turmoil within the squads. He first had to deal with the changing experience level of his unit, making certain that he distributed those who had been in battle most frequently throughout the platoon. But each time he made a change within squads, the unit cohesion of the fire teams was destroyed. Determining the optimum level of experienced combat veterans within each section of his platoon was a major part of his responsibility, and one that would directly affect his relationship with the men. This latter point was critical to combat efficiency, because psychologists and sociologists have confirmed the importance of the leader in unit cohesion.

Morris Janowitz describes the competence of the leader as most critical to unit cohesion. In studies of soldiers and leadership in past wars, the level of respect for the leader was in direct correlation with unit cohesion; hence there was an impact on combat effectiveness. British units that had been surveyed in World War I were found to have had respect for their leaders even when the leaders did not carry weapons and fight.[9] But in Vietnam, the platoon leader was a rifleman, machine-gunner, squad leader, compass man, RTO, and forward observer, because of the nature of small-unit tactics. Yet he was subjected to an even more stringent rotation policy than were his

Months in Country	Army	Marines	Navy	Air Force	Totals
First three months	11,502	3,692	367	237	15,798
Second three months	7,489	2,013	225	172	9,899
Third three months	5,045	1,349	113	138	6,645
Fourth three months	1,714	569	52	70	2,405
Over twelve months	653	176	47	15	893
Unknown — not reported	32	3,110	422	81	3,645
Totals	26,435	10,909	1,226	715	39,285

Source: Office of the Assistant Secretary of Defense (Comptroller), Directorate for Information.

soldiers, because platoon leaders were pulled from the field after six months in combat.[10] Most lieutenants were brought back to a firebase to perform battalion- or brigade-level staff duties, and a new, inexperienced lieutenant was brought in as a replacement.[11] "Generals like to have junior grade officers of recent front-line experience close to them. It provides them with a perspective on what the troops in the trenches are thinking."[12] Thus the platoon leader who survived his first six months was usually given an S-2 (Intelligence) or S-3 (Operations) job in the rear, enabling him to impart wisdom to those more senior officers who had not had combat experience. But the platoon that he left in the field would have to train a new leader, one who would arrive without combat experience and who would lack knowledge as to the qualities each soldier possessed in battle. He would also not have the confidence of the troops he was about to lead.

Lack of experience caused mishaps not only among the troops in the platoon but among the platoon leaders themselves. As an example of bad leadership, Patrick Lyons talked about the "2nd lieutenant who got killed trying to rescue me — shined a lite [*sic*] and a sniper got him!"[13] But the battlefield was an exceptionally dangerous place, particularly for leaders. "Lieutenant Cleveland's platoon was engaged in a firefight. He raised his head to look around and he was killed. 'He shouldn't have stuck his head up,' someone said. Sometimes . . . when you're the leader, you've got to."[14] Whether from inexperience or from proving to the troops that they were "one of them," junior officers had to determine the level of risk they were willing to take to create a combat-effective unit.

Since senior leaders expected the junior officer to represent them and their orders in the field, a platoon leader had to be cognizant of his dual role. "The officer in the tactical unit is also the final representative of coercive higher authority. For him to over-identify with his men would impair the system of authority. . . . Junior officers would like to enhance their authority but they are not prepared or permitted to display the direct contact with enlisted men that such increased authority would require."[15] Stated in soldiers' terms, is the platoon leader more of a "grunt" or an officer and a gentleman?

Gabriel Kolko writes in *Anatomy of a War*, "If an officer pressed his men, he was not likely to succeed in motivating them without taking their instinct of self-preservation into account. The most popular officer was the unambitious lieutenant who took no unnecessary risks and was responsible to his men and not his superiors. Such units had high morale and solidarity and minimum losses."[16] Was the goal to avoid enemy contact because doing so reduced the risk of losing men? "An infantry lieutenant's proudest boast was, 'I didn't send anyone home in a bag.'"[17] But a reluctance to engage the enemy did not mean a unit would not sustain casualties, particularly if it entered areas where troops were often ambushed. A junior officer's greater concern was how his troops perceived what the platoon was doing in the day-to-day operations that were being directed from battalion or company headquarters, and how the platoon leader responded to his superiors. Was he "gung-ho," or did he question the tactical significance of an order? Troops were usually willing to follow a leader who could explain why an operation was being conducted. "He was not gung-ho, not a man in search of a fight. It was more or less an Aristotelian ethic that Mad Mark practiced: Making war is a necessary and natural profession. It is natural, but it is only a profession, not a crusade. . . . He did what was necessary in war, necessary for an officer and platoon leader in war; he did no more or less."[18] Soldiers could sense the difference between leaders who followed orders so that they could improve their status as officers and those who followed orders to improve the status of survival, or the status of material gratification: stand-down time, in-country R&R, beer and steaks in the field, or whatever incentives the unit's hierarchy was offering.

None of the aforementioned considerations have dealt with ideology, because sociologists believe that patriotism or lack thereof is at the very bottom of the scale when dealing with the needs of combat soldiers. But the Vietnam

War was unique in American history because a strong antiwar sentiment developed in the United States during the war. Did this ideological event have an impact on the soldier's ability to fight effectively? Charles Moskos believes that there is always a certain decline in military order at the end of any war, but the military establishment in Vietnam, after 1968, drafted and received by enlistment soldiers who had been exposed to "an anti-war milieu that contrasted markedly with that of the early years."[19] However, the moral and political arguments against the war were not as significant as the growing pragmatic attitude toward the American "no-win" strategy and distress over the rising American casualties.[20] Thus soldiers began to react negatively to the orders of junior officers, probably as a result of soldiers' antipathy toward what they perceived as growing discontent by the society that sent them into battle rather than because of any change in their belief in the cause for which they had been sent to fight. And, notes Moskos, "the American Army in Vietnam did not disintegrate, it did not suffer mass defections, and it was not receptive to subversive political forces."[21]

So contrary to Kolko and others, much of the credit for the lack of disintegration lies with junior officers. Gen. William DePuy, who commanded the 1st Infantry Division in Vietnam, believed that the role of a lieutenant in combat was unique:

> Within a rifle platoon, the lieutenant finds himself within a body of fighting men some 30–40 strong, of varied skills and backgrounds, involved in a hazardous, often unpleasant task. The lieutenant is in charge because presumably he is a natural leader as well as a trained officer. But at that level, the UCMJ [Uniform Code of Military Justice] on which he must stand legally is rarely the instrument through which he exercises command. He is concerned about the lives and fears and hopes of his men and he feels very much a part of that small body. To the extent that he understands them and yet does not surrender to them, to that extent he will become a great leader. . . . No matter what the generals may think, there is an equalitarian aspect to the rifle platoon.[22]

DePuy believed that junior officers were the best soldiers to lead men into combat because they were so much like those they were asked to lead. But they would be challenged to perform these duties, particularly after 1969, when the army suffered drug and alcohol use problems, experienced racial tension, and discovered a new term for expressing discontent with authority: "fragging."

The extent to which soldiers in Vietnam used drugs was debated in the military press as well as in America's newspapers: "At least 50 percent, and probably more, of our troops in Vietnam are taking some form of drugs,"[23] wrote Col. R. D. Heinl Jr. in the *Detroit News*. Concern about the abuse of illegal drugs by American soldiers reached all the way to the White House in 1970. While preliminary military studies indicated that drug use by soldiers was no more extensive than by stateside American society, even the army recognized that there had been increased convictions of drug use since the early days of the war. President Nixon sent Egil "Bud" Krogh to Vietnam to investigate the problem, since the Department of Defense was not providing answers to the administration.[24] He went to several firebases, including Charlie 2, just south of the DMZ:

> I just went out, wandered around, and found a group of guys sitting around smoking marijuana. I said "Hi, I'm Bud Krogh from the White House." They just looked at me and one of them said, "Yeah man, and I'm from Mars." I said, "Look, nobody's gonna get punished, but I just want to get an idea of the availability of drugs over here." He said, "Well, what kind of shit do you want?" That was replicated in more or less the same vein on firebases all over the country! You don't have a drug problem, you have a drug condition. It's available everywhere, it's cheap, and you get guys who are sick and tired and bored and unhappy and scared and they're going to make use of these substances.[25]

"Bored" and "scared" were both appropriate words for describing the conditions under which soldiers turned to drugs. For the junior officer, supervising his soldiers' activities to ensure compliance with the unit's drug policies was a major task. Did he allow the use of illegal drugs in base camp, where the danger from an enemy attack was less, or must he enforce the rules to make certain that his troops understood that unit policies had to be carried out? And what about the senior NCOs who got drunk consistently on Jack Daniels bourbon, which was so cheaply accessible from the base PX (post exchange)?[26] "It's like you could drink until you passed out. I never passed out but I came pretty close. . . . You could go to the EM Club and buy a shot of good whiskey, whatever the best whiskey was that they had, for a quarter. You could buy a triple, three shots in the same glass, for seventy-five cents and that's going to give you pure whiskey, whatever you're drinking. You could go to the main PX in Chu Lai and buy a fifth of whiskey or a quarter whiskey probably for a dollar and a half, a dollar seventy-five. So alcohol was cheap."[27] This was a dilemma for platoon leaders, because they knew the value of quality stand-down time for soldiers, and most were recent arrivals from a society that had become more tolerant of drug use. But the army recognized that drug use was increasing and made an effort to determine the extent of the problem. General Westmoreland believed that the drug problem had "caught the command by surprise. A serious dilution over the war years in the caliber of junior leaders contributed to this and other disciplinary problems."[28] This comment was made after he had been promoted to the chief of staff position in April 1968 and therefore had responsibility for all theaters. So the general blamed the lieutenants for allowing drugs to become a problem. Late in the war, the army investigated the matter in several divisions to determine if it was as serious as some reporters had implied or whether it was similar to the issues associated with abuse of alcohol. The army wanted to know if combat effectiveness was being affected by such drug abuse or if the problem was being managed at the unit level.

Perhaps General Westmoreland was correct about the drug problem catching the army by surprise, because the first institutionwide study was not done until late 1969 and was published in February 1970. If the problem caught commanders by surprise, it was on Westmoreland's watch, since he was commander of MACV and responsible for the theater where careful observation would have advanced his knowledge of the existence of at least a "funny-smelling" odor at firebases around the country. Once he became chief of staff in 1968, he did initiate studies, but by then the problem had manifested itself widely. These first studies were global in nature and were not conducted by behavioral scientists and subject to the rigors of scientific investigation. Instead, surveys were sent to units, and soldiers were required to fill out forms anonymously, but with the "brass" often looking on. The first armywide studies indicated that the rate of marijuana users in 1969 had doubled that of 1968, which meant that the number in 1969 was four times that in 1967. So-called "hard narcotics," defined as opium, heroin, and morphine, had doubled, thus tripling the 1967 numbers, and "dangerous" drugs, defined as LSD, barbiturates, amphetamines, hallucinogens, depressants, and stimulants, had followed the same general patterns.[29] But the army did not believe the problem was theirs alone, because data showed that most soldiers were drug users before they joined the service, and of those who went to Vietnam, fewer identified themselves as users in the war zone than in CONUS or Europe.[30] It was not until 1969 that drug use in Vietnam drew even with that in Europe.[31]

But the armywide study did not explain the entire problem, because with the Vietnam War "winding down" through Vietnamization and removal of U.S. combat forces from the field, the number of combat support and combat service support troops increased as a percentage of the deployed forces. The effect of these changes placed more U.S. troops in the rear echelon, at firebases, with fewer troops operating on search-and-destroy missions, on patrol, and on ambushes. Boredom began to set in among the troops, and fear for their own safety or that of their fellow soldiers diminished, thus increasing the desire to escape from tedious details by consuming drugs.

The issue of how prevalent drug use was among soldiers in Vietnam has perplexed military historians, sociologists, and journalists since the war ended. The comparison is usually made of contemporary American society and the army, with the claim of drug use equally prevalent on college campuses. Among journalists who typically interviewed soldiers at firebases rather than on combat operations, the perception was that drug use was rampant among all soldiers, all the time. However, drug use was much more common in the rear and was rare among infantry soldiers in the field.

> Well, there was drug and alcohol use. I think that not in the field. On the firebase it existed and in the rear areas it existed. It kind of existed within groups. . . . In the field, if there was somebody out in the field and they were using drugs or alcohol in the field, they'd probably be dealt with. . . . They'd say, "You need to get this guy out of here because he's dangerous." Firebases were a little bit more relaxed than that, and the rear area was more relaxed than that but I never used any drugs. I will have to admit to being over the line on alcohol a few times but that was always in the rear area.[32]

"I know a lot of vets are depicted as drug addicts and junkies. But when I was there, nobody did drugs or alcohol in the field. That was the wrong time and place. You needed everything you had to stay alive, and doing drugs wasn't one of them. Word was that if you were doing drugs, you might get shot out in the field during a firefight. They didn't need to have you screw up and maybe get the whole squad killed."[33] But the Hollywood image of the infantrymen lighting up or shooting up while on patrol has been accepted by many Americans since the war ended and has been perpetuated by Vietnam veterans who used drugs after their return. "Only a fool would jeopardize himself further by anesthetizing his senses."[34] The need to be fully aware of one's surroundings, of trip wires rigged to booby traps, potential ambush sites, snakes, leeches, or the sound of incoming mortar rounds exceeded that of the desire to escape reality. "There weren't any drugs in my platoon out in the field. It just did not happen, and we wouldn't have let it happen if a new guy would have brought drugs with him."[35] But the drugs did exist in the base camps. "There was marijuana. I never saw it used in our unit in the field. Again, it seemed to be an aspect of base camp life. When we prepared our company for an inspection in September 1968, we found enough marijuana stashed in the barracks buildings to fill a GI wastebasket (about 5 gallons)."[36] Edwin Frazier, interviewed by Stephen Maxner of the Vietnam Archive, was asked about the biggest problem as far as drugs were concerned in his unit in Vietnam. He said, "Hooch maids bringing drugs into the unit, into the area, having to constantly be on the alert to watch for symptoms or signs that troops were using it: marijuana, heroin . . . that was basically the two. They had them in little vial caps that they would come in and they were buying them for a dollar. The hooch maids would slip them in. They were selling them to the troops."[37]

For the junior officer, enforcing unit and army drug rules presented a dilemma. If he knew that his men were self-policing drug use in the field, as the previously quoted soldiers have stated, then he could save his leadership capital for the times when his troops occupied the firebase during periods of defensive assignment or a stand-down situation. As platoon leader Michael Lee Lanning wrote, "Drugs were common in the rear areas — however, not much more so than on the streets in the states. In the field, drugs of any type were not tolerated. Everyone recognized that safety depended upon the actions of everyone's working as a team."[38] And as time in firebases replaced time in the field for most infantrymen, the leadership of the junior officer became more important. Leading men in a garrison was more challenging than leading them on a combat patrol into enemy territory. "The drug epidemic that followed was to some extent related to the sheer boredom among enlisted men, as long days on bases replaced search-and-destroy missions."[39]

Though the army had completed an extensive internal investigation of drug use, the study raised as many questions as it answered. Unit research in the various infantry divisions in Vietnam would reveal that the problem in rear areas was even more extensive than originally believed. The 25th Infantry Division concluded that the main problem was due to the "climatic and soil conditions within the division AO which allowed the sustained cultivation of highly potent hemp and poppy plants from which marihuana and opium are produced."[40] And since the growing of such plants was not illegal and provided income to peasant farmers, there was no effective way to control the supply. The burden for curtailing use would reside with the platoon leaders.

To assist junior officers in this daunting task, the 25th Infantry conducted a behavioral science field survey not just to determine the extent of drug use at Cu Chi and the surrounding firebases but also to provide a demographic study to aid in identifying who was most likely to become a hard drug addict. Peter S. Cookson, a sociologist at Long Binh who was assigned to the 20th Preventive Medicine Unit, conducted the study. Since enlisted men served as survey administrators, rather than the junior officers who had acted in the same capacity in previous studies, "experimenter bias" was expected to be held to acceptable levels.[41] The study showed that most drug users were white, came from small-town America, had some college background, and had been drafted into the army. Thus the typical drug user was the typical American soldier.[42]

The most revealing aspect of the study dealt with the soldiers' perception of their leader's attitude toward drug use. While not defining "leader," which thus could have been construed as a junior officer or an NCO, 44 percent reported their leader's attitude as one of indifference toward the use of marijuana, and 28 percent viewed their leaders as indifferent about hard drug usage.[43] And a similar study conducted by the brigade psychological technician for the 173rd Airborne found similar results, with one corroborating point that would appear to be in conflict with some of the previously cited information. "Field duty personnel used marijuana at a 'slightly higher' frequency than administrative personnel."[44] But this can logically be explained by recognizing that field personnel had no incentive not to use drugs when in base camp if the penalty for an infraction was jail time, which would thus deprive them of the "opportunity" to go back out on patrol after their stand-down time had been completed. And since the boredom of base camp was so opposite to the adrenalin rush of combat or fear of enemy contact, drugs were a substitute for the "high" of search-and-destroy or ambush missions.

Platoon leaders had a choice: look the other way in base camp and let their troops relax with their drug of choice, be it marijuana, alcohol, or hard drugs, or be a "hard ass" and enforce the unit rules. Since his NCO's drug of choice was probably Jack Daniels, Cutty Sark, or Budweiser, a platoon leader had to decide if there was a difference between "juicers and heads" or "drunks and dopers."[45] "Druggers can smell each other. I don't know how they do it, but they always seem to run in little cliques. You just monitor that stuff and keep tight on them. I don't think and I may be wrong. I don't ever remember a urinalysis in Vietnam until I myself was leaving and had to stand there and piss in a tube before I left. In the field I don't think there was any of that."[46]

> No. Usually, he would allow both escape mechanisms to occur, in separate quarters, as long as his platoon's combat efficiency was not affected. Since most junior officers were young, and had been exposed to drugs in college, they tended to be less judgmental about those who used them. I don't know if they looked the other way, or if they didn't think there was much going on in the unit. I think the biggest problem, grass wasn't the big thing. The alcoholism was the big thing. Everybody drank heavily, to forget the problems, forget the war. . . . Us infantry guys; we were a bunch of alcoholics.[47]

What he could not allow, however, was the disintegration of his unit even in base camp if the drugs or alcohol use led to fights or racial slurs, which often happened when soldiers drank, smoked, or injected to excess.

IF THE ARMY COMMANDERS did not see the drug problem coming, as suggested by General Westmoreland, no such claim can be made regarding the existence of racial tension. And while the army would eventually conduct studies to determine the extent to which drugs affected combat effectiveness, it needed no such surveys to verify the existence of a racial "powder keg" ready to destroy the foundations of many units.

The assumptions made about racial harmony by the senior officers in Vietnam were correct during the first days of the buildup. Units that trained in the States and deployed together were truly integrated, with African Americans holding NCO leadership positions consistent with their minority status in the army. Many of these men had combat experience gained from action in Korea, and their expertise on the battlefield was valued by the army. Junior officers who lacked such experience were fortunate to have such men as platoon sergeants and squad leaders. Leading white, black, Hispanic, and Native American men into battle was usually not accompanied by any issues regarding the color of one's skin.

Such a battlefield scenario did not change throughout the war, as long as American soldiers were killing VC or PAVN soldiers. "The jungle warfare was so intense that it trumped all the pressures and prejudices that divided them, and they struggled through it as units irrelevant of race."[48] Colin Powell served two tours in Vietnam, and although he saw differences in the racial attitudes that existed in 1964 versus 1968, he still believed that the battlefield was the place where soldiers did not notice skin color. "There was my friend Tony Mavoudis, dead these many months, on the screen. 'Race did not matter out here,' Tony said. 'It doesn't exist. . . . We're all soldiers. The only color we know is khaki and green. The color of the mud and the color of the blood is all the same.' . . . Scholars could take pages to express the wisdom Tony had captured in a few blunt words."[49] Such feelings were expressed consistently by veterans interviewed after the war, which was a way for white soldiers to pay respect to the black soldiers with whom they had served. Writes Ron Spector in his book *After TET: The Bloodiest Year in Vietnam*, "It was one of the many ironies of the Vietnam War that the greater the degree of danger and discomfort for the combatants, the greater the racial harmony and solidarity."[50] However, focusing on the positives of racial harmony in the field highlights the racial tension that existed at the firebases.

Observations about racial separation varied among junior and field-grade officers:

> On completion of each forage into the "boonies" the company was ex-
> tracted, usually by helicopter and taken back to the base camp for a three
> to five day stand down, spent in rest, recreation and cleaning up and
> preparing for the next mission. Befitting their positions, the NCOs would
> collectively set themselves apart during a stand down. But I was somewhat
> surprised to observe the line soldiers self-segregated immediately. Blacks
> staked out their territory in one part of the rest area while whites occupied
> another. Perhaps I was in error, but I sensed that the segregation was
> instigated primarily by the black troops and that the white soldiers were on
> the whole, indifferent to the arrangement.[51]

This was the environment that would require junior officers to exert their most important leadership skills. All of those sociology, psychology, and communication skills learned in ROTC or in the few humanities courses taken at West Point would be tested in the rear. The decisions made there affected how the troops would respond to the leaders and to one another once they were back in the field after the stand down. And it is reasonable to assume that black soldiers felt the need to band together, to form a subunit within the context of the larger primary group to protect themselves from what they saw as a racist army that only needed them when there was killing to be done.

African American marine, H Company, 2nd Battalion, 3rd Marines, ten miles north-west of Da Nang Air Base (photo courtesy of Brig. Gen. Edwin H. Simmons Collection, Texas Tech University, The Vietnam Archive, VA020955)

"Junior officers, black or white, were probably the most knowledgeable about the actual state of race relations in their units, but they were distracted by many other urgent tasks."[52] And since they had just left college campuses where they were most likely afforded exposure to liberal, open-minded thinking, they were in the best position to deal with racial tension. But the society they had just departed was seeking its own acknowledgment of the rights of black citizens. Riots had recently erupted in Los Angeles, Newark, Washington, and Detroit, so the junior officer brought these feelings of turmoil with him to Vietnam. He had to supervise his men in the rear in such a way as not to create more friction and thus affect the unit's ability to be combat ready, or at least to protect one another on subsequent operations. This could be accomplished by allowing the troops to form subprimary groups that were not inconsistent with the needs of the platoon. These affiliations often were based on geographical residence and affection toward the South. "We are fighting and dying in a war that is not very popular in the first place and we still have some stupid people who are still fighting the Civil War. Black soldiers should not have to serve under the Confederate flag or with it. We are serving under the American flag and the American flag only."[53] Thus junior officers had to be cognizant of the concerns of black soldiers about the sensitive matter of flying a flag. While such an issue was addressed by MACV in a directive that banned the flying of flags other than unit and American, congressmen would occasionally send state flags to troops, and many of the southern flags in 1968 contained replicas of the Confederate flag.

> Some of the African American soldiers were upset because some guys, I've forgotten which troop it was, had painted this big Confederate flag on the side of their A Cav. . . . I said, "Okay Sergeant Major, that's what sergeant majors are for." The next thing I knew there wasn't any flag on that thing. I can't tell you exactly how he took care of it, but he took care of it and that was the end of that. The military mirrors what's going on in the country. We were just beginning to get into I guess what you would call major racial tensions in the States.[54]

Perceptions by both black and white soldiers about their respective roles in the unit frequently affected soldiers' mutual respect. Black soldiers often felt that white officers put them on "point," the most dangerous position in a formation, more frequently than they should have been relative to their numbers in the platoon. Black soldiers, more than whites, may have believed that they were asked to carry "the pig" and, as Goff and Sanders stated in Chapter 5, exposed themselves to more danger than reasonable.[55] The weapon also required ammo bearers to carry the heavy bandoliers of 7.62 mm linked cartridges, and if the load was not shared proportionally throughout the platoon, racial tension could develop. White soldiers may have believed the rumors that VC and PAVN soldiers would not kill black soldiers in a fire-fight because they felt sorry for their plight in racist America.[56] "To play on the sympathy of the black soldier, the Viet Cong would shoot at a white guy, then let the black guy behind him go through, then shoot at the next white guy. It didn't take long for that kind of word to get out. And the reaction in some companies was to arrange your personnel where you had an all-black or nearly all-black unit to send out."[57] And white soldiers cried "reverse discrimination" when they saw black soldiers break unit rules on dress, haircuts, or drug use with impunity while white officers refused to act because of the fear that they might appear racist to other black soldiers.

In the field we didn't have racial tension. There's no such thing as racial tension in the field because everybody's armed, everybody's on equal ground. You have to get along because if you don't your own guys would blow you away. In the base camps is what I remembered, not in Cu Chi, the 25th Infantry division. . . . That's where I saw it more because there was more blacks and there was more soldiers . . . and racial tension was there but it was not in the field to the best of my knowledge and experience, not out in the combat areas. It just didn't exist because there was no . . . it just didn't exist. You could be right next to the black guys and the white guys, and everybody was your friend, everybody was your brother, because you had to be because you've got to deal with the enemy, you've got to deal with your buddies. So base camps, I remember there being some hostile situations but nothing that you could say that was a riot; not during the time that I was there.[58]

While the job of the junior officer regarding race relations was "easier" in the field, it was not perfect, because there were always some soldiers who could not leave their hatred in the rear: "I heard of blacks and whites being real close to each other in the bush. But I know a black kid, a grunt, whose unit was hit bad. A white guy got hit, was hurt bad. And this young brother he risked his life going back in to get him. He carried this white dude out who was hurt bad, and the gooks firing at them, and this guy kept saying, 'Put me down, nigger.' "[59]

A platoon leader had to work with all of the men in his platoon, from the southern racist to the black power radical, and solving a racial problem in the jungle did not guarantee that the camaraderie would carry over to the rear echelon:

The buddy system has to happen. You start realizing that you can't get through not communicating. Guys started opening up. Blacks realize, "I'm stuck out here in the boonies, and the white guy from the South is stuck out here, and it's life and death, we'd better begin to erase all this coloration immediately." At first, guys are strangers: They're from different backgrounds. Their parents taught them that a nigger ain't shit, a nigger can't do shit. You can see it in their eyes. They look at you as though you're supposed to ask them, "What can I do for you?" You know? It's as if they're saying, "This is what I want you to do, boy."[60]

In an interview with Richard Verrone of the Vietnam Archive at Texas Tech University, Stephen Dant discussed the difficulty that platoon leaders had in dealing with REMFs (rear-echelon mother fuckers) and combat soldiers during stand down:

SD: We came back to the rear on a three-day stand down after being out in the field for I don't know how many weeks, you lose track. We had only been there for about a day and a couple of our guys were over at the EM club, there was a lot of racial tension in the rear as well. I was back catching a nap at the hooch and I got waken up by a couple of guys in my squad and said, "What's going on?" He said, "Well," I've forgotten his name, "just got the shit kicked out of him by a bunch of black guys in the EM club." I said, "What'd they do that for?" He goes, "I guess because they can."

RV: This was a racial thing?

SD: This was a racial thing. And when I got a rear job I saw a lot of that. Anyway here's a whole company of infantry, guys that had just come down on stand down and they take your weapons away from you when you come in or you lose all your ammunition because officers don't want to be fired on by the grunts. So you know we didn't have any guns or anything to take over there. We would have fired on these guys I'm sure. So we're taking apart the cots and we're on our way in force headed over to the EM club. There are about 20 other guys standing there waiting for us. The MPs show up in a deuce and a half and start waving their nightsticks around and managed to get us corralled and back to our quarters on the beach there. Then they turned right around and said hook them up guys; you're heading back out.

RV: Oh really?

SD: Yes.

RV: They're going to get rid of you?

SD: We got suited up and got all of our gear and the helicopters were out on the pad within an hour and a half and we were back out in the field.

RV: Was that planned?

SD: I think they wanted us out of there because we were going to hurt some people. You just don't fuck with a guy who's coming out of the field.

RV: Right. And the guys who beat up your friend, they were rear personnel?

SD: They were rear personnel. Yes they were REMFs. You know it's probably a good thing that they sent us back to the field because we would have found them and hurt them.[61]

Thus the platoon leader had to deal with the disparaging remarks, looks, attitudes, and actions of desperate soldiers who did not like one another but who had to rely on one another to stay alive. These problems were similar to those faced by white supervisors and black employees in the American workplace — except that every decision made by the junior officer in Vietnam was a matter of life and death. If he made the wrong decision on the battlefield, men died. If he made the wrong decision in the rear, men might die at the hands of American soldiers.

A PLATOON LEADER'S GREATEST fear, other than losing men to enemy fire, was losing men to friendly fire. Usually associated with artillery falling short or soldiers accidentally firing a round from an M-16 while on patrol, these accidents were frequent because of the inherent risk in thousands of armed men doing dangerous things. While the exact causes of death were difficult to determine, 3,363 men died in accidents during the Vietnam War.[62] Some of these statistics did not represent accidental death, however, but the intentional destruction of a superior officer or an NCO.

The killing or attempted killing of members of one's own platoon was the most heinous crime one could commit, because it was not only murder but an attack on authority. In Vietnam it was an ever-increasing risk as the war wound down, and junior officers were in the direct line of fire. And while soldiers have killed or threatened to kill their superior officers or NCOs in every American war, the act became so notorious in Vietnam that a word was created to describe it: fragging. The term became synonymous with the murder of superiors, but it was derived from the word "fragmentation," an adjective for a type of grenade. Combat soldiers in Vietnam routinely carried six to ten fragmentation grenades on their web gear, either the baseball-style M-67 that was easier for American soldiers to throw or the World War II–style MKII, which was shaped like a pineapple. The infantryman also carried smoke, incendiary, and white phosphorous grenades, but the fragmentation grenade was the most lethal because five seconds after the pin had been pulled and the lever had left the casing, an explosion took place that shattered the fragment case into as many as 2,000 pieces and could kill or maim everything within a thirty-three-foot radius.[63] The beauty of the weapon when used in an attempted murder was that it left no fingerprints.

The act of fragging one's superiors has been studied extensively since the Vietnam War ended, and psychologists and sociologists have generally concluded that the magnitude of the attempts was a phenomenon unique to the

Vietnam War. Between 1969 and 1972, there were 800 recorded incidents, with a peak of 1.8 assaults per 1,000 servicemen in Vietnam.[64] These statistics do not include the attempted murder of superiors using knives or guns, which combat soldiers also routinely carried. Such incidents happened less frequently because anonymity was less likely if the bullet could be traced by a criminal investigation division or if the victim could fight back. The fragmentation grenade was indeed the weapon of choice when trying to eliminate a superior:

> Bosum watched it all for one week, then ordered that the LRRP units, after making contact, were not to withdraw, but were to stay where they were and harass the enemy. They were to set up ambushes and keep after Charlie until the units fixed were hit. . . . They were getting just as tired as they were getting tough. Still, the number of casual mistakes and booby-trap injuries began going down. Men quit smoking grass on patrol and began leaving things behind that might jingle. . . . Three days after Bosum issued the orders, a patrol was ambushed, and the relieving patrol got pinned down. He committed another company, then two. The fighting spread. . . . Over a thousand men were fighting, most within three or four meters of each other, in jungle so thick you couldn't even see who was firing at you. It went on for hours. . . . Whole platoons were wiped out. Squads of North Vietnamese were killed where they lay. . . . Boys killed one another in the dark, shredded apart by automatic fire from no more than a meter away. . . . The wounded, lying broken on the ground, whispered hoarsely to passing figures, only to be killed. . . . The orders were for prisoners, but the bitter and exhausted survivors shot them down where they found them. It had been an expensive victory. Division was a bit concerned about the casualties, but they decided to wait to see what effect these new tactics had on the enemy before they passed judgment. As for himself, Bosum was impressed. For the first time, the area was clear of NVA, not because the communists had decided to move, but because they had to. The next night, after he had gone to sleep, somebody rolled a grenade into his tent. Bosum died on the ground, waiting for the Dust Off.[65]

The senior officer who fell victim to this fragging incident was doing the job he had been sent to do, but a soldier believed his behavior was dangerous to the long-term survival of himself and probably others. Who committed these acts against whom and why? A study by Dr. Thomas C. Bond, chief of the psychiatry division and directorate of mental hygiene at the U.S. Disciplinary Barracks at Fort Leavenworth, Kansas, revealed that most of the perpetrators were members of combat support units rather than fighting units, and virtually none of the convicted soldiers were in combat situations when the incident took place. Such a finding is consistent with drug and racial conflict issues previously discussed; a firefight is not conducive to any activity other than killing the enemy, because you never knew whose assistance you might need to survive. The study also indicated that in most cases the perpetrator was responding to what he perceived to be "scapegoating" by the victim for infractions committed by many other soldiers. And more than 90 percent of those examined were intoxicated on alcohol or drugs at the time the murder or attempted murder took place.[66]

Racial tension was not usually cited as a cause in most fragging instances, but the attempt often took place within three days of a personal altercation with the victim. But the most frequently cited reason for the commission of the act was that the victim was "insensitive to the frustrations of the men."[67] There were usually more men involved than the one who was caught, and discussions about the crime had been going on for several days. Seldom was the victim blamed for the death of soldiers in combat, the previous incident notwithstanding; rather, the superior was blamed for causing discomfort and an adherence to rules that the soldiers believed to have little importance in a combat setting. The perpetrators admitted to boredom, monotony, and inactivity; thus the commission of fragging was something to do at a time when the soldiers needed a rush of excitement.[68]

The most frequent victims of fragging were captains and 1st sergeants, since they were most responsible for implementing disciplinary action. The 1st sergeant was the "lifer" who handed out work details, passes, and recommendations for promotions.[69] "He tried to frag our First Sergeant. He tried to kill him with a frag. He threw it up on top of a hooch. It rolled off and went down and broke and blew up, and they witholded him for the inquiry and the first Shirt comes in there and this is before I made corporal, he said, 'Padgett, are you trying to kill my ass?' I said, 'No sir.' He said, 'I knew that.' He said, 'We just got to go through the strokes.' 'No sir, but we know who did.' 'Get your ass out of here!' "[70] Lieutenants were not as frequently targeted, because they were not seen as the final decision-makers. Among combat troops, the platoon leader was seen more often as "one of the boys." It was usually captains who insisted on troops wearing flak jackets and steel pots, taking malaria pills on a daily basis, and digging foxholes at night to make defensive perimeters more secure against enemy mortars.[71] "No, you would be pretty pissed off at either a sergeant or at a lieutenant or captain who you felt was out to make a name for himself, who was more gung-ho than he was smart. You know, I don't know this for sure but I remember having a conversation about how some lieutenant, and it wasn't in our company, but it was in one of the other companies in the battalion, I guess woke up in the morning with a hand grenade down at the bottom of his poncho liner. That's what I heard."[72] The lieutenants were responsible for these same protective measures, but they often let them slide to appease the troops. To many junior officers, these were issues that aggravated troops and did little to improve the combat efficiency of the unit. While it is unimaginable to think that troops would lash out at those who were making rational decisions regarding their security, troops have historically created havoc against those who upset them, in an atmosphere where violence is the SOP and life is cheap.[73] Trained killers, used to killing, are not the rational human beings that exist in a society where people are not all armed and where every decision made does not put lives in jeopardy.

If platoon leaders made decisions in the rear that were not in keeping with best military practices and thus not supported by more senior officers, it was not necessarily because they wanted to be accepted by their troops. Since many of these junior officers were the same age as the men they led into battle, and since soldiers who had recently left campuses were more inclined to question the wisdom of both the war and tactics within the war, one can assume that junior officers would have often supported their troops against the wishes of senior officers. In many cases, these lieutenants were college graduates, and their captains above them were not. "I remember when I got to Ba Xuyen nearly all the MAT teams were officered by lieutenants and nearly all the staff positions in the province were the same. Toward the end of '70 and early '71, captains began to arrive and they were not nearly as educated and (dare I say?) as smart as the lieutenants who all wanted to get out but who also didn't mind saying what they thought."[74] Senior officers might have construed this behavior as fear of troop reprisals, which was alluded to in the senior officer evaluations in Chapter 4, but it is more likely that these lieutenants sided with the soldiers on race and drug issues because the soldiers were right.

For whatever reasons, the fragging of junior officers appears from the records to have been a rare occurrence, although it is evident that it did happen. It is unlikely that the fear of fragging led to poor decision making insofar as platoon leaders made decisions that were abhorrent to senior officers. These junior officers did the best they could to protect their troops from poor decisions at the top. And for these decisions, they were often berated as not being officers and gentlemen.

NINE CONCLUSION: ONE CALLEY

> *Warriors need a way to distinguish what they must do out of a sense of duty from what a serial killer does for the sheer sadistic pleasure of it. Their actions, like those of the serial killer, set them apart from the rest of society. Warriors, however, are not sociopaths. . . . They want to be seen as proud defenders and representatives of what is best about their culture: as heroes, not "baby-killers." . . . Warriors exercise the power to take or save lives, order others to take or save lives, and lead or send others to their deaths.*[1]
>
> ■
>
> *Our officer corps takes pride in embracing the higher expectations that our country has of their character and conduct, even if there are occasional and perhaps inevitable failures to meet those expectations.*[2]
>
> ■

The U.S. military establishment blamed the junior officer corps, in part, for America's defeat in the Vietnam War. However, the lieutenants who served in combat performed their duties with efficiency and aplomb, and the criticism afforded them after the war contrasted sharply with the reports and evaluations made during the war. The change in attitude coincides with the revelations of My Lai. But the evidence shows that there was not "a thousand Calleys" — there was only one.

To support this statement, I have presented information about and discussed the circumstances that created the Vietnam War–era junior officer corps, focusing on army infantry platoon leaders. Candidates for positions as lieutenants were mostly draft-dodgers who ran out of time, or enlistees who wanted to have some control over their military fate. American society was ambivalent or, in the case of academia, hostile to the needs of the military. Since the army depended on the support of society to accomplish its recruitment goals, it had to create its own leaders through a ramp-up of its own schools. In the process of choosing who should attend those schools, it never lowered its admittance standards, even though in the USAIS alone it increased the number of students from 716 per year in FY1962 to 10,161 in FY1968.[3] The army also tried incessantly to recruit candidates who had college degrees, or at least had some college background, but some institutions refused to admit recruiters, even though corporations and other government agencies were allowed on campus. Lt. William Laws Calley, however, was recruited and even selected to attend OCS in 1967, along with 10,048 other candidates.

The army was cognizant of the diverse array of candidates in its schools, and it attempted to change the curriculum to reflect both the needs of the prospective officers and the type of war they were about to fight. Humanities courses were introduced at West Point, and cadets in ROTC were allowed to substitute psychology and sociology for science courses, in an attempt to improve the platoon leader's interactions with soldiers and civilians. But in the words of Lieutenant Calley, "One thing at OCS was nobody said, 'Now there will be innocent civilians there.' "[4] As the RETO study confirmed, you can only do so much with training if the student cannot comprehend the lesson.

The army was concerned as to whether it was preparing its officers for the rigors of combat, and it studied the results through internal boards and commissions, as well as through outside private studies. It made necessary changes, such as reestablishing the requirement that USMA graduates attend IOBC after commissioning, because evaluations of commanders indicated that newly commissioned officers were not ready to lead troops in combat. And ongoing studies on attrition and the reasons for failure indicated that OCS did not get easier during the war, even though demand for platoon leaders increased. But one notable exception in the attrition statistics was that Lt. William Laws Calley did not make the bottom five of his OCS platoon's bayonet sheet.

To fully understand the environment that junior officers faced in combat, Part II of this study focused on the war that was fought in the Republic of Vietnam. Lieutenants were treated like any other soldier upon arrival at the repo-depo, and they had little choice as to their assignment if their MOS was 1542, or small-unit infantry commander. Most went to Vietnam as replacements, although some were fortunate to have been deployed with their unit after having trained together in CONUS or Hawaii. But effective combat leadership required training in jungle warfare. As platoon leaders, junior officers had to teach their men to respect VC mines and booby traps, to appreciate the awesome firepower of the M-60 machine gun, and to constantly clean their

M-16A1 rifles. Training with your unit was preferable to being sent out to the field as a replacement, because as a replacement platoon leader you were immersed into a unit that consisted of experienced combat veterans. Lt. William Laws Calley had an advantage because he served in Hawaii with his unit, C Company, First Battalion, 20th Infantry, prior to deploying with the reconstituted 23rd Infantry Division (Americal). "We were taught how to assault them (mountains), how to take base camps, how to kill the enemy: for Charlie was really made for war! We were mean! We were ugly! We never conceived of old people, men, women, children, babies: of Vietnamese being near us. Never did anyone tell us."[5] Calley and his men were afforded benefits of unit cohesion and training that most soldiers did not have.

The fact that the U.S. armed forces had rules of engagement to which it tried to adhere in its conduct of the war might be challenged by some historians; but such directives were established by MACV, and commanders and soldiers were expected to follow them. However, with the measure of success being the body count, and with the creation of free-fire zones to enable search-and-destroy missions to be more successful, the rules were not always followed. And the reluctance of PAVN commanders to engage the United States in large battles after the Ia Drang Valley confrontation in November 1965 caused a steady erosion of contact between large units, an increase in small-unit operations, and a more stealthy approach to killing by the PAVN and VC. The U.S. response to this change was the creation of the free-fire zone and the use of H&I, as well as air operations that destroyed many villages. And the United States began to execute its own small-unit operations to achieve a higher body count.

> After my second, my third, my fourth, my fifth, my tenth, my twelfth, my twentieth—ambush, I still hadn't had a VC in my killing zone, and I had had perfect ambush sites, too. . . . We want to kill! Not half as much as our colonel did. He kept asking us, "Any body count?"
> "No sir."
> "No body count?"
> "Nobody there to shoot at."
> "You better get on the stick sometime."
> "Yes sir."[6]

Lieutenant Calley would "get on the stick" at My Lai (4).

In what is considered arguably the most abhorrent U.S. military action in modern times, C Company, 11th Infantry Brigade, 23rd Infantry Division

(Americal), and particularly the 1st and 2nd platoons, massacred hundreds of elderly men, women, and children on March 16, 1968. The behavior of American soldiers that day was not based on any training they had received in CONUS or Vietnam, and the actions of their platoon leader were inconsistent with leadership training provided at OCS:

> "Did Lieutenant Calley change magazines?"
> "Yes, between 10 and 15 times."
> "Did you see anybody alive when you left?"
> "Like I said, I couldn't tell whether they were mortally wounded or not."[7]

Every soldier knows that ten or fifteen magazines represent between 180 and 270 rounds of ammunition fired, and considering that those being fired upon were unarmed, the magnitude of the atrocious behavior is unconscionable. Lt. William Laws Calley's actions cannot be excused by political, social, or moral explanations about the nature of the Vietnam War, or by the comparison of actions by pilots. He looked his victims in the eye, and he murdered them.

A junior officer's responsibilities did not end when he returned from the field, and supervising soldiers in garrison is more challenging than in combat. The junior officer's actions in "the rear" often determined whether his men survived their tour or went home in body bags, because it was during that stand-down time that his men used drugs and alcohol to relieve the boredom. These activities affected the way the members of the platoon interacted with one another and how bellicose they became when racial and ethnic issues confronted them. The platoon leader had to mold a primary group that might have included a member of the Black Panther Party carrying an M-60 machine gun and a member of the Ku Klux Klan bearing his ammo. The ability to meld such individuals into an effective fighting unit and keep them from killing each other in the rear would also determine whether the platoon leader survived his tour or became a victim of his men's anger. Lieutenant Calley was not a strong disciplinarian, and his pre–My Lai massacre behavior does not appear to have earned him the respect of his men. But on March 16, 1968, his men respected his position to the extent that they followed his example and mimicked his actions.

The army desired to commission only men who could become officers and gentlemen, even in a war that was unlike what any of its leaders had experienced. The one-year tour of duty, the lack of real estate objectives resulting in a war without fronts, and the drafting of only those in society who had nothing "important" to do with their lives all led to a war that placed a great deal of importance on the lowest level of commissioned leadership. "Vietnam was a lieutenant's war. One-year tours and heavy casualties required a constant flow of new officers. The demand was met by waiving the stringent peace-time commissioning requirements, by increasing the number of Officer Candidate School graduates."[8] Michael Lanning was partially correct with this statement about casualties and the ramp-up of ocs, but the requirements for admittance into ocs did not change during the war. The army did, however, relax the college diploma requirement for certain periods.

One can only speculate about the reasons why junior officers received so much of the blame for the U.S. defeat in Vietnam. There were more lieutenants serving in combat than any other officer rank; however, there were more field-grade officers who stayed in the army after the war. Those who sat on the commissions and boards were majors, lieutenant colonels, and colonels, but most of the lieutenants returned to civilian life. Few of them wrote books, and those who did wrote of their experiences with the soldiers they led, with little analysis of the politics or leadership pitfalls above them.

The infantry junior officers in Vietnam were grunts, like the men they led into battle. Consequently they tended to listen to the same music, cheat a little on the haircut regulations, look the other way when drugs were being used in the rear, and ignore the shaving and dress code in the boonies. This led field-grade officers to develop a belief that lieutenants did not take their jobs seriously, even though in most cases they had to do so to stay alive. "Junior officers, in many ways, were more responsible than senior commanders, for the closer you were to actual combat the less concerned you were with your career."[9] Or stated another way, field-grade officers seldom were involved in ground combat operations and seldom wore muddy boots. But looking at junior officers who did was frightening, particularly when those platoon leaders had reasonably good relationships with the soldiers they were commanding.

Even the commanding general of MACV, William Westmoreland, looked askance at those who did not appear clean and shaven, even in combat situations:

I had been in the field, on the run for 2 ½ weeks and was a mess, very tired, and hungry. It was a cloudy, misty day, about 0830. The landing zone was muddy. At that time I was awarded the Vietnamese Cross of Gallantry with

Silver Star and it was personally given to me by the Vietnamese President, General Kahn. I was the only Caucasian in a group of over 150 Vietnamese. Westmoreland made eye contact with me but would not come within 50 feet of me. I figured he might have wanted to stay clean and not get his shiny boots muddy. I have detested the man ever since.[10]

This was not the only time that the commanding general faced troops and appeared uncomfortable with their appearance, even though the situation was perilous:

So here we are in the building [the U.S. Embassy, Saigon, after leading a company assault to help protect the embassy during TET, 1968]. We made it in. My first thought is . . . how many people are in the corridors down here that I have to clear out. . . . Then, the last one is killed. . . . We went into a defensive position. . . . About that time General Westmoreland shows up. I expected [him] to say where are your automatic weapons, where is your reserve, how are your communications? I expected a very professional discussion because this is a high priority target. The guy took one look at me and said, "Captain, you haven't shaved and your men haven't either. You look like Hell!" He scowled at me, turned on his heel and walked away. I stood there stunned, absolutely stunned. I said this is the kind of jerk that's leading this thing and I concluded we were losing the war.[11]

Neither Lt. Jack Cummings nor Captain O were, at those moments, shining examples of officers and gentlemen. But they had performed their duties efficiently, as combat leaders are trained to do. Still, the image of the disheveled soldier, whether before, during, or after combat, did not sit well with many general-grade officers, who seldom got dirty carrying out their assignments. Only the grunts got dirty, which included the junior officers who led them.

Perhaps the My Lai massacre was the final blow in reinforcing the perception General Westmoreland had of junior officers: "Judging from the events at My Lai, being an officer in the United States Army exceeded Lt. Calley's abilities. Had it not been for educational draft deferments, which prevented the army from drawing upon the intellectual segment of society for its junior officers, Calley would probably never have been an officer. Denied that usual reservoir of talent, the army had to lower its standards. Although some who became officers under those conditions performed well, others such as Calley failed."[12]

Chief Warrant Officer Hugh Thompson (see Chapter 8), Lt. Rick Rescorla (see Chapter 1), and Lt. Robert Ferguson (see Chapter 1) did not fail, nor did thousands of other junior officers who reluctantly went to war. They did their duty and came home to an ungrateful nation. And 5,069 junior officers were killed; all of them volunteered to be officers.[13]

Dr. Charles D. McKenna, currently a professor at the Command and Staff College, U.S. Marine Corps at Quantico, Virginia, was present at a meeting at Fort Benning, Georgia, in which General Westmoreland, chief of staff, talked about the current personnel situation in the U.S. Army. He told the students of the Infantry Officer Advanced Class that since the Vietnam War was winding down (1972), the army would have a chance to purge or cleanse itself of the "crud" it had accumulated during the war. When pressed by the students about who the "crud" actually was, Westmoreland backpedaled, but everyone in the room knew to whom he was referring.[14]

Roy R. Grinker and John P. Spiegel wrote that men in World War II "seem to be fighting more for someone than against somebody."[15] The infantry junior officers in the Vietnam War were the protectors of their men, because they were grunts like their men, and they absorbed the pain and suffering of each soldier. The majors and the colonels were not there when the privates and corporals were screaming in agony from a gunshot wound, an injury from an explosive device, or a puncture by a booby-trapped punji stick. To criticize the platoon leader for fighting for someone rather than against somebody fails to recognize human instincts in battle. When one of your soldiers dies in your arms, muddy boots, beards, drugs, and politics are not at the forefront of your thoughts — nor is the morality of war. The junior officer at that moment is not a gentleman, but just another soldier in a war that was not a gentleman's war.

Appendix One Glossary

MILITARY ABBREVIATIONS AND ACRONYMS

AIT	advanced individual training
AO	area of operations
ARVN	Army of the Republic of Vietnam
AWOL	absent without leave
BCT	basic combat training
CAP	Combined Action Platoon
CO	commanding officer
CONUS	continental United States
DMZ	Demilitarized Zone
FM	field manual
FY	fiscal year
GVN	Government of Vietnam
H&I	harassment-and-interdiction fire; artillery fired into an area without visual sighting of the enemy
HumRRO	Human Resources Research Office
IOBC	Infantry Officer Basic Course
KIA	killed in action
LAW	light antitank weapon
MACV	Military Assistance Command, Vietnam
MAT	Mobile Advisory Team
MOS	Military Occupational Specialty
NCO	noncommissioned officer
NDP	night defensive perimeter
NLF	National Liberation Front (Viet Cong)
NVA	North Vietnamese Army, also known as PAVN, Peoples Army of Vietnam
OBC	Officer Basic Course
OCS	Officer Candidate School
PAVN	Peoples Army of Vietnam (North Vietnam), also known as NVA, North Vietnamese Army
POI	program of instruction
POW	prisoner of war

R&R	rest and relaxation
RA	Regular Army
RETO	Review of Education and Training for Officers
ROTC	Reserve Officer Training Corps
RTO	radio, telephone operator
SOP	standard operating procedure
TAC	tactical (i.e., TAC officer)
USAIS	U.S. Army Infantry School
USMA	U.S. Military Academy at West Point
VC	Viet Cong
WIA	wounded in action

MILITARY TERMS

11-B: An MOS designation of infantryman, "grunt," typically the worst job in the military. The addition of a (P) designated Airborne qualified.

1542: The officer equivalent of 11-B, a "grunt platoon leader." The addition of a (7) designated Airborne qualified.

Plebe: A freshman at the U.S. Military Academy.

Repo-depo: Replacement facility where incoming and departing troops were processed.

Stand down: When a unit returns to a firebase after days or weeks in the field, to clean equipment, change clothes, and relax.

Steel pot: Helmet worn by U.S. soldiers.

UNOFFICIAL MILITARY ACRONYMS

BT	barbiturates
FNG	fucking new guy
REMF	rear-echelon mother fucker

UNOFFICIAL MILITARY TERMS

Bouncing Betty: A Viet Cong explosive device that explodes in the groin area of the unfortunate soldier who trips it.

Chi-com grenade: An explosive device detonated on command and manufactured in Communist China.

Punji pit: A Viet Cong booby trap designed to impale the unfortunate soldier who falls into it, made of sharpened bamboo stalks dipped in animal or human excrement.

Toe popper: A Viet Cong explosive device designed to blow away half of a soldier's foot, disabling him and causing other soldiers to come to his aid.

Appendix Two **Historiographical Essay**

In order to fully comprehend the magnitude of belief that existed among the military brass and, to a certain extent, the general public, a review of the literature produced by and consumed by participants in the war must be accomplished. These studies were conducted late in the war right after Saigon fell in 1975, and in subsequent years. All gave credence to the army's own BDM study that junior officers were, in part, responsible for America's defeat.

In 1968 Ward Just, a *Washington Post* correspondent, wrote *To What End: Report from Vietnam*, which questioned U.S. motives for engaging in the conflict.[1] His 1970 book, *Military Men*, was one of the first to question the resolve of those who were fighting the war.[2] With revelations of the My Lai incident having first burst on the scene just months before his publication date, Just interviewed officers at West Point, many of whom were instructors. They believed that reports of My Lai were credible, given the rules of engagement, and this was before the Peers Commission recommended that charges be brought against two generals and twelve lesser officers.[3] The startling revelation in *Military Men* was Just's conclusion that cadets at West Point had already begun to write off Vietnam as a "chicken-shit war" that would interfere with their careers in an honorable profession.[4] Lieutenant Calley had not yet been convicted, and no end to the war was in sight; yet these future junior officers questioned American leadership and willingly shared these views with a reporter.

Over the next few years, but before America's involvement had ended in March 1973, books appeared that were usually written by retired lieutenant colonels. Most of these authors had completed a tour in Vietnam and had become disillusioned with the war and the military establishment. The abbreviation "Ret." added to an author's title lent a degree of credibility to a book critical of the military establishment that could never be gained by a reporter or academician. Several books fit this category; the first chronologically was Edward L. King's *The Death of the Army: A Pre-Mortem*.[5] The retired lieutenant colonel focused most of his criticism on the West Point Protective Association, the unofficial graduates of the USMA who, he alleged, will always protect one of their own. While not criticizing junior officers as a group, this Korean War combat veteran believed that the army had appointed William Peers as investigator of the My Lai incident because he was a non–West Pointer; his was a dead-end job, since no member of the West Point Protective Association ever supported the promotion of an ROTC-commissioned officer.[6] From King's perspective, the Vietnam War continued because there was too much incentive for aggressive combat performance built into the promotion system. He blames the Hamburger Hill episode on Maj. Gen. Melvin Zais's desire to earn a third star; the only way to achieve this was to lead a division on a significant real estate acquisition operation.

This is a strong indictment. King's conversation with Zais prior to another tour in Vietnam supposedly gave King insight into the general's motivation. Zais said, "You know if I'm ever going to make a third star I need to have command of a division."[7] Hill 937, the military terminology for what later would be known as Hamburger Hill, would be assaulted by elements of the 101st Airborne Division, and the ten-day battle would result in the deaths of 56 American soldiers and 600 PAVN troops. (Zais would later say that his third star had been approved before the operation and that the report of the battle had been written by an inexperienced Associated Press reporter who based his entire story on an interview with one private.) The story made headlines in the U.S. papers, and Zais was denounced on the Senate floor by Senator Ted Kennedy. King agreed with the senator's assessment that the operation was done for the glory of "commander seeking advancement and promotion."[8] This early "angry colonel book" was also on target with its prediction that only a young, inexperienced lieutenant would be found guilty at My Lai.[9]

The next significant angry colonel book was *The Tarnished Shield: A Report on Today's Army*, by Col. George Walton (Ret.).[10] Walton took on the entire army, including junior officers, whom he described as "ambitious, but far from able."[11] Quoting Ward Just, Walton stated, "It was common knowledge in Vietnam that men coming from Officer Candidate School (Lt. Calley was an OCS man), were not the army's best quality."[12] Thus, Walton made the case against junior officers by quoting another author's generalization. Walton also wrote, again quoting another author, that "the more expensive young academy graduate is no better an officer than one from ROTC or OCS."[13] This pattern of former field-grade officers quoting one another or anonymous sources who make platitudinous statements about thousands of officers will be repeated as often as historians debate the performance of young leadership in Vietnam. Few of the angry colonels will cite primary sources to prove their point, other than that Lt. William Laws Calley was an officer and that the military establishment had commissioned him to lead a platoon into combat.

The last of the significant books to be written by angry colonels during the war was *America's Army in Crisis: A Study in Civil-Military Relations*, by William L. Hauser, lieutenant colonel.[14] Notice there is no "Ret." after his title. Hauser, at the time of publication, was an active-duty army officer who had served time as a battalion commander of an artillery unit in the Mekong Delta of Vietnam. Writing as a research associate of Johns Hopkins University's Washington Center for Foreign Policy Research, he focused on the problems the army encountered in fighting a war that was not supported by society. This was particularly consequential for recruiting junior officers, since the army had to compete with business, academia, and other branches, which could offer more safety, money, and prestige than could an institution that was being shunned by the very society that it represented. ROTC was particularly highlighted, and Hauser delved into the statistics regarding the precipitous drop in enrollment.[15] Hauser's book focused on solving the problems that the army faced in a post–Vietnam War world, rather than criticizing the institution without a plausible remedy.

Not qualifying as an angry colonel book only because the author does not use his "retired" title is William R. Corson's *Consequences of Failure*.[16] Corson wrote *Betrayal* in 1968, and his 1974 book addressed the issue of incompetent junior officers. He concluded that those who fought in the early days of the war, defined by Corson as 1966 through early 1967, were an elite group of young men who shared their civilian contemporaries' views on race, foreign affairs, and other modern-day societal ills. But as the war intensified, these attributes became liabilities to effective combat performance as these men began to question military decisions and disillusionment set in.[17] Then, according to Corson, the military lowered its standards and began to take anyone into the officer corps, "the epitome being Lieutenant William Calley."[18] However, as discussed in Chapter 2, the army's selection process does not show a diminution of standards as the war progressed; rather, the OCS classes in 1968 through 1970 were overwhelmingly populated by College Option candidates, and as reported in Chapter 4, many of these candidates were never commissioned because they could not meet the leadership standards set by the army. Again, Corson accepted the "Calley is bad, therefore standards were lowered" thesis, which does not appear to have happened.

The previously mentioned books were all written when America's actions were being criticized throughout society, but before actual defeat was known — before the fall of Saigon in April 1975. Once the humiliation of a Communist victory was realized, several authors published books that analyzed America's defeat, whereas previous books discussed America's poor performance in a war that most authors predicted would end in a stalemate like Korea. One of the best and most quantitatively researched volumes was *The War Managers: American Generals Reflect on Vietnam*, written by Brig. Gen. Douglas Kinnard.[19] Kinnard served two tours in Vietnam, and his interest in the war went beyond soldier performance. As a social scientist, he was interested in quantifying the responses to a series of questions directed to all of the generals who served in Vietnam. While attitudes toward junior officers were a small part of his study, the significance of his work was that he proved that the majority of those who directed the activities of combat soldiers doubted the leadership that was coming from the politicians in Washington. Questioning the objectives of the war itself, these commanders also revealed their distaste for the horrendous decision not to call up the reserves, thus failing to bring the war to all facets of society.[20]

Another book that was published during the late 1970s and which addressed the war from the political, military, and social aspects was Guenter Lewy's *America in Vietnam*.[21] Lewy, a political scientist, was among the first authors to challenge some of the conventional wisdom about America's failures of both strategy and tactics and to question whether lack of leadership was one of the overriding issues in the U.S. defeat. Like others before him, he cited the same anonymous colonel in the "thousand Calleys" quotation and blamed the junior officer corps for the lack of troop discipline, which he concluded led to some of the atrocities that were committed. His conclusion, unlike that of most previous authors, was that the records did not indicate that American soldiers committed atrocities at a rate greater than that of previous wars. And he excused many of the actions as part of the nature of a "guerilla war without fronts."[22] One of his theses was that "the sense of guilt created by the Vietnam War in the minds of many Americans is not warranted and that the charges of officially condoned illegal and grossly immoral conduct are without substance."[23] However, Lewy opined that if such actions did take place, it was probably because of the lack of leadership at the junior officer level.

One of the most captious of the postwar studies was *Crisis in Command: Mismanagement in the Army*, by Richard A. Gabriel and Paul L. Savage.[24] As retired staff and intelligence officers, they indicted the entire officer corps, including junior officers, which they believed "grew in inverse proportion to its decline in quality."[25] Central to the Gabriel and Savage thesis is the premise that not enough officers died when compared to enlisted men, and compared to other wars. They believed that the troops being led observed this lack of total commitment on the part of officers and drew conclusions about the officers' self-interests when issuing operations orders. Citing "available evidence" but not referencing where the data was found, they wrote that "the number of officers who actually died in combat in Vietnam was smaller proportionately compared to the number of Americans killed in other wars and to officer losses suffered by other armies."[26] Their book also endorsed the thesis that the junior officer corps diminished in quality as the war wound down, evidenced by William Laws Calley's actions.

One of the most scathing indictments of the officer corps, but most critical of field- and general-grade officers, was *Self-Destruction: The Disintegration and Decay of the United States Army during the Vietnam Era*.[27] Written by "Cincinnatus," a pseudonym adopted by a field-grade officer on the Pentagon staff who has since been identified as Cecil B. Curry, the book's jacket proclaimed that "the old refrain that the army failed because of political softness and social unrest at home is still the theme song of the upper ranks. The fact is that the military disaster in Vietnam grew out of ineptitude at the top."[28] His analysis of the My Lai massacre, unlike that of many of the previously noted works, is that it was not an isolated incident and that "Vietnam had been turned into a gigantic My Lai."[29] Because of the rules of engagement, guerilla-type warfare, and civilians on the battlefield, incidents like My Lai were bound to occur. But the leadership did nothing to work within the context of such a war, develop appropriate plans, or proceed to accomplish the mission. Had the senior officers understood the environment, My Lai and other incidents like it could have been avoided.[30]

As a military history book, *The Rise and Fall of an American Army: U.S. Ground Forces in Vietnam, 1965–1973*, by Shelby L. Stanton, has been generally considered one of the classic chronological studies of the war.[31] Based on after-action reports and military historians' contemporaneous accounts, the book describes battle after battle and frequently comments on failures and leadership mistakes in operations. But since most of the battles were won decisively by the American forces, his criticism is reserved more for the political decisions made in Washington. The book received very positive reviews by both the general press and military reviewers, but Stanton's status as an author was diminished when his military résumé was recently questioned.[32]

Virtually all of the books that have been discussed here have been critical of both senior and junior officer leadership. After the successful completion of the Gulf War in 1991, books began to appear that cast a more positive light on leadership in Vietnam. Norman Schwarzkopf's *It Doesn't Take a Hero*,[33] Colin Powell's *My American Journey*,[34] and James Kitfield's *Prodigal Soldiers*[35] all compared the political aspects of Vietnam to the Gulf War and drew stark distinctions between the operational plans. Kitfield's book gave credit to the military's superb performance in Desert Storm and to the leadership shown by generals who had served as lieutenants in Vietnam.

In 1993, historian Ronald H. Spector published *After TET: The Bloodiest Year in Vietnam*, which questioned many of the stereotypes of the 1970s studies about soldiers in the Vietnam War.[36] "Vietnam GIS of 1968 were not simply a collection of ill-educated, impoverished youths from the bottom rungs of society. Rather they represented the solid middle of American Society."[37] This book, coupled with Christian Appy's seminal work, *Working Class War*,[38] began to question the findings of previous scholars who had stated that the war was fought by the impoverished youth of America. Spector also identified the American soldier and officer as more educated than the soldier in World War II or Korea. And this education was a positive attribute for both soldiers and officers. Spector's analysis of the problems with the American military in Vietnam minimizes the deficiencies of the junior officer corps and lays most of the blame on Saigon and Washington.

A more recent book by Peter S. Kindsvatter, *American Soldiers: Ground Combat in the World Wars, Korea, and Vietnam*,[39] took a position similar to that of Spector by identifying the Vietnam leaders as more educated than their predecessor wartime officers but afflicted with a set of problems different from those of officers of previous wars. "Even for those junior leaders who did their best to carry out their assigned missions, and the majority undoubtedly fell into this category, the yardstick for measuring success increasingly became a low number of friendly casualties, not damage done to the enemy."[40] Thus, these officers had a set of motives different from those of the officers in World War II, because this war was so different.

Finally, no historiographical essay on junior officers in Vietnam would be complete without reference to those officers who wrote their memoirs. For many years, books like Philip Caputo's *A Rumor of War*,[41] David Donovan's *Once a Warrior King*,[42] James McDonough's *Platoon Leader*,[43] and Michael Lee Lanning's *The Only War We Had*[44] were the only publications that gave scholars a sense of the problems inherent in leading men in combat in Vietnam. Each of these authors was able to focus on his specific leadership issues, depending on what job he was doing and where he was located in-country. Their individual accounts are valuable to the study of junior officer leadership.

Appendix Three OCS Leadership Qualities and Traits

Initiative: The quality of doing more than is required.

Physical ability: The ability to handle strenuous duties with both stamina and coordination. Exercises such as drill and ceremony and bayonet practice were used to measure these skills.

Tact: Everyday diplomacy.

Moral courage: Standing up for correct convictions. The ability to advise superiors, then accept their command if your advice is not accepted.

Enthusiasm: Advancing with zeal and vigor.

Judgment: Weighing choices with expected results, then acting without hesitation.

Decisiveness: Weighing all factors, but also to instill confidence in peers, subordinates, and superiors.

Attitude: Having a positive approach to any task, not being satisfied in just getting by.

Deportment: The manner in which an individual conducts himself publicly and privately.

Knowledge: The body of facts accumulated through training and experience that can be utilized.

Loyalty: Faithfulness to duty, supporting both subordinates and superiors to the best of your ability.

Adaptability: The ability to adjust rapidly to meet new requirements or changing situations. This is absolutely essential to performing effectively in combat.

Command presence: These are intangibles that the army broke into four components:

— appearance: confident air, shined shoes, "the spit shine syndrome"[1]

— poise: voice commands, air of composure

— bearing: physical and mental posture

— command voice: strictly the physical sound of one's command.

Cooperation: The ability to work with others to achieve a common goal.

Expression: The manner in which thoughts are conveyed to others.

Instructional ability: Officers must teach their men; thus they must be able to convey instructions in a coherent manner.

Orders: Must be clear and concise.

Organizational ability: Develop and control necessary resources to accomplish mission in the most efficient manner.

Supervision: The ability to oversee effective use of resources in accomplishment of assigned tasks.[2]

Appendix Four Questionnaires and Interviews

Many Vietnam veterans have been interviewed in books such as James Ebert's *A Life in a Year*, Mark Baker's *'Nam*, Stanley Beesley's *Vietnam: The Heartland Remembers*, and Peter Kindsvatter's *American Soldiers*. I began my process in 2002 by researching former officers and enlisted men who had voluntarily submitted their names to the Vietnam Veterans National Memorial in Angel Fire, New Mexico (now the Vietnam Veterans Memorial State Park). The "Keep in Touch" project contains the names of thousands of veterans who have visited the memorial since 1976 and have chosen to leave some personal information behind. I obtained a random sample of 135 of those names and addresses, including approximately 50 percent junior officers and 50 percent noncommissioned officers.

In March 2003, I sent letters to all 135 identified veterans asking them to participate in the "Not a Gentleman's War" research project (see letter 1, below). By returning a postcard and checking one of three options, 77 percent of the former officers and 79 percent of the noncommissioned officers responded positively to either a phone or in-person interview and agreed to participate in my project.

I became aware of the U.S. Army Military History Institute's Vietnam War Era Service Survey Questionnaire Project at Carlisle Barracks, Pennsylvania, and sought their permission to use their form to obtain factual information about these former soldiers as well as to seek attitudinal information. Twelve pages in length, it asks very detailed questions about their Vietnam service. With their permission to use this form they provided me with 200 copies along with return mailing envelopes. These surveys will ultimately be returned to the Military History Institute and be placed alongside those of veterans for use by future generations. Their assistance in my research is appreciated.

The questionnaire was mailed to sixty-one former officers and seventy-four former noncommissioned officers, all of whom had agreed to participate in the project. Fewer veterans responded to this request than had previously agreed to participate. Perhaps the length of the questionnaire or the very personal questions that were asked caused some veterans to decline. Twenty-six percent of the former officers and 15 percent of the former noncommissioned officers responded positively by returning the completed questionnaire.

Interviews were set up with several of the project participants. Each session lasted approximately 1½ hours, and a variety of topics were discussed. The information gathered from both the interviews and the questionnaire has been valuable in support of this research process.

Keep in Touch (courtesy of David Westphall Veterans Foundation, Vietnam Veterans Memorial State Park, Angel Fire, N.M.)

_____ PLEASE CONTACT ME TO ARRANGE A MEETING.

_____ I WOULD LIKE TO TALK TO YOU BY PHONE.

_____ THANK YOU, BUT I AM NOT INTERESTED.

Postcard (author's personal archive)

LETTER ONE

Ron Milam
1703 Copperwood Lane
Richmond, Texas 77469
(281) 341-0809
JRMilam54@yahoo.com

Name
Address
City, State, Zip Code

Dear Fellow Veteran:

I am a Vietnam Veteran (Infantry Advisor, MACV, MAT 38, Pleiku Province, Phu Nhon District, 1970–1971). I am also presently a graduate student in military history at the University of Houston.

In fulfillment of the requirements for the Ph.D. degree, I am completing my dissertation entitled "Not a Gentleman's War: Junior Officers in the Vietnam War." Interviews with both officers and non-commissioned officers are critical to my research.

I obtained your name from the "Keep in Touch" registry at the Vietnam Veteran's Memorial at Angel Fire, New Mexico, and I would like to include you in my study. The enclosed post card offers several options for you to participate. The interviews will be conducted by phone and in person, with initial meetings being held between May 1 and September 1, 2003.

I look forward to receiving your response, and talking with you soon.

Sincerely,
Ron Milam
Encl.

LETTER TWO

May 20, 2003

Ron Milam
1703 Copperwood Lane
Richmond, Texas 77469

Name
Street Address
City, State, Zip Code

Dear Fellow Veteran:

Thank you for responding to my request for assistance in my dissertation research. The next step in the process is to obtain some preliminary information regarding your Vietnam experiences, which will enable subsequent interviews to be conducted expeditiously.

Enclosed is a questionnaire prepared by the U.S. Army Military History Institute at Carlisle, Pennsylvania. I have received permission by the Institute to use their survey, which is part of their ongoing effort to record for history the facts and opinions of veterans of *all* wars. We have, in fact, encouraged our students at the University of Houston to solicit data from their relatives who served in World War II, and the Vietnam survey is now available similarly. If you approve, and you do not have to make this decision prior to our interview, these surveys will ultimately be placed alongside those of your fellow Vietnam Veterans for use by future generations.

I have provided a self-addressed and stamped envelope for your use in returning the form. The form is lengthy, so complete it at your leisure. I would, however, appreciate having it returned by June 10, at which time I will contact you about setting a scheduled phone or personal interview.

If you have any questions about this next step, please contact me by phone at (281) 341-0809 or by e-mail at JRMilam54@yahoo.com.

Thank you,
J. R. Milam
Encl.

Notes

ABBREVIATIONS

In addition to the abbreviations used in the text, the following appear in the notes.

CMH   Center of Military History, Fort McNair, District of Columbia
DRL   Donovan Research Library, Fort Benning, Georgia
ID   Infantry Division
LBJ Library Lyndon Baines Johnson Presidential Library, Austin, Texas
MHI   Military History Institute, Carlisle Barracks, Pennsylvania
NARA   National Archives, College Park, Maryland
Peers Report Peers, William R., Burke Marshall, and Jack Schwartz. *The My Lai
             Massacre and Its Cover-Up: Beyond the Reach of Law? The Peers
             Commission Report*. New York: Free Press, 1976.
USAIS   U.S. Army Infantry School, Fort Benning, Georgia

CHAPTER ONE

1. Puller, *Fortunate Son*, 185–86. Puller served as a platoon leader in the 2nd Battalion, 1st Marine Regiment of the 1st Marine Division near Phu Bai in I Corps, in 1968. Three months after he arrived in-country, he tripped a wire that was attached to a howitzer round that inflicted the damage herein described. In 1994, after twenty-six years of dealing with his wounds and post-traumatic stress disorder, he committed suicide.

2. Harry G. Summers interview, quoted from Summers, *On Strategy*, 21.

3. Heinl, "Collapse of the Armed Forces," 8.

4. The origin of "officer and a gentleman" appears to be from the European military. The use of the term in America is attributed to John Paul Jones; see File Reference Card, September 29, 1964, CMH Archives. The card cites a letter that Jones wrote to the Marine committee, January 21, 1777, and is located in the Library of Congress, per Lovette, *Naval Customs*, 346: "None other than a Gentleman, as well as a Seaman, both in theory and practice, is qualified to support the character of a commissioned officer in the navy, nor is any man fit to command a Ship of War who is not also capable of communicating his ideas on paper in language that becomes his rank." Since the navy was created after the army in colonial America, it is reasonable

to assume that George Washington adopted the same attitude toward the officers in the Continental Army.

5. Alexander Hamilton letter to John Jay, as quoted in Millis, *Arms and Men*, 21, from Kemble, *Image of the Army Officer in America*, 22.

6. George Washington, "To the President of Congress," 12, from Kemble, *Image of the Army Officer in America*, 22.

7. The best account of this battle is in Moore and Galloway, *We Were Soldiers Once*.

8. Military jargon and acronyms are explained in Appendix 1.

9. Appy, *Working-Class War*.

10. See Chapter 7.

11. The infrastructure that supported the REMFs was incredible. For example, the 25th ID at Cu Chi had enlisted men's clubs, dances, and even a sauna. While these comforts could be enjoyed by "grunts" when "standing down" between operations, the field-grade officers lived in this luxury all the time, at least as perceived by infantry soldiers. See Bergerud, *Red Thunder, Tropic Lightning*, 35.

12. The manual designation was changed in 1999 to FM6-22. See Bonn, *Army Officer's Guide*, 67.

13. Ferguson letter to Gen. Harold K. Johnson, Johnson Papers, MHI Archives. These records were in the "personal papers" section.

14. This term has general usage in military history, and its origin is unknown. It has been adopted here from Connelly, *On War and Leadership*, 1.

15. I do not choose to disparage those who served their tours of duty in helicopter service — be they crew or pilots — as will be understood in other sections of this book. But field- and general-grade officers were *relatively* safe when compared with the platoon and company leadership on the ground.

16. Department of Defense Records indicate 40,389 deaths by hostile fire through 1971. Of this total, 2,388 held the rank of 2nd or 1st lieutenant. With one platoon leader for approximately every thirty soldiers, their proportionate deaths should have been 3.3 percent, or 1,333. Thus, these junior officers were killed at a rate nearly twice that which might have been anticipated. See Geog V Vietnam, 704 — Casualties, 1961–1971, 228.01, CMH Archives.

17. Moore, "After Action Report," USAIS, DRL Archives.

18. Currey, *Victory at Any Cost*, from Connelly, *On War and Leadership*, 210.

19. Stewart, *Heart of a Soldier*, 14.

20. Ibid., 183.

21. Bilton and Sim, *Four Hours in My Lai*, 49–50.

22. Sack, *Lieutenant Calley*, 25.

23. Moore and Galloway, *We Were Soldiers Once*.

24. Bilton and Sim, *Four Hours in My Lai*.

CHAPTER TWO

1. Wonsick interview. Wonsick was a platoon leader with the 198th Light Infantry Brigade, which merged with other units to become the 23rd ID (Americal) and served from 1967 to 1968.

2. John F. Kennedy's Inaugural Address, January 20, 1961, from the John F. Kennedy Presidential Library and Museum, Boston, Mass.

3. Total battle casualties through October 1962 were eighteen killed in action and seventy-six wounded in action, of which 50 percent were officers. The high percentage of officer casualties was due to the number of company-grade officers who were assigned as advisors to South Vietnamese Ranger and Airborne units, and to the officers involved in aviation. Helicopter combat was a new tactic, and casualty rates in the beginning were high. See Geog V Vietnam, 704—Casualties, 1961–1971, 228.03, CMH Archives.

4. Cooper, "Day It Became the Longest War." Cooper was the "human easel" for the presentation to Johnson, and he believes McNamara had orchestrated the meeting's logistics to belittle the chiefs' presentation. This included having no chairs or easels and positioning Marine Corps Commandant Wallace Green and Army Chief of Staff Harold K. Johnson as far away from President Johnson as possible. They would have been most affected by his acceptance of the plan, since they had the most troops on the ground and would ultimately sustain the most casualties.

5. Bruen, "Repercussions from the Vietnam Mobilization Decision."

6. Westmoreland, *Soldier Reports*, 143.

7. Herring and Knight, "Are Reserve Component Officers Ready?," MHI Archives. Studies later in the war when the Reserve Mobilization Issue was again a concern would confirm these fears of junior officer readiness.

8. Contrary to common beliefs, 5,977 reservists and 101 National Guard soldiers were killed in Vietnam. Most of those identified as reservists were officers who did not hold Regular Army commissions. However, all of the guardsmen held special MOSs needed by the army. See Department of Defense records, CMH Archives.

9. Hall, "Wailing Walls?," 22.

10. Executive Order 11360, 32 Federal Register 9787, Administrative History for Department of Defense, vol. 4, Manpower, 1969, box 2, A.3b Draft Policies, LBJ Library, 92.

11. Davis, "Does ROTC Have a Place on the College Campus?," 4.

12. Neiberg, *Making Citizen-Soldiers*, 171.

13. Ibid.

14. Office of the Chief of Staff, "Recruiters on College Campuses," CMH Archives. ("Hippie types" is their term.)

15. Chief of Procurement Division, "Report of Colleges and Universities Which

Bar On-Campus Recruitment," CMH Archives. Each of the referenced colleges sent letters to the army, all of which are contained in this memorandum.

16. Chief of Staff, U.S. Army, memo regarding "Proposal on On-Campus Military Recruitment," CMH Archives.

17. Office of Personnel Operations, "Survey Estimate of Opinions on the Image of the Army as Expressed by Active Duty Male Personnel," CMH Archives, 15–21.

18. The study does not define "Spanish American," and since the government did not begin to categorize Hispanics until 1972, this was probably a grouping that interviewers established based on skin color and perceived ethnic characteristics.

19. "Negro" was the Department of Defense term for African Americans in 1969.

20. United States Army Recruiting Command, "Summary of Findings," CMH Archives.

21. Records of college graduates in OCS are difficult to procure, because individual battalion histories are the only records available. By definition, USMA- and ROTC-commissioned officers were college graduates, but this was not necessarily so with OCS. Having perused such records as OC 17-66, 64th Company, and OC 17-66, 64th Company, Candidate Brigade, Fort Benning, Georgia, NARA, I extrapolate that each class contained between 50 percent and 75 percent college graduates.

22. "Officer Training to Be Limited to College Graduates."

23. Sack, *Lieutenant Calley*, 24. Lieutenant Calley will be discussed in Chapter 7.

24. Manpower and Reserve Affairs, "Coffee Houses and Union Movement," CMH Archives. It is noteworthy that the actual accessions for FY1969 turned out to be only 10.2 percent, which not only was a function of more draftees and enlistees than predicted in August 1968 but also occurred because college students figured out other ways to avoid service. But the numbers are significant: 44,795 in FY1969, 31,687 in FY1970, and 17,178 in FY1971. See Office of the Deputy Chief of Staff for Personnel, "Utilization of Increased College Graduate Accessions," CMH Archives.

25. Office of the Deputy Chief of Staff for Personnel, "Utilization of Increased College Graduate Accessions," CMH Archives.

26. "Army Makes a New Point," 132.

27. Atkinson, *Long Gray Line*, 555.

28. Office of the Deputy Chief of Staff for Personnel, "Annual Historical Summary," FY1966, CMH Archives, 19.

29. Office of the Assistant Secretary of Defense for Public Affairs, "Army to Expand Officer Candidate Program," NARA.

30. Annual Command Histories, "Build-up of U.S. Forces," NARA, 290.

31. MacDonald, "Outline History," CMH Archives, 65–66.

32. Carney, "OCS to Graduate 21,000 in FY67."

33. Office of the Deputy Chief of Staff for Personnel, "Annual Historical Summary," FY1968, CMH Archives, 28.

34. Ibid., 212.

35. Newman letter to Marvin Watson, LBJ Library.

36. Ulman, "Changing Point," 1.

37. The figures for KIAs are as follows: 1965, 25; 1966, 29; 1967, 29; 1968, 20; 1969, 18; and 1970, 4. See Ron Meier, USMA, Class of '66, "In Memory of our classmates who fell in Vietnam," <www.academybiznet.org/VietnamMemorial .html>.

38. Atkinson, *Long Gray Line*, 137.

39. Moore interview. Moore served with the 23rd ID (American Division) and saw few West Point–commissioned junior officers assigned there, although Norman Schwarzkopf was assigned to the unit as a major. The graduates of West Point were typically assigned to the 173rd Airborne Brigade, the 101st Airborne Division, or the 1st Air Cavalry Division.

40. Keatley, "ROTC Ranks Expand Despite Antagonism on Many Campuses."

41. Faber interview. Faber served in Vietnam in 1964–65 as an army pilot after having been commissioned through ROTC.

42. BDM Corporation, *Strategic Lessons Learned in Vietnam*, NARA.

43. Norton letter to Col. W. E. Showalter, NARA. The letter is in response to a request to advertise within ROTC for cadets to choose the infantry. Norton informed Showalter that army regulations precluded such advertising but that other avenues of "coercion" were possible.

44. Horton interview. Horton served in Vietnam in 1971 with the 1st ID, after having been commissioned in armor through ROTC.

45. Coffman, *War to End All Wars*, 17.

46. McPherson, *Ninety-Day Wonders*, iv.

47. Vitucci, "Bradley Set Up the First OCS at Fort Benning."

48. Greene, "Infantry OCS Has Its Roots in Expansion of 1930s."

49. Turner, *Practice for Officer Candidate Test*, 40.

50. "Army Officer Candidate Program."

51. Talbott, "Role of the U.S. Army Infantry School in Training Infantrymen," USAIS, DRL Archives.

52. BDM Corporation, *Strategic Lessons Learned in Vietnam*, NARA, 1:37.

53. Appy, *Working-Class War*, 24.

54. Fallows, "What Did You Do in the Class War, Daddy?"

55. Barnett, Stanley, and Shore, "America's Vietnam Casualties."

56. Fallows, "Low-Class Conclusions."

57. Ibid.

58. Terry, *Bloods*, xiv.

59. Young, *Vietnam Wars*, 320.

60. Baskir and Strauss, *Chance and Circumstance*, 8.

61. Appy, *Working-Class War*, 33.

62. U.S. Casualties in Southeast Asia by Grade and Military Service, Geog V Vietnam, 704—Casualties, 1961–1971, 228.01, CMH Archives.

63. Sherrill, *Military Justice Is to Justice as Military Music Is to Music*, 219.

64. Fahy Committee Report, 439, and Department of Defense, *Task Force*, 1:55, from Westheider, *Fighting on Two Fronts*, 120.

65. Westheider, *Fighting on Two Fronts*, 123.

66. Westmoreland, *Report of the Chief of Staff*, CMH Archives, 65.

67. My OCS class, OC 66 Graduation June 1969, commissioned 8 black officers from a class of 189. All were College Option enrollees, and none had been recycled from previous classes.

68. Roberto Munoz was the only known Hispanic commissioned in OC 66.

69. Just, "Soldiers."

CHAPTER THREE

1. Cook interview. Cook graduated from OCS in 1966 and served with the 23rd ID (American) in Vietnam from 1967 to 1968. He is referring to the process of spit-shining floors with a buffing machine, which was my experience, versus hand polishing. The debate about the relative merits was frequent.

2. "Army Makes a New Point," 136.

3. Creighton interview. Creighton was a graduate of the USMA class of 1954 and achieved the rank of major general. He served with the 9th ID, 25th ID, and other units in 1967 and 1968.

4. Robert A. Doughty and Theodore J. Crackel, "The History of History at West Point," in Betros, *West Point*, 390–434.

5. Creighton interview.

6. Ulman, "Changing Point," 4.

7. "Army Makes a New Point," 134.

8. Ulman, "Changing Point," 1.

9. *Army Field Manual*, FM22-100 (Washington, D.C.: Government Printing Office, 1965).

10. "Manuscript of FM22-100 Military Leadership," USAIS.

11. Atkinson, *Long Gray Line*, 9–41.

12. Ibid., 39. Atkinson's book is exclusively about the West Point class of 1966, but the 25 percent figure is consistent with other studies, such as Prashker's *Duty, Honor, Vietnam*.

13. Creighton interview.

14. Atkinson, *Long Gray Line*, 26.

15. Ibid., 37.

16. Ibid., 398.

17. Boone interview in Prashker, *Duty, Honor, Vietnam*, 20.

18. Dickinson, Mackmull, and Merritt, "West Point Study Group," MHI Archives.

19. "Analysis of Current Army System of Officer Schooling," Annex D, Appendix 1, "Officer Recruitment and Retention," from *Final Report of the Haines Board*, 1967, CMH Archives, 418. The Haines Board Report is dealt with extensively in Chapter 4.

20. Mataxis interview. Mataxis was commissioned through ROTC and served multiple tours in Vietnam in 1969, 1970, 1971, and 1972.

21. Donnelly, "Why Graduates of the U.S. Military Academy from 1964 to 1966 Did Not Attend a Branch Officer Basic Course," 1.

22. Ibid., 2.

23. Johnson, "Memorandum for ACSFOR," CMH Archives.

24. "CONUS Assignments for Newly Commissioned Second Lieutenants Prior to Assignment to Vietnam," CMH Archives, SEA-RS-121.

25. Neiberg, *Making Citizen-Soldiers*, 138.

26. Moon, "ROTC on the Rebound."

27. Neiberg, *Making Citizen-Soldiers*, 94.

28. Macdonald letter to Brig. Gen. William Lindley, University of Texas President's Office Records, VF37/c.b, Air Force Science 1960–1968 folder, from Neiberg, *Making Citizen-Soldiers*, 107.

29. Neiberg, *Making Citizen-Soldiers*, 110.

30. Letter from Robben Fleming to John Pemberton, Executive Director, American Civil Liberties Union, March 19, 1969, University of Michigan Archives, Bentley Historical Library, President's Papers, box 10, ROTC folder, from Neiberg, *Making Citizen-Soldiers*, 136–37.

31. Neiberg, *Making Citizen-Soldiers*, 139.

32. National Security Information Center, Inc., "Summary Report: 1968–1973," New York University/National Security Information Center, Inc., May 1973, from Neiberg, *Making Citizen-Soldiers*, 142.

33. Assistant Commandant, "Policies, Combat Platoon Leader Course," USAIS, DRL Archives.

34. Ibid., 3

35. "Report of the Combat Platoon Leader Course (5 weeks) Curriculum Review Committee," USAIS, DRL Archives, 4.

36. Faber interview.

37. Forsythe letter to Brig. Gen. Leon H. Hagen, NARA.

38. Assistant Commandant, "Policies, Combat Platoon Leader Course," USAIS, DRL Archives.

39. Woolnough, "Teacher to an Army in a War."

40. Woolnough letter to Army ROTC programs nationwide, NARA.

41. Benson, "Academic World and Military Education," 6, quoted in Neiberg, *Making Citizen-Soldiers*.

42. Neiberg, *Making Citizen-Soldiers*, 134.

43. "Personal Histories of Officers in My Lai (4)," CMH Archives.

44. *Infantry Officer Candidate Manual*, 6-3 (1968), DRL.

45. Ibid.

46. Hutton interview. Hutton taught Platoon and Company Tactics as a captain, after his tour with the 23rd ID (Americal) in Vietnam.

47. "Analysis of Current Army System of Officer Schooling," Annex B, Appendix 3, "Pre-commission Military Schooling," from *Final Report of the Haines Board*, 1967, CMH Archives, 147.

48. Lovejoy interview and Ryan interview. Both Lovejoy and Ryan served with the 23rd ID (Americal) in 1967–68.

49. *Infantry Officer Candidate Manual*, 7-4 (1968), DRL.

50. Ibid., 2-5.

51. I recall one candidate who had thirteen years of prior service and had been awarded the Medal of Honor for his service as a medic in Vietnam. He was recycled because he could not run a mile in less than eight minutes. I don't know if he was ever commissioned.

52. Hiett interview. Hiett was commissioned through OCS, became a helicopter pilot, and served in Vietnam in 1968.

53. Piper, "OCS Today," 42.

54. *Tactical Officer's Guide*, January 1968, DRL, 1-3.

55. Ibid., 3-1.

56. Piper, "OCS Today," 42. The average age, education, and prior service changed as the war progressed, as was discussed in Chapter 2. However, Piper's snapshot in early 1970 probably reflects the College Option candidates who no longer had the protection of college and chose to enlist.

57. Ibid., 44.

58. Candidates had numerous terms for these sheets, "bayonet sheets" being the most common. A more colorful term, from personal experience, was the "Fuck Your Buddy" report.

59. "Fragging" as a form of eliminating individuals from a unit is discussed in detail in Chapter 8.

60. Hiett interview.

61. *Tactical Officer's Guide*, January 1968, DRL, 4-1.

62. While not mentioned in any formal guide or handbook, this could include "Drop down and give me ten" (push-ups), running down the stairs and around the barracks, or any number of demeaning and morale-lowering tactics.

63. *Tactical Officer's Guide*, January 1968, DRL, 4-2.

64. Ibid., 4-8.

65. Linster interview. Linster was a graduate of OCS and served in Vietnam in 1967–68 as a helicopter pilot.

66. Frazier interview. Frazier was a graduate of OCS and served in Vietnam in 1966–67 as a helicopter pilot.

67. Piper, "OCS Today," 45.

CHAPTER FOUR

1. Moore interview. Moore was an instructor at the USAIS from February 1967 until June 1968 in the platoon tactics department and taught OCS candidates.

2. DePuy, "Army Leadership Moves Upward on Performance," 1.

3. Office of the Commandant letter to Gen. Mark Clark, USAIS. Though this quote and letter are from the Korean War era, they illustrate the issue confronting the training of civilians in OCS.

4. Smith letter to Army Commanders World-wide, "Department of the Army Board to Review Army Officer Schools," NARA.

5. Ibid., 2.

6. Ibid., 4.

7. Edwards letter to Captain Porter, "USAIS Position Paper on Army School System," NARA, 2.

8. "Analysis of Current Army System of Officer Schooling," Annex D, Appendix 1, "Officer Recruitment and Retention," from *Final Report of the Haines Board*, 1967, CMH Archives, 430.

9. York letter to Commanding General, U.S. Continental Army Command, NARA, 19.

10. "Analysis of Current Army System of Officer Schooling," Annex D, Appendix 1, "Officer Recruitment and Retention," from *Final Report of the Haines Board*, 1967, CMH Archives, 431.

11. York letter to Commanding General, U.S. Continental Army Command, NARA, 14.

12. Ibid., 19.

13. Johnson letter to Company Tactics Department, "Haines Board Briefing," NARA, 2.

14. "Analysis of Current Army System of Officer Schooling," Annex D, Appendix 1, "Officer Recruitment and Retention," from *Final Report of the Haines Board*, 1967, CMH Archives, 148.

15. Ibid., 425.

16. Ibid., 572.

17. Ibid., 150.

18. Ibid., 14.

19. Ibid., 399. Costs from National Security Information Center, "Summary of Activities," June 1969, University of Michigan Archives, Bentley Historical Library, Vice-President for Academic Affairs Papers, box 40, ROTC-Air Force 1972 folder, from Neiberg, *Making Citizen-Soldiers*, 132. Costs: USMA, $48,917; OCS, $5,880; ROTC, $4,250.

20. "Analysis of Current Army System of Officer Schooling," Annex D, Appendix 1, "Officer Recruitment and Retention," from *Final Report of the Haines Board*, 1967, CMH Archives, 422.

21. Ibid., 423.

22. Ibid., 424.

23. Ibid., 405.

24. Ibid., 418.

25. Ibid., 420.

26. Ibid., 155–56.

27. Allen to Review Army Officer Schools, "Provision of Document," MHI Archives, 5.

28. Ibid. Interestingly, there was a handwritten note in the margin: "Good words to put in our study." These words do not appear in the final document, perhaps because they belittle the need for the study, or because the word "input" would make more sense if it were "output."

29. Wickham memorandum, "Report of the Department of the Army Board to Review Army Officer Schools," MHI Archives.

30. Review of Education and Training for Officers (RETO Study), MHI Archives, III-22.

31. Ibid., V-2.

32. During the Vietnam War, the percentage fluctuated between 7 at the beginning to less than 5 at the peak, even though the total number was higher. See Atkinson, *Long Gray Line*, 555.

33. There had been other critics of West Point before the scandal broke. J. Arthur Heise's *Brass Factories* questioned whether such institutions were necessary, particularly in light of the cost of educating an officer at ROTC or OCS. And using the war in Vietnam as a benchmark, Heise quoted some officers who said anonymously that West Pointers in Vietnam tended to support whatever senior officers wanted done, whereas ROTC-commissioned officers tended to question why; see 163–64. This anonymous source: *Newsweek*, July 10, 1967.

34. Dickinson, Mackmull, and Merritt, "West Point Study Group," MHI Archives, 1.

35. Quarterly Progress Report, USAIS, DRL Archives.

36. Jacobs et al., "Analysis of Seven U.S. Army Officer Candidate Schools," USAIS, DRL Archives.

37. Demographic information regarding OCS is difficult to decipher, but some information can be found in Peterson, "Comparison of Behavioral Styles." In his study, done during the same period as the HumRRO report, Peterson found that 20 percent of the OCS candidates were college graduates and 45 percent had some college; that the modal age was 21, with an average age of 21.5; and that most had only six months of active duty prior to becoming candidates.

38. Jacobs et al., "Analysis of Seven U.S. Army Officer Candidate Schools," USAIS, DRL Archives, iv.

39. Ibid., v.

40. Kern and McFann, "Confidence Development during Training," NARA, 2.

41. Jacobs et al., "Analysis of Seven U.S. Army Officer Candidate Schools," USAIS, DRL Archives, 58.

42. Analysis and Review Branch Office, "Report on Survey of Military Knowledge and Skills," USAIS, DRL Archives.

43. Ibid., 2. The titles of the other two exams were the Military Knowledge Survey Tests and the Officer Candidate Comprehensive Examination.

44. Ibid., 4.

45. Atkinson, *Long Gray Line*, 555.

46. The army was so confident that soldiers who achieved a score of 115 on the Officer Candidate Test could succeed in the academic aspects of the program that it stated this qualification in advertisements for OCS: "The fact that you received 115 or above on the OCT indicates that you can comprehend the academic instruction. The subjects are presented starting with the basics and then proceeding to the advanced. Officer Candidates do not normally encounter problems with academics during the course" (*Facts for the Prospective Infantry Officer Candidate*, DRL Archives, 3–4).

47. Vallo interview and response to questionnaire, November 27, 2003, Houston, Texas. Ed served with the Headquarters, Headquarters Battery, 4th ID, in Pleiku from January to April 1970 and also served in support of the 25th ID's incursion into Cambodia from April to November 1970.

48. Office of Assistant Commandant, "Review and Analysis, 4th Quarter," FY62–73, DRL Archives. The Ranger School had an attrition rate of between 12 and 15 percent during the Vietnam War era, and the Noncommissioned Officer Candidate Course School had attrition rates in the range of 20–25 percent.

49. Izenour memorandum, "Pre-OCS Dropouts," CMH Archives.

50. Ron Milam's personal experience.

51. Office of Assistant Commandant, "Review and Analysis, 4th Quarter," for each year between 1962 and 1972, DRL Archives.

52. Most graduates of OCS remember the demanding course of physical training. Larry Tritle recalls his company commander, Capt. Larry Moore, being so strict on

candidates that more than 50 percent failed to graduate. Captain Moore was a combat veteran of the Battle of Dak To, as a platoon leader with the 173rd Airborne Brigade. See Tritle, *From Melos to My Lai*, 144, and personal e-mail (ltritle@lmumail.lmu.edu), November 20, 2003.

53. Engelhardt, "OCS Status Report."

54. Linster interview.

55. Hiett interview.

56. This very GI term has its origin in World War II, at least as it relates to the military. Paul Fussell described the term as "behavior that makes military life worse than it need be: petty harassment of the weak by the strong; open scrimmage for power and authority and prestige; sadism thinly disguised as necessary discipline" (Fussell, *Wartime*, 80). All military units operate with a certain degree of this, but it is particularly acute in periods when troops are being trained to go to war.

57. Complimentary letters in the NARA files included those from Maj. Gen. Jonathan O. Seaman, Commanding General of the 1st Infantry Division, Fort Riley, Kansas, August 18, 1965; Brig. Gen. Charles W. Fernald, Commanding General of the Arizona National Guard, Phoenix, July 30, 1965; Maj. Gen. B. E. Powell, Commanding General of the 101st Airborne Division, Fort Campbell, Kentucky, July 26, 1965; and Maj. Gen. Autrey J. Maroun, Commanding General of the 5th Infantry Division (Mechanized), Fort Carson, Colorado, August 5, 1965.

58. Mabry letter to Robert H. York, Commandant, NARA. Mabry opined that junior officers "felt lacking in the knowledge of platoon control and integration of tank elements." He was, however, complimentary as to the general training received by junior officers.

59. Lawrie letter to Maj. Gen. Robert H. York, NARA. More maintenance courses and a need to stress the importance of maintenance were imperative.

60. Carver letter to Maj. Gen. Robert H. York, NARA.

61. Foery letter to Maj. Gen. John A. Heintges, NARA.

62. Forsythe letter to the Commanding General, United States Army Continental Army Command, "Liaison Visit to Viet Nam," NARA.

63. Hitchcock letter to Col. Herbert E. Wolff, NARA.

64. Comments of B. G. DePuy, J-3, MACV, in "Report of Staff Visit" from Col. Towsor, USCONARC Training Team, Republic of Vietnam, March 22, 1966, p. 3, USAIS, DRL Archives, DS556.1, T4, dU.

65. Report of the Liaison Visit to Vietnam, December 13, 1966, p. 3, USAIS, DRL Archives, DS556.1, V2, dU.

66. Report of USCONARC Training Team Visit to Republic of Vietnam, December 1–December 14, 1966, January 13, 1967, p. 1, USAIS, DRL Archives, DS556.1, W8, dU.

67. The 25th had only been in Vietnam since March 1966, only nine months before the liaison visit. See Kelley, *Where We Were in Vietnam*, B-15.

68. Report of USCONARC Training Team, January 13, 1967, p. 3, USAIS, DRL Archives, DS556.1, V2, dU.

69. Ibid., 5.

70. Report of USCONARC Training Team Visit to Republic of Vietnam, April 19, 1967, p. 7, USAIS, DRL Archives, DS556.1, V2, dU.

71. Report of USCONARC Training Team, January 13, 1967, p. 3, USAIS, DRL Archives, DS556.1, V2, dU.

72. Ibid., 8.

73. Moore and Galloway, *We Were Soldiers Once*, 257.

74. RVN Liaison Training Visit, July 17–28, August 30, 1968, p. 21, USAIS, DRL Archives, DS556.1, l5, dU.

75. Ibid., 28.

76. The 25th Infantry Division suffered the highest casualties during the war, with the 1st Cavalry Division experiencing the most deaths (25th Infantry Division: KIA, 4,102, and WIA, 30,368; 1st Cavalry Division: KIA, 4,432, and WIA, 2,579). However, the 25th Infantry Division was in-country nearly one year less than the 1st Cavalry Infantry Division. Many of these deaths were attributable to the period around TET, February 1968. See "Battle Casualties by Organization RVN," Geog V Vietnam, 704 — Casualties, 1961–1971, 228.03, CMH Archives.

77. Two officers per rifle company would represent 40 percent strength, according to the Army Infantry Division Table of Organization and Equipment. Each platoon would normally be assigned one officer as platoon leader and one officer as a weapon's platoon leader. See *Infantry Reference Data*, July 1968, USAIS.

78. Report of USCONARC Liaison Visit to RVN, USAIS Representative, February 25, 1969, p. 2, USAIS, DRL Archives, DS556.1, P93, dU.

79. Ibid.

80. Ibid.

81. Kinnard, *War Managers*, 111.

82. Ibid., 112–13.

83. Nadal interview.

CHAPTER FIVE

1. Peers speech before the University of Delaware ROTC Commissioning Exercise, Peers Papers, MHI Archives.

2. "Training," chap. 4, 101st Airborne Division, DVSCOM, NARA, 270/030/34/6.

3. Anderson, *The Grunts*, 8.

4. Lovejoy interview. A few soldiers experienced alternative modes of transportation to Vietnam, such as military transport aircraft or ocean liners commandeered as troop ships by the military. For example, the 198th Light Infantry Brigade, which eventually became part of the 23rd ID (Americal), was transported entirely by rail, then by ship from Fort Hood, Texas, to Vietnam. Few units were transported en masse; most soldiers went over as individual replacements.

5. Givhan interview.

6. *Platoon*.

7. Caputo, *Rumor of War*, 52.

8. Faber interview.

9. Cook interview. Cook describes the arrival of the 198th Light Infantry Brigade near Chu Lai in 1967 as "surreal," because the troops had "locked and loaded" for a D-Day type assault. Instead, beautifully dressed Vietnamese women in traditional *Ao Dais* walked into the water and greeted the soldiers.

10. My memories were of the intense heat and humidity, and I had described such in letters home. But I had lived and trained in northern states, departing from Detroit, Michigan. Upon my return to Vietnam in 2001, I did not notice the heat, nor did my wife, since we had lived for fifteen years in Houston, Texas, where the heat and humidity are similar.

11. Willbanks interview.

12. Mataxis interview.

13. Mathiak interview. Mathiak served as an NCO in Vietnam in 1970 and 1971.

14. Linster interview.

15. Dant interview. Dant served as a rifleman in Vietnam in 1970 and 1971.

16. Leppelman, *Blood on the Risers*, 13.

17. Kelley, *Where We Were in Vietnam*, F-57.

18. Ibid., 5–129.

19. Schultz interview in Ebert, *Life in a Year*, 92.

20. Keeling interview in Ebert, *Life in a Year*, 93.

21. Thayer, *War without Fronts*, 115–16. The book details deaths by province and military region and states that 53 percent of American combat deaths occurred in I Corps between 1967 and 1972. However, the Central Highlands area of II Corps experienced greater casualties between 1965 and 1967; this is the region where the Battle of the Ia Drang Valley was fought, as chronicled in Moore and Galloway, *We Were Soldiers Once*.

22. "Chief of Staff Guidance," Headquarters of the 1st Infantry Division, February 6, 1969, NARA, 270/029/15/1.

23. McDonough, *Platoon Leader*, 15.

24. "Personnel Processing: Orientation for Newly Arrived Personnel," Headquar-

ters, 25th Infantry Division, January 22, 1966, NARA, 270/030/16/6. Among the agenda items for this hour-long program was "the Division Band Plays Appropriate Music," "History and Traditions of the Division," and "Law and Order."

25. "Education and Training: Attendance at the Lightning Replacement Training Course," Headquarters, 25th Infantry Division, July 22, 1967, NARA, 270/030/16/5.

26. "Commanding General's Welcome to Newly Joined Officers and Non-commissioned Officers of the 25th Infantry Division," Appendix I to Circular Number 4612-3, April 20, 1966, 3, NARA, 270/030/16/6.

27. "Education and Training: Proficiency Training," United States Military Assistance Command, Vietnam, Directive Number 350-3, April 18, 1966, 2, NARA, 270/075/25/5.

28. "Commanding General's Welcome to Newly Joined Officers and Non-commissioned Officers of the 25th Infantry Division," Appendix I to Circular Number 4612-3, April 20, 1966, 1, NARA, 270/030/16/6.

29. "Division Replacement Training Program," Training Circular Number 61-5, Headquarters, 25th Infantry Division, June 24, 1966, I-1, NARA, 270/030/16/6.

30. "Education and Training, Revolutionary Development Training," Headquarters, United States Military Assistance Command, Vietnam, Directive Number 350-5, October 24, 1966, 1, annex A, NARA, 270/075/25/5.

31. "Education and Training, Major Unit Training," Regulation Number 350-1, Headquarters, 1st Infantry Division, January 19, 1969, A-1–B-1, NARA, 270/029/15/1.

32. An example of poor design was the first issued weapon's flash suppressor, which had three slots (which could be used expeditiously to cut the wires encasing C-rations) that would occasionally break the suppressor or bend the barrel. Eventually, the flash suppressor was enclosed, which did not lessen the efficiency of concealing the muzzle pyrotechnics.

33. Westmoreland, *Soldier Reports*, 158.

34. Handouts provided each soldier at the repo-depo, Ron Milam's personal archives.

35. The strongest indictment of the weapon was made by Col. David Hackworth, documented in *About Face*. Hackworth tested the weapon very early in the process and stated that it required "surgical cleanliness" and "was not GI proof" (435).

36. The M-14 could be fired fully automatically, but its reliability and accuracy were diminished when this option was selected. The recoil and rise were difficult to control as compared with the M-16A1.

37. Bradbury interview, September 15, 2003. Bradbury served as a rifleman in Vietnam in 1967 and 1968.

38. Marshall, *Men against Fire*, 54. Subsequent investigations by military historians and psychologists have questioned Marshall's research methodology, thus requiring

some discounting of his findings. Nevertheless, the book had an important impact on America's post–World War II weapons training.

39. Mathiak interview.

40. Glenn, *Reading Athena's Dance Card*, ix.

41. Drill sergeants and weapons instructors in AIT who had served in Vietnam were constantly stressing the need to fire low because of the coupled tendencies of VC to crawl low in combat and the M-16A1's natural rise.

42. Spawr interview. Spawr served two tours in Vietnam in 1967, 1968, and 1969, one of them as an interpreter.

43. Goff and Sanders with Smith, *Brothers*, 73.

44. Franklin interview. Franklin served as an RTO in Vietnam in 1968 and 1969.

45. Personal experience of Ron Milam. The weapons characteristics cited in this chapter are from *Infantry Reference Data*, July 1968, USAIS, 400–404.

46. Meringolo interview in Ebert, *Life in a Year*, 178.

47. Thayer, *War without Fronts*, 117.

48. Lanning, *Only War We Had*, 22.

49. The Iraq War generated the acronym "IED," for "improvised explosive device," although this was not known to us in Vietnam, perhaps because mines and booby traps were such a common form of weaponry to the Viet Cong.

50. Mataxis interview.

51. O'Kelley interview. O'Kelley served in Vietnam in 1967 and 1968 as a marine officer after graduating from OCS.

52. O'Brien, *If I Die in a Combat Zone*, 122.

53. Lanning, *Only War We Had*, 71. More graphic but expressive of the concern soldiers had for their private parts was the passage in James Webb's *Fields of Fire*, 6. After a lieutenant had stepped on a mine and had half of his leg traumatically amputated, he asked the medic, "Snake, is my dick all right? Tell me the truth, is it?" "Course it is, unless you're hung halfway to your knees." Though Webb's book is fiction, it is representative of diaries and journals written by combat veterans. (Both of these citations were provided in Kindsvatter, *American Soldiers*, 81).

54. O'Kelley interview.

55. Bergerud, *Red Thunder, Tropic Lightning*, 111.

56. Ryan interview and follow-up personal e-mail (bory450@hotmail.com), September 29, 2003. Bob mentioned his wound in the initial interview, and I asked him to provide more detail in writing. His wounds were very significant, and he spent more than a year in various overseas and stateside hospitals. Promoted to captain after his hospital time, he served as an instructor at OCS and IOBC classes at Fort Benning, Georgia, teaching search-and-destroy methods in the small-unit tactics department.

57. "Operational Report—Lessons Learned," 101st Airborne Division (Airmobile), period ending April 30, 1971, RCS CSFOR-65, 9, NARA, 270/030/28/28.

58. "British Army Jungle Warfare School," Headquarters, United States Military Assistance Command, Vietnam, Directive Number 350-1, January 2, 1964, 2, NARA, 270/075/25/5.

59. "Operations Report—Lessons Learned 6-67—'Observations of a Brigade Commander,'" AGAM-P(M) (22 December 67) FOR OT RD, December 27, 1967, MHI Archives, 57.

60. "Education and Training—Lightning Ambush Academy," 25th ID, Regulation Number 350-7, July 5, 1966, II-1–5, NARA, 270/030/16/6.

61. Thayer, *War without Fronts*, 117. The only uniformed woman killed by hostile fire in Vietnam was 1st Lt. Sharon Lane, a nurse at the 312th Evacuation Hospital in Chu Lai who died in a mortar attack on June 8, 1969. Seven other uniformed women died from accidents or other causes, and several female civilians died while serving in various capacities in support of the war. See Norman, *Women at War*, 57.

62. McMamers, *Ultimate Special Forces*, 141.

63. Mataxis interview.

64. Garland, *Infantry in Vietnam*, 159.

65. McDonough, *Platoon Leader*, 17–18.

CHAPTER SIX

1. Bernhardt interview in Appy, *Patriots*, 350. Bernhardt was a member of Charlie Company, 1st Battalion, 20th Infantry, and 11th Light Infantry Brigade of the 23rd (American) Division stationed at My Lai on March 16, 1968, when the massacre occurred. Not firing his weapon because he had been ordered to guard the command post for Captain Medina, he entered the village after all of the killing had been accomplished.

2. Lemak response to questionnaire. Lemak was a member of a Marine CAP operating in I Corps, near Da Nang, from November 1967 to December 1968.

3. Jordan, *Oxford Companion to Military History*, 789.

4. Herring, *America's Longest War*, 145.

5. Taylor, *Swords and Plowshares*, 344.

6. Weigley, *History of the United States Army*, 562.

7. Not all military experts supported the airmobile concept, writes Gabriel Kolko in *Anatomy of a War*, 192. Although Kolko cites neither references nor individuals, he claims that "the helicopter revealed troop numbers and location, thus enabling the enemy to ambush the deplaning troops." While this assessment is technically accurate, the Cobra gunships flying in support of the troop-carrying UH-1 "Huey" heli-

copters also killed many enemy soldiers who shot at the choppers. Generally, the military supported airmobile operations, and virtually all infantry divisions possessed aviation units by 1966. Helicopters also ferried thousands of soldiers to hospitals, usually in less than thirty minutes, which allowed most of the injured to escape death. The statement that "the industry kept pushing new designs on the Pentagon, which showed no great interest in the air mobility concept" is oversimplifying the concerns about guerilla warfare and fails to recognize the ability for troop delivery. Developments since Vietnam in helicopter technology have resulted in Blackhawks replacing Hueys and Apaches replacing Cobra gunships. Thus, the army was and is committed to the helicopter.

8. Moore and Galloway, *We Were Soldiers Once*, xxi. There is no more complete and accurate account of the Battle of the Ia Drang Valley than that found in *We Were Soldiers Once*. The battle has recently been adapted for the screen by Mel Gibson with the title *We Were Soldiers*, with technical advice by both Galloway and Moore. Both the book and the film are a reasonably accurate account of the battle when compared to Moore, "After Action Report," USAIS, DRL Archives.

9. Cash, Albright, and Sandstrum, *Seven Firefights in Vietnam*, 2.

10. Sheehan, *Bright Shining Lie*, 573.

11. Nadal interview. Nadal was a graduate of the USMA and served two tours in Vietnam.

12. Weigley, *History of the United States Army*, 562.

13. Sheehan, *Bright Shining Lie*, 574.

14. Thayer, *War without Fronts*, 46.

15. "Tactical Initiative in Vietnam," study in CMH Archives, SEA-RS-122— Ground Combat, 8. (No date is on the document, but the period October 1966–May 1968 is covered in the report.) Other sources verifying such data include Kolko, *Anatomy of a War*, 180, which states that more than 80 percent of contacts were initiated by the enemy.

16. Weigley, *History of the United States Army*, 564.

17. Westmoreland, *Soldier Reports*, 83.

18. Ibid.

19. Alexander and Sasser, *Taking Fire*, 91.

20. Westmoreland, *Soldier Reports*, 273.

21. Ibid., 161.

22. Tzu, *Art of War*, 77. At the world's largest museum of military history in Beijing, China, Sun Tzu's words are displayed above an exhibit portraying his men's capture, but not destruction, of an enemy force.

23. Westmoreland, *Soldier Reports*, 273: "Sgt. Betty Reed told me years later that the only time during several years in my office she ever heard me swear was when somebody mentioned 'body count.' "

24. Kinnard interview in Appy, *Patriots*, 322. The supervision of a squad-level action by a colonel instead of a sergeant means that an officer whose regular responsibility was the supervision of 1,500 men was on an operation with fewer than 10 men.

25. Thompson, DSA for PSYOPS, Tay Ninh, from the Donald Seibert Papers, MHI Archives, 1166. Also found in CMH Archives, SEA-RS-122m — Ground Combat.

26. K interview.

27. Johnson letter to DePuy, Johnson Papers, MHI Archives. In Chief of Staff Johnson's letter, the reference to Holly is to Brig. Gen. James F. Hollingsworth, assistant division commander of the 1st Infantry Division.

28. MACV Directive 381-21, December 26, 1967, Tab B to Appendix 1 to Annex A, cited in Lewy, *America in Vietnam*, 78.

29. Caputo, *Rumor of War*, 169.

30. Merrill interview in Ebert, *Life in a Year*, 273. Merrill served with the 4th ID, B/1-14th Infantry, from November 1968 until November 1969.

31. Yushta interview in Ebert, *Life in a Year*, 272. Yushta served with B/1/5th Marines from August 1969 until May 1970.

32. Goldman and Fuller, *Charlie Company*, 71.

33. Haseman interview.

34. Mangold and Penycate, *Tunnels of Cu Chi*, 77–78. These burial processes were confirmed by a personal visit to these tunnels in the summer of 2001 and again in 2006, 2007, and 2008, when several guides affirmed how bodies were prepared for "wall burial."

35. Ninh, *Sorrow of War*, 21. While this work is a novel, one can surmise that because it was written by a combat veteran who served for ten years in the PAVN, it contains factual information regarding handling of the dead. In my interviews with Bao Ninh in 2006, 2007, and 2008, I became convinced that his novel is historically accurate, but because it contains some negative comments about the PAVN, he chose to write the book as fiction.

36. Ninh interview, June 9, 2008. Bao Ninh served for ten years in the PAVN, mostly with the Glorious 27th Youth Brigade.

37. The after-action report filed by the 1/92nd Field Artillery Unit can be found online at <http://www.bravecannons.org/History/hist—phy-n.html>.

38. Good interview in Ebert, *Life in a Year*, 274. Good served with the 101st Airborne Division from December 1969 to November 1970.

39. Gadd, *Line Doggie*, 220, from Ebert, *Life in a Year*, 274.

40. Thayer, *War without Fronts*, 5.

41. "Allocation of Ground Force Efforts in SVN," September 1967, study in CMH Archives, SEA-RS-122h — Ground Combat, 10–11.

42. Young, *Vietnam Wars*, 186.

43. Leepson, *Webster's New World Dictionary of the Vietnam War*, 159.

44. Miller, *Whattaya Mean I Can't Kill 'Em?*, 95. Miller claims that the army and marines refused to use small units such as those led by Navy Seals to infiltrate enemy positions, and thus the lives of many soldiers were endangered.

45. "Combat Operations After Action Report (RCS: MACV J3-J2)," 4th Infantry Division, March 14, 1969, NARA, 270/075/25/5.

46. Unit 379, tape 3, side 1, Sp4 Dennis R. Moss, RA68009559, CMH Archives, SEA-RS-122n — Ground Combat. This interview was done shortly after the operation in which most of this enlisted man's unit was killed or wounded. The extraction could not be done by air due to fog and haze, so it was done by navy patrol boats. Six of his men drowned because of poor execution by the officer in charge of the boat.

47. "Handbook for Military Support of Pacification," Headquarters, USMACV, February 1968, 49, Ron Milam's personal archives.

48. Westmoreland, *Soldier Reports*, 152.

49. OSDA, "SEA Report," November 1967, from Krepinevich, *Army and Vietnam*, 201.

50. Unexpended ordnance still exists, even in 2006, in the jungles of Cambodia, Laos, and Vietnam. American veterans' groups have launched programs to assist the Vietnamese government in the recovery of these dud shells. They are particularly damaging to children, who remove the shells from their embedded grounds, attempt to remove the firing mechanisms, and blow themselves up. On a trip to Vietnam in the summer of 2001, my wife and I learned that our Pleiku Hotel maid's husband had been killed, two days before we arrived, by an unexploded bomb on a coffee plantation near Buon Me Thuot. On subsequent trips in 2006, 2007, and 2008 I found the situation less critical because of the efforts of American veterans' groups and extensive "urban sprawl."

51. Lacombe, *Light Ruck*, 159.

52. Hickey, *Window on a War*, 34.

53. Graves, "Operations Report," MHI Archives, 11.

54. Kinnard, *War Managers*, 40.

55. Westmoreland, *Soldier Reports*, 166.

56. Ibid.

57. Metzner, *More Than a Soldier's War*.

CHAPTER SEVEN

1. Lovejoy interview. Lovejoy was a 1st lieutenant with Company E, 3rd Battalion, 1st Infantry, 11th Light Infantry Brigade of the 23rd Infantry Division (Americal) and was in the My Lai area before the massacre occurred. He was Lieutenant Calley's CO for a few days after the March 16, 1968, operation.

2. Boltz response to questionnaire. Boltz was a 1st lieutenant infantry advisor to the ARVN 2nd Ranger Group near Ben Het, Bu Prong, and Dak Pek.

3. Kahalekulu response to questionnaire. Kahalekulu was a 1st lieutenant helicopter pilot who served two tours: at Vung Tau with the 54th Aviation Company with the 16th Aviation Group at Da Nang and with the 2nd Recon Airplane Company at Chu Lai.

4. Moore response to questionnaire and interview. Moore served two tours in Vietnam, the second as Bn S-3 of the 1-46th Infantry, 23rd ID (American) at Chu Lai, and was involved in the administrative matters associated with the My Lai massacre investigation.

5. Brinkley, *Tour of Duty*, 347.

6. Michelson, "Bringing the War Home."

7. Office of the Director, Judge Advocate Division, Headquarters USMC, Winter Soldier Investigation files, cited in Lewy, *America in Vietnam*, 317.

8. Michelson, "Bringing the War Home," 22.

9. Walzer, *Just and Unjust Wars*, 304. This quotation is taken from chap. 19, "War Crimes: Soldiers and Their Officers," and absolves both of any responsibility for the decision to go to war, if that decision is not part of their soldiering responsibilities. If one were both the king and the general, like Alexander the Great or Adolf Hitler, the responsibilities were blurred.

10. Prugh, *Law at War*, 73.

11. Sutherland letter to Commanders, "Treatment of the Enemy Dead," CMH Archives.

12. Grossman, *On Killing*, 194.

13. Ibid. Some of this material originally appeared in Milam, "Extreme Violence in War," in *Paisano* (online).

14. Victor Davis Hanson, "Hoplite Technology in Phalanx Battle," in Hanson, *Hoplites*, 71.

15. Thucydides, *Peloponnesian War*.

16. Moore, "After Action Report, Ia Drang Valley Operation, 1st Battalion, 7th Cavalry, 14–16 November, 1965," USAIS, DRL Archives.

17. Pisor, *End of the Line*, 260.

18. Wheeler memo to President Lyndon B. Johnson, LBJ Library. In a previous study I could find no evidence that the use of nuclear weapons was strongly considered, with only President Johnson having authority to direct their use. There were none in the theater, although tactical "nukes" were warehoused in nearby Okinawa.

19. Worley, *Hippeis*, 169.

20. Tzu, *Art of War*, 77.

21. Shay, *Achilles in Vietnam*, 106.

22. For good examples of colonists' attitudes toward Native Americans, particu-

larly in early wars such as King Philip's War, see Lepore, *Name of War*; Bourne, *King's Rebellion*; and Richter, *Facing East from Indian Country*.

23. Shay, *Achilles in Vietnam*, 106.

24. Charland response to questionnaire. Charland was an infantry NCO who served with A Company, 1 Bn, 26th IR, 1st ID, at Phuoc Vinh from December 1966 until November 1967.

25. Lyons response to questionnaire. Lyons served as an NCO with a Long Range Reconnaissance Patrol unit assigned to the 1st Cavalry ID and was wounded, cutting short his tour.

26. Patterson response to questionnaire. Patterson served two tours as a helicopter pilot with the 1st Air Cavalry Division, July 1968–July 1969 and August 1971–February 1972.

27. Chang, *Rape of Nanking*, 41.

28. Bartov, *Hitler's Army*, 7.

29. Steedle, *Mark Freedom Paid*, 79. One of the veterans interviewed in this anthology, Col. Fred G. Rand, was a student of mine in the College of Lifelong Learning, and he told me about the massacre.

30. Ambrose, *Band of Brothers*, 206.

31. Olson interview quoted from Ebert, *Life in a Year*, 284. Olson served with the 1st Bn, 1st Marine Division, from June 1967 until February 1968.

32. My personal experiences with sappers seldom indicated suicide, even though the task was exceptionally dangerous and usually resulted in the death of the soldier carrying the satchel charge.

33. Ed Austin, letter to his parents and diary kept in training and in Vietnam. Photocopies in private collection of James Ebert. Quoted from Ebert, *Life in a Year*, 285.

34. McDonough, *Platoon Leader*, 106–7.

35. Bradford, *Some Even Volunteered*, 63.

36. Thayer, *War without Fronts*, 202.

37. "Report of Investigation Concerning Alleged Improper Treatment of Prisoners," CMH Archives, 3.

38. Boehm interview in Ebert, *Life in a Year*, 286. Boehm served with D Company, 5-46th Inf. of the 23rd ID (Americal) from August 1968 to March 1969.

39. TeCube, *Year in Nam*, 217.

40. Grossman, *On Killing*, 201.

41. Thucydides, *Peloponnesian War*, 5.116.3.

42. Tritle, *From Melos to My Lai*, 119–23.

43. Bilton and Sim, *Four Hours in My Lai*, 1.

44. TeCube, *Year in Nam*, 99. Sgt. Leroy TeCube was a member of Bravo Company that was sent to My Lai as a blocking force on March 16, 1968, and he witnessed the

retreating soldiers of Charlie Company after the assault. "How did you guys do? With all the shooting, did you kick some ass?" None of them seemed willing to share any information. All one said was "We shot a bunch of them."

45. Goldstein, Marshall, and Schwartz, *My Lai Massacre and Its Cover-up*, 58.

46. Ibid., 59.

47. Ibid., 60.

48. Ibid., 61. Also substantiated in Bilton and Sim, *Four Hours in My Lai*, 85. The Peers Report was emphatic that villagers participated in the laying and maintaining of booby traps, although hard evidence is lacking. But the soldiers of the Americal Division believed this to be true, and it is logical that the villagers did participate, since the village sympathized with the VC more than with Americans.

49. Peers Report, 79.

50. Ibid., 82.

51. "Background of Officers at My Lai," CMH Archives, 2. This document appears to be the first official inquiry regarding the massacre and focuses on the commission sources of each officer in the chain of command. Prepared by Arthur Sussman and endorsed by John Kester, acting deputy assistant secretary of the army, the memo traces the personal backgrounds of each officer as well as officer efficiency report data.

52. Ibid., 3.

53. Ibid., 1–2.

54. Ibid., 7.

55. Peers Report, 331.

56. Bilton and Sim, *Four Hours in My Lai*, 114.

57. Ibid., 115.

58. Ibid., 129.

59. Ibid., 131.

60. Ibid., 121. The narrative in the Bilton and Sim book is taken from the My Lai Trial Records, which were, at the time of the writing of the book, housed at the Federal Records Center at Suitland, Maryland. Records were also obtained from the Clerk of Court at Military Review in Falls Church, Virginia.

61. Peers Report, 342.

62. Bilton and Sim, *Four Hours in My Lai*, 123.

63. Greenhaw, *Making of a Hero*, 153.

64. Brinkley, *Tour of Duty*, 358.

65. Ibid., 359.

66. "War Crimes Allegations Against U.S. Army Personnel, Other Than Son My (as of June 15, 1975)," from U.S. Department of the Army, Office of the Judge Advocate General, International Affairs Division, from Lewy, *America in Vietnam*, 348.

67. A recent series of articles in the *Toledo Blade* has uncovered the likelihood of the

murder of noncombatants in the same province, Quang Ngai, eighteen months before My Lai. The unit, Tiger Force, was a reconnaissance unit of the 101st Airborne Division, and it was given the responsibility of spying on enemy forces. From May to November 1967, they allegedly murdered hundreds of unarmed civilians. This story was being "hinted at" when I was completing my research at NARA in June 2003. As with My Lai, the army apparently investigated this matter for four and a half years, then dropped it without issuing any findings. The secretary of defense when it was dropped was Donald Rumsfeld. The most recent *Toledo Blade* article has mentioned a reopening of the case by the Pentagon, which is a good thing. The entire investigation can be found at <http://www.toledoblade.com/apps/pbcs.d11article?AID=/20031019/SRTIGERFORCE/110190168>. The authors are Michael D. Sallah, Mitch Weiss, Joe Mahr, and Andy Morrison.

68. William Peers, Oral History, MHI Archives. Peers was deputy commanding general, 8th Army, of Korea after he conducted the investigation of My Lai (4). He came back to the States to receive his fourth star, and he was "passed over." My observation, not substantiated by any evidence, was that President Nixon refused to allow his promotion because of his thorough report on the My Lai massacre, in which he recommended the court-martial of thirty officers. Only thirteen were indicted. Only Calley was convicted.

69. Schoppes, "Lessons from My Lai," 5.

70. Dower, *War without Mercy*, 64.

71. "Investigation of Alleged War Crime," CMH Archives.

72. Prugh, *Law at War*, 73.

73. Leppelman, *Blood on the Risers*, 59.

74. "Report of Investigation," Headquarters, 101st Airborne Division (Airmobile), CMH Archives.

75. Baker, *NAM*, 84.

76. Endicott interview. Endicott graduated from ROTC at the Citadel and served in Vietnam as a lawyer. He later was involved in the Calley trial at Fort Benning, Georgia.

77. Estes, *Field of Innocence*, 180.

78. Some of these pictures made it into U.S. press stories and were publicized around the world to show the inhumanity of the American soldier. One such picture was published by the *New York Times* and shows a group of soldiers smiling, with body parts of VC soldiers spread before them. This picture is on display in the War Remnants Museum, Ho Chi Minh City, Vietnam.

79. "Visit to the United States Army Infantry Center and School, Fort Benning, Georgia," MHI Archives.

80. Sack, *Lieutenant Calley*, 75.

81. McDonough, *Platoon Leader*, 62.

CHAPTER EIGHT

1. Alloy response to questionnaire. Alloy served in the Marine Corps at Don Ha, with Headquarters, Group Lima 4/12, 1970–71, and part of an artillery battery.

2. Trujillo, *Soldados*, 148.

3. Janowitz and Little, *Sociology and the Military Establishment*, 93.

4. Ibid., 94.

5. Marshall, *Men against Fire*, 42.

6. Charles Moskos, "Surviving the War in Vietnam," from Figley and Leventman, *Stranger at Home*, 73.

7. Ibid., 77.

8. Thayer, *War without Fronts*, 114.

9. Janowitz and Little, *Sociology and the Military Establishment*, 102.

10. Gabriel and Savage, *Crisis in Command*, 11.

11. Hollywood was partially responsible for the myth that the life span of a lieutenant in Vietnam was fifteen minutes. While no records exist regarding such a statement, the fact that so many platoon leaders were new in their job would account for the likelihood of an early WIA or KIA situation for many, until they could achieve experience, and before they were rotated back to the rear.

12. McDonough, *Platoon Leader*, 186.

13. Lyons questionnaire, 5.

14. Bradford, *Some Even Volunteered*, 45.

15. Janowitz and Little, *Sociology and the Military Establishment*, 103.

16. Kolko, *Anatomy of a War*, 362.

17. Bradford, *Some Even Volunteered*, 39.

18. O'Brien, *If I Die in a Combat Zone*, 82.

19. Moskos, *Public Opinion and the Military Establishment*, 81.

20. Schuman, "Two Sources of Anti-War Sentiment in America."

21. Moskos, *Public Opinion and the Military Establishment*, 82.

22. DePuy, "Army Leadership Moves Upward on Performance," 2–3.

23. Heinl, "Service Morale, Discipline at Low Ebb." This article is significant because Colonel Heinl was a military analyst who wrote extensively during the Vietnam War and was a critic of the lack of discipline he saw in the U.S. military. His biography included marine service before World War II; presence at Pearl Harbor on December 7, 1941; combat experience on Guam and Iwo Jima; and command experience during the Korean War.

24. Krogh interview in Appy, *Patriots*, 438. Krogh was eventually convicted of assisting with breaking into and entering the office of Daniel Ellsberg's psychiatrist, and he served four and a half months in prison. "Asking how many addicts there were in the military, a senior officer replied: 'about a hundred.' I said 'How did you come up

with that number?' He said, 'Well, that's how many people we've been able to prose-
cute and convict.' "

25. Ibid.

26. Jack Daniels bourbon sold for $1.75/quart, and each soldier had a ration card
that allowed him to buy four quarts per month. Whiskey and scotches of lesser
quality, such as Cutty Sark and Jim Beam, respectively, sold for $1.25/quart. Drugs
were also cheap, so the decision of which drug or alcoholic beverage to choose was not
usually made on the basis of economics.

27. Noller interview. Noller served as an enlisted soldier in Vietnam with the 23rd
ID (Americal) in 1970 and 1971.

28. Westmoreland, *Soldier Reports*, 371.

29. Kerwin memo to General Palmer, "In-depth Analysis of Drug Problem in U.S.
Army," CMH Archives, 1.

30. Ibid., 7.

31. Ibid., 9.

32. Noller interview.

33. Bowman interview in Bergerud, *Red Thunder, Tropic Lightning*, 285. Bowman
was with the 25th ID at Cu Chi and Tay Ninh during the TET Offensive, 1968.

34. Ibid.

35. Julian interview in Bergerud, *Red Thunder, Tropic Lightning*, 284. Julian was with
the 25th ID at Cu Chi during the last days of the war for U.S. troops, a time when
drug use was at its zenith. Yet in this interview he challenged the characterization of
soldiers in combat using drugs.

36. Sincock interview in Bergerud, *Red Thunder, Tropic Lightning*, 284.

37. Frazier interview. Frazier served two tours in Vietnam as a helicopter pilot.

38. Lanning, *Only War We Had*, 198.

39. Kolko, *Anatomy of a War*, 363.

40. "Marihuana and Drugs," CMH Archives.

41. Cookson, "Marijuana and Drug Abuse in the Twenty-fifth Infantry Division,"
CMH Archives. An interesting sidelight to the issue of experimenter bias that also
must have told the survey administrators something about the perception by the
soldiers about the drug issue was the footnote stating, "In one company surveyed
during off-duty hours a large number of respondents appeared to be drunk. Many
respondents took great delight in throwing beer cans, salt and pepper shakers, and
even questionnaires at the survey administrators."

42. Ibid., 6.

43. Ibid., 9.

44. Sellards and Urban, "Marijuana in a Tactical Unit," CMH Archives.

45. Stoddard, *What Are They Going to Do?*, 25. Various units had different names for

those who used drugs or alcohol to excess, and it was somewhat of a generational issue, with the younger enlisted personnel choosing drugs and NCOs choosing liquor.

46. Mataxis interview.

47. Baltazar interview. Baltazar served as an RTO with the 101st Airborne in Vietnam in 1969 and 1970.

48. Wright, *Soldiers of Freedom*, 241.

49. Powell with Persico, *My American Journey*, 125. Powell was referring to an NBC documentary titled *Same Mud, Same Blood*, dealing with blacks in the military in Vietnam.

50. Spector, *After TET*, 259.

51. Hayward interview in Astor, *Right to Fight*, 430. Hayward was a white officer who served as a brigade commander with the 101st Airborne Division.

52. Spector, *After TET*, 248.

53. Eddie L. Kitchen interview in *Jet*, from Spector, *After TET*, 245.

54. Creighton interview.

55. Goff and Sanders with Smith, *Brothers*, 61–71.

56. "This Paper Can Save Your Life," Viet Cong propaganda leaflet, reprinted in House Committee on Internal Security, *Investigation of Attempts to Subvert*, 6806, from Westheider, *Fighting on Two Fronts*, 157. A VC propaganda flier that was circulated in Vietnam opened with "Everyone's heard stories of black GIs being let through ambushes" and went on to assure readers that if they go AWOL because they don't want to fight or because they can't put up with the army racism, "the NLF will get you out of the country." Westheider's account of black soldiers being enticed by the VC not to fight is compelling. However, he accepts the argument that VC appeared to try not to kill black soldiers because blacks often walked point, and therefore they escaped the killing zone since the VC knew to fire on the center of the patrol, not on the lead elements. However, VC killed everyone in the killing zone, as did Americans when setting ambushes, because you never knew if the one who got away would be the one who could bring reinforcements or firepower from available artillery or gunships.

57. Browne interview in Terry, *Bloods*, 167.

58. Gutierrez interview. Gutierrez served in Vietnam as an enlisted man with the 25th ID in 1968.

59. Bridges interview in Beesley, *Vietnam*, 16. Bridges was a Fire Direct Control man with the Third Marine Division of Dong Ha, from 1967 to 1968.

60. Goff and Sanders with Smith, *Brothers*, 23.

61. Dant interview.

62. Thayer, *War without Fronts*, 118.

63. McMamers, *Ultimate Special Forces*, 162.

64. Bond, "Fragging."

65. Glasser, *365 Days*, 181–88.

66. Ibid., 47. Personal experience can verify the effect of drugs and alcohol on such incidents. In March 1971 while on district business in Nha Trang, another lieutenant and I were told to "shut the fuck up, or I'll frag you!" by a very drunk NCO who was staying in the room next to us. We turned him in and we were called to Nha Trang in May to testify against him at his court-martial. My recollection is that we did not want to see him convicted, which he wasn't, but the return trip was an opportunity to get out of the field for a few days.

67. Gillooly and Bond, "Assaults with Explosive Devices on Superiors," 701.

68. Ibid.

69. Ibid., 703.

70. Padgett interview. Padgett served in Vietnam as an enlisted marine in 1968 and 1969.

71. Holmes, *Acts of War*, 330.

72. Dant interview.

73. Holmes, *Acts of War*, 330.

74. Larry Tritle, personal e-mail (ltritle@lmumail.lmu.edu), November 20, 2003.

CHAPTER NINE

1. French, *Code of the Warrior*, 5.

2. John McCain, U.S. Senator, in the foreword to ibid., x.

3. Office of Assistant Commandant, "Review and Analysis, 4th Quarter," FY62–73, DRL Archives.

4. Sack, *Lieutenant Calley*, 28.

5. Ibid., 29.

6. Ibid., 47.

7. Greenhaw, *Making of a Hero*, 132.

8. Lanning, *Only War We Had*, 205.

9. Arnold Daxe and Victor J. Stemberger, "Vietnam Assessment," Fort Leaven-worth, USACGSC student paper (1976), quoted from Cincinnatus, *Self-Destruction*, 162.

10. Cummings response to questionnaire. Cummings served as a marine advisor to the ARVN, 1964–65.

11. O interview.

12. Westmoreland, *Soldier Reports*, 380.

13. William F. Abbott, "Vietnam War Casualties — Officer Deaths by Rank," American War Library, 1988 (retrieved January 15, 2004), <http://www.american warlibrary.com/vietnam/vwc4.htm>. Statistics include W-1 through O-3 for Army and Marines.

14. Dr. Charles D. McKenna, personal e-mail (mckennad@teom.usmc.mil), June 17, 2003.

15. Janowitz and Little, *Sociology and the Military Establishment*, 94.

APPENDIX TWO

1. Just, *To What End*.

2. Just, *Military Men*.

3. Ibid., 20.

4. Ibid., 19.

5. King, *Death of the Army*.

6. Ibid., 122.

7. Ibid., 99.

8. Melvin Zais interview as part of Oral History Project #77-3, MHI Archives, 579–84.

9. Ibid., 122.

10. Walton, *Tarnished Shield*.

11. Ibid., 169.

12. Ibid., 169. Quoted from Just, "Soldiers."

13. Walton, *Tarnished Shield*, 163.

14. Hauser, *America's Army in Crisis*.

15. Ibid., 153.

16. Corson, *Consequences of Failure*.

17. Ibid., 83.

18. Ibid., 84.

19. Kinnard, *War Managers*.

20. Ibid., 117.

21. Lewy, *America in Vietnam*.

22. Ibid., 309.

23. Ibid., vii.

24. Gabriel and Savage, *Crisis in Command*.

25. Ibid., 10.

26. Ibid., 16. This data was challenged by Russell Glenn in *Reading Athena's Dance Card*. His Department of Defense data indicates that officers, particularly lieutenants and captains, died at a much greater rate in Vietnam than in all other twentieth-century wars. All of these authors were using the data to support different theses, and there were certainly more rear-echelon officers who died in Vietnam versus other wars because of the lack of a front, but the data itself is supportable through Department of Defense records.

27. Cincinnatus, *Self-Destruction*.

28. Ibid., jacket cover.

29. Ibid., 99.

30. Ibid., 96.

31. Stanton, *Rise and Fall of an American Army*.

32. One of the first authors to question Stanton's credibility was B. G. Burkett, in *Stolen Valor*. It is difficult now to determine truth from fiction in his accounts. But most of the factual reports of the various battles he describes have not been challenged by participants.

33. Schwarzkopf, *It Doesn't Take a Hero*.

34. Powell with Persico, *My American Journey*.

35. Kitfield, *Prodigal Soldiers*.

36. Spector, *After TET*.

37. Ibid., 38.

38. Appy, *Working-Class War*.

39. Kindsvatter, *American Soldiers*.

40. Ibid., 149.

41. Caputo, *Rumor of War*.

42. Donovan, *Once a Warrior King*.

43. McDonough, *Platoon Leader*.

44. Lanning, *Only War We Had*.

APPENDIX THREE

1. Brassford, *Spit-Shined Syndrome*. Brassford criticized this attribute because the army considered it to be more important than all others. His thesis held that the army could measure this quality by observation, but that the others took more evaluation; thus commanders dealt with what they could see. This was particularly true in Vietnam.

2. *Tactical Officers Guide*, January 1968, DRL, 3-2, 3.

Bibliography

PRIMARY SOURCES

Manuscript Collections and Government Documents

Center of Military History, Fort McNair, District of Columbia
Geog V Vietnam, 704,228
　MacDonald, Charles B. "An Outline History of U.S. Policy toward Vietnam."
　　Part 2, 228091, HRC Geog V VN Policy, US 008.
Haines Board Reports
Office of the Deputy Chief of Staff for Personnel. "Annual Historical Summary."
　　FY1966, FY1968.
Southeast Asia Collection of Ron Spector
　"Background of Officers at My Lai." Memorandum for the Secretary of the Army.
　　December 22, 1969. SEA-RS-251.
　Chief of Procurement Division. "Report of Colleges and Universities Which Bar
　　On-Campus Recruitment." June 19, 1969. SEA-RS-289m.
　Chief of Staff, U.S. Army. Memo regarding "Proposal on On-Campus Military
　　Recruitment," by Dr. Edwin D. Etherington. September 5, 1969. SEA-
　　RS-289n.
　Cookson, M. S. "Marijuana and Drug Abuse in the Twenty-fifth Infantry Divi-
　　sion, Republic of Vietnam, 1970." SEA-RS-11c.
　"Investigation of Alleged War Crime." Submitted by the Staff Judge Advocate
　　Office, 199th Infantry Brigade. SEA-RS-126m.
　Izenour, Brig. Gen. Frank M., Director of Man-Power, DCSPER-PD. Memoran-
　　dum to Acting Deputy Chief of Staff for Personnel. "Pre-OCS Dropouts."
　　August 12, 1965. SEA-RS-289d.
　Johnson, Harold K. "Memorandum for ACSFOR, Subject: West Point." SEA-
　　RS-121.
　Kerwin, LTG Walter, Jr., Deputy Chief of Staff for Personnel. Memo to General
　　Palmer. "In-depth Analysis of Drug Problem in U.S. Army." February 20,
　　1970. SEA-RS-37.
　Manpower and Reserve Affairs. "Coffee Houses and Union Movement." Au-
　　gust 1, 1968. SEA-RS-240a.
　"Marihuana and Drugs." Fact sheet. August 30, 1970. SEA-RS-11b.

Office of Personnel Operations, Personnel Management Development Office, U.S. Dept. of the Army. "Survey Estimate of Opinions on the Image of the Army as Expressed by Active Duty Male Personnel." August 31, 1969. SEA-RS-237.

Office of the Chief of Staff. "Recruiters on College Campuses." April 21, 1969. SEA-RS-2890.

Office of the Deputy Chief of Staff for Personnel. "Utilization of Increased College Graduate Accessions." February 23, 1997. SEA-RS-240b.

"Personal Histories of Officers in My Lai (4)." Memorandum for the Secretary of the Army. SEA-RS-251.

"Report of Investigation." Headquarters, 101st Airborne Division (Airmobile). November 10, 1969. SEA-RS-126h.

"Report of Investigation Concerning Alleged Improper Treatment of Prisoners by Members of the 11th Aviation Battalion and Others on or about February 15, 1969." February 20, 1970. SEA-RS-126L.

Sellards, Capt. Robert R., and Sgt. Laurence E. Urban. "Marijuana in a Tactical Unit." SEA-RS-11d.

Sutherland, Lt. Gen., Commanding General, XXIV Corps. Letter to Commanders. "Treatment of the Enemy Dead." November 6, 1970. SEA-RS-126K.

United States Army Recruiting Command. "Summary of Findings: Quantitative Phase, Army Recruiting Study." May 1969. SEA-RS-281a.

Westmoreland, Gen. William. *Report of the Chief of Staff.* 1969.

Donovan Research Library, Fort Benning, Georgia

Analysis and Review Branch Office of the Director of Instruction. "Report on Survey of Military Knowledge and Skills of Recently Commissioned 2nd Lieutenants." January 1965.

Haines Board Files

Infantry Officer Basic Course File

Infantry Officer Candidate Manuals

Office of Assistant Commandant, FY Review and Analysis

Officer Candidate School Files

Tactical Officer's Guides

U.S. Army Infantry School

    Assistant Commandant. Letter to Officer Students. "Policies, Combat Platoon Leader Course (Infantry Officer Basic Course)." July 28, 1965. U422,l51,dU.

    Facts for the Prospective Infantry Officer Candidate. February 1966. U408.2i1511,dU.

    Jacobs, T. O., et al. "An Analysis of Seven U.S. Army Officer Candidate Schools." September 1967. HumRRO Division 4, Fort Benning.

Moore, Col. Harold G. "After Action Report, Ia Drang Valley Operation."
 December 9, 1965.
Quarterly Progress Report, July–September 1965. HumRRO Division 4.
"Report of the Combat Platoon Leader Course (5 weeks) Curriculum Review
 Committee." May 1967. U422,I51,dU.
Talbott, Maj. Gen. Orwin C. "The Role of the U.S. Army Infantry School in
 Training Infantrymen." Speech before the Royal Military College of Aus-
 tralia. U422,T14,d4.
USCONARC Reports of Staff Visits to Vietnam

Lyndon Baines Johnson Presidential Library, Austin, Texas
Cabinet Meetings File
Clark L. Clifford Papers
Tom Johnson's Meeting Notes
Meeting Notes File
Newman, Guy D., President, Howard Payne University. Letter to Marvin Watson,
 Special Assistant to the President. March 4, 1968. National Security Files,
 D.O.D., box 182.
Wheeler, Gen. Earl. Memo to President Lyndon B. Johnson. February 3, 1968. Na-
 tional Security Files, Khe Sanh Reports, A–S, box 49.

Military History Institute, Carlisle Barracks, Pennsylvania
Allen, Rolfe L., Educational Advisor to Brigadier Gen. Babcock, President of the
 Army Board, to Review Army Officer Schools. "Provision of Document:
 Trained Manpower in the U.S. Army." October 22, 1965.
Company Grade Officer Project
Corcoran, LTC Kevin. "Maneuver Company Commanders and Their Battalion
 Commanders in Vietnam: No Shared Value." Project #84-60. U.S. Army War
 College Military Studies Paper. March 20, 1989.
Davis, LTC Oscar R. "Does ROTC Have a Place on the College Campus?" U.S.
 Army War College. December 7, 1971.
Dickinson, Maj. Gen. Hillman, Maj. Gen. Jack V. Mackmull, and Brig. Gen. Jack N.
 Merritt. Letter to Gen. Bernard W. Rogers, Chief of Staff of the United States
 Army. "West Point Study Group."
Graves, 1st Lt. Patrick H., Jr. "Operations Report—Lessons Learned 1-67 'Obser-
 vations of a Platoon Leader.'" AGAM-P(M), January 24, 1967, FOR OT RD,
 Department of the Army, Office of the Adjutant General.
Herring, Col. Kenneth G., and LTC Daniel B. Knight. "Are Reserve Component
 Officers Ready?" Group Study Project at U.S. Army War College. March 8,
 1973.

Harold K. Johnson Papers

    Ferguson, Maj. Gen. R. G., Commander, U.S. Army, Berlin. Letter to Gen. Harold
        K. Johnson, Army Chief of Staff. December 27, 1967. Close Hold file, box 128.

    Johnson, Harold K. Letter to William E. DePuy. May 6, 1966.

    Oral Histories

      William DePuy

      Ralph Haines

      Bruce Palmer

      William Peers

      William Rossen

      James Woolnough

      Melvin Zais

William Peers Papers

    Peers, Lt. Gen. W. R. Speech before the University of Delaware ROTC Commis-
        sioning Exercise, Newark. June 7, 1970.

Review of Education and Training for Officers (RETO Study). 1978.

"Visit to the United States Army Infantry Center and School, Fort Benning,
    Georgia." Department of the Army, Headquarters, United States Continental
    Army Command, Fort Monroe, Virginia, Liaison Office, Pentagon, Wash-
    ington, D.C. April 27, 1972.

Wickham, Maj. Gen. Kenneth G., Adjutant General. Memorandum to Comman-
    dants of Various Schools and West Point. "Report of the Department of the
    Army Board to Review Army Officer Schools." December 9, 1970.

National Archives, College Park, Maryland

1st Infantry Division: 270/029/15/1

23rd Infantry Division (Americal): 270/30/11/1&2

25th Infantry Division: 270/030/16/5&6

101st Airborne Division: 270/030/34/6

173rd Airborne Brigade: 270/31/06/5

Annual Command Histories, Command History. "Build-up of U.S. Forces, 1965
    Records of U.S. Forces in S.E. Asia, Headquarters, MACV." FRG472.

BDM Corporation. *Strategic Lessons Learned in Vietnam.*

Carver, Maj. Gen. George A., Commanding General, Alaska. Letter to Maj. Gen.
    Robert H. York. October 8, 1965. FRG472.

Edwards, Col. I. A., Director, Ranger Department. Letter to Captain Porter.
    "USAIS Position Paper on Army School System." July 22, 1965. FRG472.

Foery, Maj. Gen. Martin H., Commanding General, New York Army National
    Guard. Letter to Maj. Gen. John A. Heintges, Commandant USAIS. August 4,
    1965. FRG472.

Forsythe, Brig. Gen. George T., Assistant Commandant, USAIS. Letter to Commanding General, United States Army Continental Army Command, Fort Monroe, Virginia. "Liaison Visit to Viet Nam." July 1, 1965. FRG472.

———. Letter to Brig. Gen. Leon H. Hagen, Asst. Adj. Gen., Army National Guard of Minnesota. October 5, 1965. FRG472.

Hitchcock, Col. Raymond H., Chief Doctrine and Concepts Division. Letter to Col. Herbert E. Wolff, Director of Instruction, USAIS. September 4, 1965. FRG472.

ISARV Regulation: 270/075/26/4

Johnson, Lt. Col. Paul E. Letter to Company Tactics Department. "Haines Board Briefing." July 26, 1965. FRG472.

Kern, Richard, and Howard McFann. "Confidence Development during Training." HumRRO Division No. 3, Presidio of Monterey, California. February 18, 1965. FRG472.

Lawrie, Maj. Gen. Joe S., Commanding General, 82nd Airborne Division, Fort Bragg, North Carolina. Letter to Maj. Gen. Robert H. York, Commandant, USAIS. August 14, 1965. FRG472.

Mabry, Brig. Gen. George L., Jr., Commanding General of the 1st Armored Division (Old Ironsides), Fort Hood, Texas. Letter to Robert H. York, Commandant, USAIS. August 17, 1965. FRG472.

MACV Directives: 270/075/25/5

Norton, Brig. Gen. John, USAIS and Assistant Commandant. Letter to Col. W. E. Showalter, Professor of Military Science at the University of Dayton. September 1, 1964. HQ DNRI File.

Office of the Assistant Secretary of Defense for Public Affairs. "Army to Expand Officer Candidate Program." June 2, 1966. HRC 352,228.01.

Record Group 472: MACV

Record Group 472: MACV Command Histories

Smith, Gen. Charles B. Letter to Army Commanders World-Wide. "Department of the Army Board to Review Army Officer Schools." July 19, 1965. FRG472.

USARV (U.S. Army, Vietnam) Memos: 270/075/26/5

Woolnough, James K. Letter to Army ROTC programs nationwide regarding change in army ROTC programs. July 1969. FRG472.

York, Gen. Robert H. Commandant of USAIS. Letter to the Commanding General, U.S. Continental Army Command, Fort Monroe, Virginia. August 10, 1965. FRG472.

U.S. Army Infantry School, Fort Benning, Georgia

Mabry, Brig. Gen. George L., Jr. Letter to Robert H. York. August 14, 1965.

"Manuscript of FM22-100 Military Leadership." Record of Comments on Publications. July 28, 1965. 69.1.

Office of the Commandant, The Infantry School. Letter to Gen. Mark Clark, Chief, Army Field Forces. April 14, 1952.

Interviews

Baltazar, Gonzalo. Interview by Stephen Maxner. March 23, 2001. Item #OH0152, The Vietnam Archive, Texas Tech University, Lubbock.

Barron, Robert. Interview by Stephen Maxner. April 21, 2001. Item #OH0163, The Vietnam Archive, Texas Tech University, Lubbock.

Bernhardt, Michael. Interview by Christian G. Appy in *Patriots*. 2003.

Boehm, Paul. Interview by James Ebert in *Life in a Year*. December 9, 1989.

Boone, Howard. Interview by Ivan Prashker in *Duty, Honor, Vietnam*. 1988.

Bowman, C. W. Interview by Eric Bergerud in *Red Thunder, Tropic Lightning*. 1968.

Bradbury, Michael. Interview by Richard Verrone. September 15, October 27, 28, 2003. Item #OH0335, The Vietnam Archive, Texas Tech University, Lubbock.

Bridges, Rudolph. Interview by Stanley W. Beesley in *Vietnam*. 1987.

Browne, Don F. Interview by Wallace Terry in *Bloods*. 1985.

Cook, Dave. Interview by Ron Milam. August 16, 2003. Frisco, Colorado.

Creighton, Neil. Interview by Stephen Maxner. November 2002. Item #OH0243, The Vietnam Archive, Texas Tech University, Lubbock.

Cummings, Gary. Interview by Stephen Maxner. April 2001. Item #OH0162, The Vietnam Archive, Texas Tech University, Lubbock.

Dant, Stephen W. Interview by Richard Verrone. March 2005. Item #OH0418, The Vietnam Archive, Texas Tech University, Lubbock.

Dodge, Charles. Interview by Richard Verrone. July 18, 2003. Item #OH0315, The Vietnam Archive, Texas Tech University, Lubbock.

Endicott, James. Interview by Stephen Maxner. September 17, 1999. Item #OH0100, The Vietnam Archive, Texas Tech University, Lubbock.

Faber, Peter. Interview by Stephen Maxner. July 19, 2000. Item #OH0024, The Vietnam Archive, Texas Tech University, Lubbock.

Franklin, Gary. Interview by Jonathan Bernstein. November 1, 2001. Item #OH0194, The Vietnam Archive, Texas Tech University, Lubbock.

Frazier, Edwin. Interview by Stephen Maxner. May 5, 2000. Item #OH0102, The Vietnam Archive, Texas Tech University, Lubbock.

Givhan, John. Interview by Stephen Maxner. September 11, 2000. Item #OH0059, The Vietnam Archive, Texas Tech University, Lubbock.

Good, Bryan. Interview by James Ebert in *Life in a Year*. March 5, 1991.

Grigsby, Bryan. Interview by Richard Verrone. May 2, 2003. Item #OH0292, The Vietnam Archive, Texas Tech University, Lubbock.

Gutierrez, Frank. Interview by Kim Sawyer. January 24, 2001. Item #OH0078, The Vietnam Archive, Texas Tech University, Lubbock.

Haseman, John. Interview by Stephen Maxner. June 21, 2000. Item #OH0105, The Vietnam Archive, Texas Tech University, Lubbock.

Hayward, Harold. Interview by Gerald Astor in *Right to Fight*. 1998.

Hiett, Russell. Interview by Stephen Maxner. May 9, 2001. Item #OH0173, The Vietnam Archive, Texas Tech University, Lubbock.

Horton, Michael. Interview by Monty Hostetler. February, March 1990. Item #OH039, The Vietnam Archive, Texas Tech University, Lubbock.

Hutton, Mike. Interview by Ron Milam. August 16, 2003. Frisco, Colorado.

Johnson, Quinton. Interview by Stephen Maxner. October 2, 1999. Item #OH0113C, The Vietnam Archive, Texas Tech University, Lubbock.

Julian, Robert. Interview by Eric Bergerud in *Red Thunder, Tropic Lightning*. 1968.

K, Lt. Col. Interview by Lt. Col. Taylor. March 20, 1989. In Corcoran, "Maneuver Company Commanders." Project #84-60. U.S. Army War College, Military History Institute Archives, Carlisle Barracks, Pennsylvania.

Keeling, Robert. Interview by James Ebert in *Life in a Year*. September 9, 1989.

Kinnard, Douglas. Interview by Christian Appy in *Patriots*. 2003.

Krogh, Egil "Bud." Interview by Christian Appy in *Patriots*. 2003.

Linster, Frank. Interview by Stephen Maxner. July 1, 2001. Item #OH0003, The Vietnam Archive, Texas Tech University, Lubbock.

Lovejoy, Vernon. Interview by Ron Milam. August 17, 2003. Frisco, Colorado.

Lyons, Patrick. Interview by Ron Milam. February 16, 2004. Houston, Texas.

Mataxis, Theodore, Jr. Interview by Stephen Maxner. April 13, 2002. Item #OH0134, The Vietnam Archive, Texas Tech University, Lubbock.

Mathiak, Marvin. Interview by Stephen Maxner. August 8, 2000. Item #OH0011, The Vietnam Archive, Texas Tech University, Lubbock.

Meringolo, Paul. Interview by James Ebert in *Life in a Year*. August 24, 1989.

Merrill, John. Interview by James Ebert in *Life in a Year*. May 1, 1989.

Moore, John. Interview by Ron Milam. August 13, 2003. Angel Fire, New Mexico.

Nadal, Ramon Antonio. Interview by Ron Milam. November 10, 2005. Item #OH0462, The Vietnam Archive, Texas Tech University, Lubbock.

Ninh, Bao. Interview by Ron Milam. July 2006, July 2007, June 9, 2008. Hanoi, Socialist Republic of Vietnam.

Noller, Gary. Interview by Richard Verrone. August 2005 to March 2006. Item #OH0440, The Vietnam Archive, Texas Tech University, Lubbock.

O. Interview by Lt. Col. Lord. March 20, 1989. In Corcoran, "Maneuver Company Commanders." U.S. Army War College, Military History Institute Archives, Carlisle Barracks, Pennsylvania.

O'Kelley, James. Interview by Stephen Maxner. August 4, 2000. Item #OH0012,
The Vietnam Archive, Texas Tech University, Lubbock.

Olson, Vince. Interview by South Dakota Veterans Oral History Project. September
16, 1985. In Ebert, *Life in a Year*.

Padgett, James. Interview by Stephen Maxner. November 29, 1999. Item #OH0115,
The Vietnam Archive, Texas Tech University, Lubbock.

Rand, Fred G., Col. Interview by Ron Milam. March 15, 2003. Houston, Texas.

Ryan, Bob. Interview by Ron Milam. August 17, 2003. Frisco, Colorado.

Schultz, Thomas. Interview by James Ebert in *Life in a Year*. March 2, 1984.

Sincock, Morgan. Interview by Eric Bergerud in *Red Thunder, Tropic Lightning*.
1968.

Spawr, Chad. Interview by Stephen Maxner. March 16, 2000. Item #OH0006, The
Vietnam Archive, Texas Tech University, Lubbock.

Summers, Harry G. Interview by Karl Fleming in "Troubled Army Brass." 1971.

Titleman, Kenneth. Interview by Ron Milam. September 25, 2003.

Vallo, Ed. Interview by Ron Milam. November 27, 2003. Houston, Texas.

Vertrees, Paul. Interview by Ron Milam. June 29, 2003. Chico, California.

Willbanks, James. Interview by Stephen Maxner. September 20, 2000. Item
#OH0063, The Vietnam Archive, Texas Tech University, Lubbock.

Wonsick, Jim. Interview by Ron Milam. August 16, 2003. Frisco, Colorado.

Yushta, Jeff. Interview by James Ebert in *Life in a Year*. August 2, 1989.

Zeller, Jim. Interview by Ron Milam. November 8, 2003. Angel Fire, New Mexico.

Questionnaires

Officers

Arkovich, Capt. David V., Ames, Iowa

Bishop, Capt. John, Coleville, California

Cook, 1st Lt. David, Lago Vista, Texas

Cummings, 1st Lt. Jack, Palm Desert, California

Harrell, Capt. Stuart J., Phoenix, Arizona

Kahalekulu, 1st Lt. Ben, Cochiti Lake, New Mexico

Lovejoy, 1st Lt. Vernon, Lakewood, Colorado

Meyers, 1st Lt. Chuck, Highland Park, Illinois

Moore, Lt. Col. John, Navarre, Florida

Patterson, Maj. Roger D., Alamosa, Colorado

Rainey, Capt. Gerald, Fountain, Colorado

Sims, C.W.O. (02) Richard, Lubbock, Texas

West, Capt. Brent, Fort Worth, Texas

Wilson, C.W.O. (02) Lucky H., Spring Branch, Texas

Enlisted Personnel

Alloy, Specialist 4th Class Mark, Rosharon, Texas
Baldwin, Platoon Sgt. David, Albuquerque, New Mexico
Boltz, PFC Farrell, Houston, Texas
Brooks, Specialist 4th Class Cecil, Port Lavaca, Texas
Charland, Sgt. Jim, Jr., Redondo Beach, California
DeLa Fuente, Platoon Sgt. Pete, Jr., New Braunfels, Texas
Dimas, Sgt. Rick, Stockton, California
Lemak, Sgt. David M., Houston, Texas
Lyons, Sgt. Patrick, Houston, Texas
Vallo, Sgt. Ed, Houston, Texas
Zeller, Sgt. Jim, Angel Fire, New Mexico

Memoirs

Alexander, Ron, and Charles W. Sasser. *Taking Fire: The True Story of a Decorated Chopper Pilot*. New York: St. Martin's Press, 2001.

Bartimus, Tad, Denby Fawcett, Jurate Kazickas, Edith Lederer, Ann Bryan Mariano, Anne Morrissy Merick, Laura Palmer, Kate Webb, and Tracy Wood. *War Torn: Stories of War from the Women Reporters Who Covered Vietnam*. New York: Random House, 2002.

Beesley, Stanley W. *Vietnam: The Heartland Remembers*. Norman: University of Oklahoma Press, 1987.

Bradford, Alfred S. *Some Even Volunteered: The First Wolfhounds Pacify Vietnam*. Westport, Conn.: Praeger, 1994.

Donovan, David. *Once a Warrior King*. New York: Ballantine, 1985.

Estes, Jack. *A Field of Innocence*. New York: Warren Books, 1987.

Gadd, Charles. *Line Doggie: Foot Soldiers in Vietnam*. Novato, Calif.: Presidio, 1987.

Goff, Stanley, and Robert Sanders, with Clark Smith. *Brothers: Black Soldiers in the Nam*. Novato, Calif.: Presidio, 1982.

Goldman, Peter, and Tony Fuller. *Charlie Company: What Vietnam Did to Us*. New York: Ballantine, 1983.

Hackworth, Col. David H. *About Face: Odyssey of an American Warrior*. New York: Touchstone, 1989.

——. *Steel My Soldiers' Hearts*. New York: Rugged Land, 2002.

Kovic, Ron. *Born on the Fourth of July*. New York: McGraw-Hill, 1976.

Lacombe, Tom. *Light Ruck: Vietnam, 1969*. Fort Valley, Va.: Loft Press, 2002.

Lanning, Michael Lee. *The Only War We Had: A Platoon Leader's Journal of Vietnam*. New York: Ivy Books, 1987.

Leppelman, John. *Blood on the Risers: An Airborne Soldier's Thirty-Five Months in Viet-nam.* New York: Ivy Books, 1991.

McDonough, James R. *Platoon Leader: A Front Line Personal Report of Vietnam Battle Action.* New York: Bantam, 1985.

Metzner, Edward P. *More Than a Soldier's War: Pacification in Vietnam.* College Station: Texas A&M University Press, 1995.

Miller, Rad, Jr. *Whattaya Mean I Can't Kill 'Em? A Navy Seal in Vietnam.* New York: Ivy Books, 1998.

O'Brien, Tim. *If I Die in a Combat Zone, Box Me Up and Ship Me Home.* New York: Broadway Books, 1975.

Powell, Colin, with Joseph E. Persico. *My American Journey: An Autobiography.* New York: Ballantine, 1996.

Puller, Lewis B., Jr. *Fortunate Son: The Autobiography of Lewis B. Puller, Jr.* New York: Bantam, 1991.

Schwarzkopf, Norman. *It Doesn't Take a Hero.* New York: Ballantine, 1996.

Steedle, Lee. *Mark Freedom Paid: A Combat Anthology.* Jeannette, Pa.: 83rd Chemical Mortar Battalion Veterans Assoc., 1997.

Stoddard, Jack. *What Are They Going to Do, Send Me to Vietnam?* Las Vegas: Sunrise Mountain Publishing, 2000.

Taylor, Maxwell D. *Swords and Plowshares.* New York: Norton, 1972.

TeCube, Leroy. *Year in Nam: A Native American Soldier's Story.* Lincoln: University of Nebraska Press, 1999.

Terry, Wallace. *Bloods: An Oral History of the Vietnam War by Black Veterans.* New York: Ballantine, 1985.

Trujillo, Charley. *Soldados: Chicanos in Viet Nam.* San Jose, Calif.: Chusma House Publications, 1990.

Van Devanter, Linda. *Home before Morning.* New York: Warner Books, 1983.

Westmoreland, William C. *A Soldier Reports.* New York: Da Capo Press, 1976.

Newspapers and Periodicals

Air Force ROTC Education Bulletin
American Journal of Sociology
Armed Forces Journal
Army
Army Digest
Army Reserve Magazine
Army Times
Atlantic Monthly
The Bayonet (Fort Benning, Ga.)
Business Week

Detroit News
Infantry
Military Medicine
New Republic
Newsweek
New York Times
Operations Research
Paisano
Parameters
Proceedings
Think
Toledo Blade
Wall Street Journal
Washington Monthly

SECONDARY SOURCES

Books

Addington, Larry H. *America's War in Vietnam: A Short Narrative History*. Bloomington: Indiana University Press, 2000.

Ambrose, Stephen E. *Band of Brothers*. New York: Touchstone, 1992.

Anderson, Charles B. *The Grunts*. Novato, Calif.: Presidio, 1976.

Appy, Christian. *Patriots: The Vietnam War Remembered from All Sides*. New York: Viking, 2003.

———. *Working-Class War: American Combat Soldiers and Vietnam*. Chapel Hill: University of North Carolina Press, 1993.

Arial, Tracey. *I Volunteered: Canadian Vietnam Vets Remember*. Winnipeg, Canada: Watson and Dwyer Publishing, 1997.

Astor, Gerald. *The Right to Fight: A History of African Americans in the Military*. Cambridge, Mass.: Da Capo Press, 1998.

Atkinson, Rick. *The Long Gray Line*. New York: Henry Holt, 1999.

Baker, Mark. *NAM: The Vietnam War in the Words of the Men and Women Who Fought There*. New York: Cooper Square Press, 1981.

Bartov, Omar. *Hitler's Army: Soldiers, Nazis, and War in the Third Reich*. Oxford: Oxford University Press, 1992.

Baskir, Lawrence M., and William A. Strauss. *Chance and Circumstance: The Draft, the War, and the Vietnam Generation*. New York: Vintage, 1978.

Bergerud, Eric M. *The Dynamics of Defeat: The Vietnam War in Hau Nghia Province*. Boulder, Colo.: Westview Press, 1991.

———. *Red Thunder, Tropic Lightning: The World of a Combat Division in Vietnam*. New York: Penguin, 1993.

Berman, Larry. *No Peace, No Honor: Nixon, Kissinger, and Betrayal in Vietnam*. New York: Free Press, 2001.

Betros, Lance, ed. *West Point: Two Centuries and Beyond*. Abilene, Tex.: McWhiney Foundation Press, 2004.

Bilton, Michael, and Kevin Sim. *Four Hours in My Lai*. New York: Penguin, 1992.

Bonn, Keith E. *Army Officer's Guide*. 49th ed. Mechanicsburg, Pa.: Stackpole Books, 2002.

Bourne, Russell. *The King's Rebellion: Racial Politics in New England, 1675–1678*. New York: Oxford University Press, 1990.

Brassford, Charles. *The Spit-Shined Syndrome: Organizational Irrationality in the American Field Army*. New York: Greenwood Press, 1988.

Brinkley, Douglas. *Tour of Duty: John Kerry and the Vietnam War*. New York: William Morrow, 2004.

Browning, Christopher R. *Ordinary Men: Reserve Police Battalion 101 and the Final Solution in Poland*. New York: Harper Collins, 1992.

Burkett, B. G. *Stolen Valor: How the Vietnam Generation Was Robbed of Its Heroes and Its History*. New York: Verity Press, 1998.

Buzzanco, Robert. *Masters of War: Military Dissent and Politics in the Vietnam Era*. New York: Cambridge University Press, 1996.

———. *Vietnam and the Transformation of American Life*. Malden, Mass.: Blackwell Publishers, 1999.

———, ed. *Vietnam and America: Readings and Documents*. Needham Heights, Mass.: Pearson Custom Publishing, 1999.

Cash, John A., John Albright, and Allan W. Sandstrum. *Seven Firefights in Vietnam*. New York: Bantam, 1985.

Chang, Iris. *The Rape of Nanking: The Forgotten Holocaust of World War II*. London: Penguin, 1997.

Cincinnatus. *Self-Destruction: The Disintegration and Decay of the United States Army during the Vietnam Era*. New York: Norton, 1981.

Coffman, Edward M. *The War to End All Wars: The American Military Experience in World War I*. Lexington: University of Kentucky Press, 1998.

Connelly, Owen. *On War and Leadership: The Words of Combat Commanders from Frederick the Great to Norman Schwarzkopf*. Princeton: Princeton University Press, 2002.

Corson, William R. *Consequences of Failure*. New York: Norton, 1974.

Cress, Lawrence Delbert. *Citizens in Arms: The Army and Militia in American Society to the War of 1812*. Chapel Hill: University of North Carolina Press, 1982.

DeGroot, Gerard J. *A Noble Cause? America and the Vietnam War*. New York: Pearson Education Limited, 2000.

Denenberg, Barry. *Voices from Vietnam*. New York: Scholastic Inc., 1995.

Dower, John W. *War without Mercy: Race and Power in the Pacific War*. New York: Pantheon Books, 1986.

Ebert, James R. *A Life in a Year: The American Infantryman in Vietnam, 1965–1972*. Novato, Calif.: Presidio, 1993

Fall, Bernard B. *The Two Viet-Nams: A Political and Military Analysis*. New York: Praeger, 1963.

Figley, Charles R., and Seymour Leventman. *Stranger at Home: Vietnam Veterans since the War*. New York: Praeger, 1980.

Fitzgerald, Frances. *Fire in the Lake: The Vietnamese and the Americans in Vietnam*. New York: Vintage, 1972.

Flynn, George Q. *The Draft: 1940–1973*. Lawrence: University Press of Kansas, 1993.

French, Shannon E. *The Code of the Warrior: Exploring Warrior Values Past and Present*. Lanham, Md.: Rowman and Littlefield, 2003.

Fussell, Paul. *Wartime: Understanding and Behavior in the Second World War*. New York: Oxford University Press, 1989.

Gabriel, Richard A., and Paul L. Savage. *Crisis in Command: Mismanagement in the Army*. New York: Hill and Wang, 1978.

Garland, LTC Albert N. *Infantry in Vietnam: Small Unit Actions in the Early Days, 1965–1966*. Nashville: Battery Press, 1967.

Glasser, Ronald J., M.D. *365 Days*. New York: George Braziller, 1971.

Glenn, Russell. *Reading Athena's Dance Card: Men against Fire in Vietnam*. Lawrence: University Press of Kansas, 2003.

Goldstein, Joseph, Burke Marshall, and Jack Schwartz. *The My Lai Massacre and Its Cover-up: Beyond the Reach of Law?* New York: Free Press, 1976.

Greenhaw, Wayne. *The Making of a Hero: The Story of Lieutenant William Calley, Jr.* Louisville, Ky.: Touchstone Publishing Company, 1971.

Grossman, Dave. *On Killing: The Psychological Cost of Learning to Kill in War and Society*. New York: Little, Brown, 1996.

Halberstam, David. *The Best and the Brightest*. New York: Ballantine, 1969.

Hanson, Victor Davis. *Hoplites: The Classical Greek Battle Experiences*. London: Routledge, 1991.

Hauser, Colonel William L. *America's Army in Crisis: A Study in Civil-Military Relations*. Baltimore: Johns Hopkins University Press, 1973.

Heineman, Kenneth J. *Campus Wars: The Peace Movement at American State Universities in the Vietnam Era*. New York: New York University Press, 1994.

Heise, J. Arthur. *The Brass Factories: A Frank Appraisal of West Point, Annapolis, and the Air Force Academy*. Washington, D.C.: Public Affairs Press, 1969.

Herr, Michael. *Dispatches*. New York: Random House, 1991.

Herring, George C. *America's Longest War: The United States and Vietnam, 1950–1975*. New York: McGraw-Hill, 1996.

Hickey, Gerald C. *Window on a War: An Anthropologist in the Vietnam Conflict*. Lubbock: Texas Tech University Press, 2003.

Holmes, Richard. *Acts of War: Behavior of Men in Battle*. New York: Free Press, 1985.

Janowitz, Morris, and Roger W. Little. *Sociology and the Military Establishment*. Beverly Hills: Sage Publications, 1971.

Jordan, David. *The Oxford Companion to Military History*. Edited by Richard Holmes. New York: Oxford University Press, 2001.

Just, Ward S. *Military Men*. New York: Knopf, 1970.

——. *To What End: Report from Vietnam*. Washington, D.C.: Public Affairs Press, 1968.

Karnow, Stanley. *Vietnam: A History*. New York: Penguin, 1984.

Karsten, Peter. *Law, Soldiers, and Combat*. Westport, Conn.: Greenwood Press, 1978.

Kelley, Michael P. *Where We Were in Vietnam*. Central Point, Ore.: Hellgate Press, 2002.

Kemble, C. Robert. *The Image of the Army Officer in America: Background for Current Views*. Westport, Conn.: Greenwood Press, 1973.

Kindsvatter, Peter S. *American Soldiers: Ground Combat in the World Wars, Korea, and Vietnam*. Lawrence: University Press of Kansas, 2003.

King, Colonel Edward L. *The Death of the Army: A Pre-Mortem*. New York: Saturday Review Press, 1972.

Kinnard, Douglas. *The War Managers: American Generals Reflect on Vietnam*. New York: Da Capo Press, 1977.

Kitfield, James. *Prodigal Soldiers: How the Generation of Officers Born of Vietnam Revolutionized the American Style of War*. Washington, D.C.: Brassey's, 1995.

Knoll, Erwin, and Judith Nies McFadden, eds. *War Crimes and the American Conscience*. New York: Holt, Rinehart and Winston, 1970.

Kolko, Gabriel. *Anatomy of a War: Vietnam, the United States, and the Modern Historical Experience*. New York: New Press, 1985.

Krepinevich, Andrew F., Jr. *The Army and Vietnam*. Baltimore, Md.: Johns Hopkins University Press, 1986.

Leepson, Marc, ed. *Webster's New World Dictionary of the Vietnam War*. New York: Simon and Schuster Macmillan, 1999.

Lepore, Jill. *The Name of War: King Philip's War and the Origins of American Identity*. New York: Vintage, 1998.

Lewy, Guenter. *America in Vietnam*. New York: Oxford University Press, 1978.

Lifton, Robert Jay. *Home from the War*. New York: Simon and Schuster, 1973.

Lovette, Leland Pearson. *Naval Customs, Traditions, and Usage*. Annapolis: United States Naval Institute, 1967.

Mangold, Tom, and John Penycate. *The Tunnels of Cu Chi*. New York: Berkley Books, 1985.

Marshall, S. L. A. *Men against Fire: The Problem of Battle Command*. Norman: University of Oklahoma Press, 1947.

McMamers, Hugh. *Ultimate Special Forces*. New York: DD Publishing, 2003.

McPherson, Milton M. *The Ninety-Day Wonders*. Birmingham: University of Alabama Printing Services, 2001.

Millis, Walter. *Arms and Men: A Study in American Military History*. New York: G. P. Putnam's Sons, 1956.

Moore, Harold G., and Joseph L. Galloway. *We Were Soldiers Once . . . and Young — Ia Drang: The Battle That Changed the War in Vietnam*. New York: Random House, 1992.

Moser, Richard. *The New Winter Soldiers: GI and Veteran Dissent during the Vietnam Era*. New Brunswick, N.J.: Rutgers University Press, 1996.

Moskos, Charles, Jr. *Public Opinion and the Military Establishment*. Beverly Hills: Sage Publications, 1971.

Moyar, Mark. *Triumph Forsaken*. New York: Cambridge University Press, 2006.

Neiberg, Michael S. *Making Citizen-Soldiers: ROTC and the Ideology of American Military Service*. Cambridge, Mass.: Harvard University Press, 2000.

Norman, Elizabeth. *Women at War: The Story of Fifty Military Nurses Who Served in Vietnam*. Philadelphia: University of Pennsylvania Press, 1990.

Olson, James S., and Randy Roberts. *Where the Domino Fell: America and Vietnam, 1945–1995*. St. James, N.Y.: Brandywine Press, 1999.

Peers, William R., Burke Marshall, and Jack Schwartz. *The My Lai Massacre and Its Cover-Up: Beyond the Reach of Law? The Peers Commission Report*. New York: Free Press, 1976.

Pisor, Robert. *The End of the Line: The Siege of Khe Sanh*. New York: Norton, 1982.

Prashker, Ivan. *Duty, Honor, Vietnam: Twelve Men of West Point Tell Their Stories*. New York: Warner Books, 1988.

Prugh, Major General George S. *Law at War: Vietnam, 1964–1973*. Washington, D.C.: Department of the Army, 1975.

Richter, Daniel. *Facing East from Indian Country: A Native History of Early America*. Cambridge, Mass.: Harvard University Press, 2001.

Sack, John. *Lieutenant Calley, His Own Story*. New York: Viking, 1970.

Santo, Al. *Leading the Way: How Vietnam Veterans Rebuilt the U.S. Military, an Oral History*. New York: Ballantine, 1993.

Shay, Jonathan. *Achilles in Vietnam: Combat Trauma and the Undoing of Character*. New York: Simon and Schuster, 1994.

———. *Odysseus in America: Combat Trauma and the Trials of Homecoming*. New York: Scribner, 2002.

Sheehan, Neil. *A Bright Shining Lie: John Paul Vann and America in Vietnam*. New York: Vintage, 1988.

Sherrill, Robert. *Military Justice Is to Justice as Military Music Is to Music*. New York: Harper and Row, 1969.

Solis, Gary D. *Son Thang: An American War Crime*. New York: Bantam, 1997.

Sorley, Lewis. *A Better War: The Unexamined Victories and Final Tragedy of America's Last Years in Vietnam*. New York: Harcourt Brace, 1999.

———. *Thunderbolt: General Creighton Abrams and the Army of His Times*. Washington, D.C.: Potomac Books, 1998.

———, ed. *Vietnam Chronicles: The Abrams Tapes, 1968–1972*. Lubbock: Texas Tech University Press, 2004.

Spector, Ronald H. *After TET: The Bloodiest Year in Vietnam*. New York: Vintage, 1993.

Stanton, Shelby. *The Rise and Fall of an American Army: U.S. Ground Forces in Vietnam, 1965–1973*. New York: Dell Books, 1985.

Stewart, James B. *Heart of a Soldier: A Story of Love, Heroism, and September 11th*. New York: Simon and Schuster, 2002.

Summers, Harry G., Jr. *On Strategy: A Critical Analysis of the Vietnam War*. Novato, Calif.: Presidio, 1982.

Taylor, Telford. *Nuremberg and Vietnam: An American Tragedy*. Chicago: Quadrangle Books, 1970.

Thayer, Thomas. *War without Fronts: The American Experience in Vietnam*. Boulder, Colo.: Westview Press, 1985.

Thucydides. *The Peloponnesian War*. Crawley translation. New York: Random House, 1992.

Tritle, Larry. *From Melos to My Lai: War and Survival*. New York: Routledge, 2000.

Trooboff, Peter D., ed. *Law and Responsibility in Warfare: The Vietnam Experience*. Chapel Hill: University of North Carolina Press, 1975.

Turner, David R. *Practice for Officer Candidate Test*. New York: Arco Press, 1966.

Tzu, Sun. *The Art of War*. Translated and with an introduction by Samuel B. Griffith. New York: Oxford University Press, 1969.

Verrone, Richard Burks, and Laura M. Calkins. *Voices from Vietnam: Eye-Witness Accounts of the War, 1954–1975*. Cincinnati: David and Charles, 2005.

Walton, Colonel George (Ret.). *The Tarnished Shield: A Report on Today's Army*. New York: Dodd, Mead, 1973.

Walzer, Michael. *Just and Unjust Wars: A Moral Argument with Historical Illustrations*. New York: Basic Books, 1992.

Weigley, Russell F. *The American Way of War: A History of United States Military Strategy and Policy*. Bloomington: Indiana University Press, 1973.

———. *History of the United States Army*. Bloomington: Indiana University Press, 1984.

West, Captain Francis J., Jr. *Small Unit Action in Vietnam, Summer 1966*. New York: Arno Press, 1967.

Westheider, James E. *Fighting on Two Fronts: African Americans and the Vietnam War*. New York: New York University Press, 1997.

Willbanks, James H. *The Battle of An Loc*. Bloomington: Indiana University Press, 2005.

Worley, Leslie J. *Hippeis, the Cavalry of Ancient Greece*. Boulder, Colo.: Westview Press, 1994.

Wright, Kai. *Soldiers of Freedom: An Illustrated History of African Americans in the Armed Forces*. New York: Black Dog and Levanthal Publishers, 2002.

Young, Marilyn B. *The Vietnam Wars: 1945–1990*. New York: Harper Collins, 1991.

Articles

"Army Makes a New Point." *Business Week*, March 27, 1965, 132–36.

"Army Officer Candidate Program." *Think*, 1966.

Barnett, Arnold, Timothy Stanley, and Michael Shore. "America's Vietnam Casualties: Victims of a Class War?" *Operations Research*, 1992.

Benson, George. "Academic World and Military Education." *Air Force ROTC Education Bulletin*, February 1971.

Bond, Thomas C. "Fragging: A Study." *Army* 27, no. 4 (April 1977): 45.

Bruen, LTC John D. "Repercussions from the Vietnam Mobilization Decision." *Parameters*, Spring–Summer 1972, 32.

Carney, Larry. "OCS to Graduate 21,000 in FY67." *Army Times* 26 (June 5, 1966): 1.

Cooper, LTG Charles G. "The Day It Became the Longest War." *Proceedings*, May 1996, 77–80.

DePuy, Maj. Gen. William E. "Army Leadership Moves Upward on Performance." *Army Reserve Magazine* 15, no. 1 (January 1969): 1–3.

Engelhardt, Lt. Robert W. "OCS Status Report." *Army Digest*, March 1970, 50.

Fallows, James. "Low-Class Conclusions: A Widely Reported New Study Claiming That All Classes Shared the Burden of the Vietnam War Is Preposterous." *Atlantic Monthly*, April 1993, 6.

———. "What Did You Do in the Class War, Daddy?" *Washington Monthly*, 1975.

Fleming, Karl. "The Troubled Army Brass." *Newsweek*, May 24, 1971, 21–23.

Gillooly, Maj. David H., and Thomas C. Bond, M.D. "Assaults with Explosive Devices on Superiors: A Synopsis of Reports from Confined Offenders at the U.S. Disciplinary Barracks." *Military Medicine*, October 1976, 700–702. In Center of Military History Archives, Fort McNair, District of Columbia, SEA-RS-125b.

Greene, SSG Larry. "Infantry OCS Has Its Roots in Expansion of 1930s." *The Bayonet*, October 4, 1968, 20.

Heinl, Robert D. "The Collapse of the Armed Forces." *Armed Forces Journal* 108, no. 19 (June 7, 1971).

———. "Service Morale, Discipline at Low Ebb." *Detroit News*, January 12, 1971.

Just, Ward S. "Soldiers," pt. 2. *Atlantic*, November 1970, 83.

Keatley, Robert. "ROTC Ranks Expand Despite Antagonism on Many Campuses." *Wall Street Journal*, July 2, 1969, 1.

Michelson, Peter. "Bringing the War Home: Veterans Testify against the Atrocity in Indochina." *New Republic*, February 27, 1971, 21–25.

Milam, J. R. "Extreme Violence in War: The Historical Treatment of Atrocities." *Paisano* (University of Texas), Spring 2002.

Moon, Gordon. "ROTC on the Rebound." *Army* 17, no. 8 (August 1967): 46–55.

"Officer Training to Be Limited to College Graduates." *The Bayonet*, September 8, 1967, 17.

Piper, Col. Robert M. "OCS Today." *Infantry*, March–April 1970, 42–45.

Schuman, Howard. "Two Sources of Anti-War Sentiment in America." *American Journal of Sociology* 78, no. 3 (November 1972): 513–36.

Ulman, Neil. "The Changing Point: U.S. Military Academy Struggles to Maintain Traditional Prestige." *Wall Street Journal*, June 18, 1969.

Vitucci, Steve. "Bradley Set Up the First OCS at Fort Benning." *The Bayonet*, March 30, 1973, 24.

Woolnough, Gen. James K. "Teacher to an Army in a War, on Move," *Army Times*, November 1968, 39.

Novels

Caputo, Philip. *A Rumor of War*. New York: Henry Holt, 1977.

Dye, Dale A. *Platoon*. New York: Charter Books, 1986.

Greene, Graham. *The Quiet American*. Berlin: Cornelsen Verlag, 1991.

Hasford, Gustav. *The Short-Timers*. New York: Bantam, 1979.

Heinemann, Larry. *Paco's Story*. New York: Farrar, Straus and Giroux, 1979.

Huggett, William Turner. *Body Count*. New York: Dell Publishing, 1973.

Ninh, Bao. *The Sorrow of War*. London: Secker and Warburg, 1993.

O'Brien, Tim. *Going after Cacciato*. New York: Broadway Books, 1978.

———. *The Things They Carried*. New York: Broadway Books, 1990.

Scott, Leonard B. *The Expendables*. New York: Ballantine, 1991.

———. *The Last Run*. New York: Ballantine, 1987.

Trujillo, Charley B. *Dogs from Illusion*. San Jose: Chusma House Publications, 1994.

Webb, James. *Fields of Fire*. New York: Bantam, 1978.

Unpublished Papers

Donnelly, William. "Why Graduates of the U.S. Military Academy from 1964 to 1966 Did Not Attend a Branch Officer Basic Course." Personal e-mail, <Will.Donnelly@hqda.Army.Mil>. In Center of Military History Archives, Fort McNair, District of Columbia. June 3, 2003.

Hall, Brian Sadler. "The Wailing Walls? LBJ and Draft Reform." Lyndon Baines Johnson Presidential Library, Austin, Texas. 1995.

Peterson, Peter Barron. "A Comparison of Behavioral Styles between Entering and Graduating Students in Officer Candidate School." George Washington University. 1967.

Schoppes, Colonel Jared B. "Lessons from My Lai." Research Element, U.S. Army War College, Carlisle Barracks, Pennsylvania. April 14, 1973.

Films

Dear America: Letters Home from Vietnam. Produced by HBO Video. 1987.

The Deer Hunter. Produced by Barry Spinkings, Michael Deeley, Michael Cimino, and John Peverall. Directed by Michael Cimino. MCA Universal. 1991.

Full Metal Jacket. Produced and directed by Stanley Kubrick. Warner Bros. 1987.

Going Back. Produced and directed by Ron and Maxine Milam. 2001.

Go Tell the Spartans. Produced by Allan F. Bodoh and Mitchell Cannold. Directed by Ted Post. HBO Video. 1978.

Hamburger Hill. Produced by Marcia Nasatir and Jim Carabatsos. Directed by John Irvin. Artisan. 1998.

Platoon. Produced by Arnold Kopelson. Written and directed by Oliver Stone. MGM Home Entertainment. 1986.

We Were Soldiers. Produced by Bruce Davey, Stephen McEveety, and Randall Wallace. Directed by Randall Wallace. Paramount. 2002.

Index

(ill.), 162; massacre at, 9–10, 41–42, 49, 58, 113, 124, 126, 128–30, 134, 136, 138, 164–65, 167, 171–72; Son My Village in, 112, 126–30, 133, 138. *See also* Thompson, W.O. Hugh; Calley, Lt. William Laws; Medina, Capt. Ernest

Nanking, China, 120
National Defense Act (1916), 25, 37
National Liberation Front (NLF). *See* Viet Cong
Ninh, Bao, *Sorrow of War,* 104
Nixon, Richard, and Vietnamization, 134, 146
Noncombatants, 115, 118, 120, 125, 133–34, 206 (n. 67); civilian casualties, 109–11, 134; prisoners (POWs), 106, 120–25, 131
Noncombat arm of OCS: Aberdeen Proving Grounds, Maryland, 20; Fort Belvoir, Virginia, 20, 63, 68; Fort Eustis, Virginia, 20, 51, 64; Fort Lee, Virginia, 20
Noncommissioned officer (NCO), 34, 69, 77, 93, 99, 128, 146, 152, 157
North Vietnamese Army (NVA). *See* Peoples Army of Vietnam

Officer and gentleman, definition of, 55, 183 (n. 4); and George Washington, 184 (n. 4); and John Paul Jones, 183 (n. 4)
Officer Candidate School (OCS), 6, 9, 30, 32–33, 56, 59, 61, 63–64, 66, 68–69, 84, 108, 172; and academics, 42–43; College Option Enlistment Program, 21–23; and leadership, 45–49; and officer procurement, 18–19; and physical stress, 42–44; and psychologi-

cal stress, 44. *See also* "Bayonet sheets"; Recycled
Officer Efficiency Report, 128–29
One-year tour of duty, 165–66
Operation ROLLING THUNDER, 97

Peers, William, 134, 171; Peers Report, 128–29, 131, 171, 205 (n. 48)
Peoples Army of Vietnam (PAVN), 84, 89, 95, 97–101, 104–7, 116–19, 122, 124, 151, 154, 158, 164
Phu Nhon, 105, 111
Physical Combat Proficiency Test, 26, 31–32, 36, 41, 44, 63
Piper, Col. Robert M., 46, 49
Platoon leader, 6, 32, 40, 42
Powell, Colin, 152, 175
Primary Group, 139–40, 152
Project 100,000, 27, 28

R&R (rest and relaxation), 93
Racial tension, 151–55, 159, 165
Ranger, 35, 40, 51–53, 56, 61–62
Rear-echelon personnel, 81, 148, 155, 157, 160, 165; and Confederate flags, 154; REMFs, 95, 156, 184 (n. 11)
Recycled, 42, 44, 64. *See also* Officer Candidate School
Repo-depo, 80–81, 139; Cam Ranh Bay, 80; Da Nang, 80, 97, 105, 111; Tan Son Nhut, 78, 80
"Report on Survey of Military Knowledge and Skills of Recently Commissioned 2nd Lieutenants," 61
Rescorla, Rick, 8, 9, 10, 168
Reserve Officer Training Corps (ROTC), 6, 14–15, 17, 20, 23–24, 28–30, 33, 37, 42, 54, 56, 58, 62, 108; and academics, 40–41; and four-year scholarships, 37; at Howard Payne Univer-